Routledge Revivals

The Mende Language

The Mende Language

Containing Useful Phrases, Elementary Grammar, Short Vocabularies, Reading Materials

F. W. H. Migeod

Routledge
Taylor & Francis Group
ROUTLEDGE REVIVALS

First published in 1908 by Kegan Paul, Trench, Trübner & Co., Ltd.

This edition first published in 2018 by Routledge
2 Park Square, Milton Park, Abingdon, Oxon, OX14 4RN
and by Routledge
711 Third Avenue, New York, NY 10017

Routledge is an imprint of the Taylor & Francis Group, an informa business

Publisher's Note
The publisher has gone to great lengths to ensure the quality of this reprint but points out that some imperfections in the original copies may be apparent.

Disclaimer
The publisher has made every effort to trace copyright holders and welcomes correspondence from those they have been unable to contact.

A Library of Congress record exists under ISBN: 9000403

ISBN 13: 978-1-138-62515-0 (hbk)
ISBN 13: 978-1-138-62519-8 (pbk)
ISBN 13: 978-0-429-46008-1 (ebk)

THE MENDE LANGUAGE

CONTAINING

USEFUL PHRASES
ELEMENTARY GRAMMAR
SHORT VOCABULARIES
READING MATERIALS

BY

F. W. H. MIGEOD

TRANSPORT OFFICER
GOLD COAST COLONY

LONDON
KEGAN PAUL, TRENCH, TRÜBNER & Co., Ltd.
DRYDEN HOUSE, 43 GERRARD STREET, W.
1908

Richard Clay & Sons, Limited,
BREAD STREET HILL, E.C., AND
BUNGAY, SUFFOLK.

INTRODUCTION

THE Mende nation is located in the eastern part of the Sierra Leone Protectorate. As to its origin I have been unable to obtain any information, but if its recent movement be any indication, the general direction of its migration would seem to have been southerly. In the fourth decade of the nineteenth century Mendes were apparently little known on the seaboard, except as slaves brought down from the interior. The late Reverend Dr. Schoen, of the Church Missionary Society, and the author of books on the Hausa, Ibo, and Mende languages, states (1882) that "it seems that the nation is pressing on to the seashore, as they occupy at present the country where, in 1839, the slave-dealers had their depôts of slaves in the Sherbro country. Their baracoons were destroyed on the banks of the great river Bum by Captain Denman, of the British Navy, in 1840 or 1841, and since that time the country is open to British commerce and missionary operations, and the Mende are the principal occupants of the place, and their language has all but superseded, and will ere long supersede, the Sherbro altogether." This movement has continued, but the Sherbro language still exists.

The imposition of peace on the country after the war of 1898, when the nation endeavoured to throw off European control, seems to have been the immediate cause of large numbers of the young men leaving their country. The suppression of local feuds deprived them of their chief activities. When there was constant local warfare the safety of the town depended on its male inhabitants being always at home. With the abolition of the necessity for their presence the young men began to look around for some direction in which to turn their energies, and finding none at home they were necessarily compelled to go abroad; and they are now to be found in all parts of West Africa, including the French and German colonies. As regards the Gold Coast, they were first introduced to that country through being brought in small numbers in the capacity either of soldiers or carriers for the local wars, beginning with the Ashanti war of 1873. For the Ashanti war of 1900 they came in larger numbers. The West African Regiment, which was sent from Sierra Leone, had many Mendes in its ranks; and of the carriers that were enlisted at Freetown for the same war probably over 4000 were Mende. About this time, too, large numbers were recruited as labourers for the Sekondi to Kumasi railway. As many as were willing to go were sent back at the expiration of their engagements, but many returned again to obtain work either from the Government or on the mines. At the present time (1907) they probably do not number much more than 1200 in the Colony, and four to five years would seem to be the average period of residence. Their number has been steadily decreasing, owing to the restrictions imposed by the Sierra Leone Government on their leaving that Colony, and those that go back home now find it difficult to come again. Unlike the Krumen, who have considerable objection to leaving the coast-line, and who work in gangs, which come and return annually, the Mendes subject themselves to no similar restrictions, and their enterprise and self-reliance take them everywhere.

They are not generally tall, but sturdy, fearless, and capable of great endurance. The following table of measurements, which I have made, gives possibly a fairly correct indication of this people's stature.

HEIGHTS OF 894 MENDES MEASURED.

	No.
Shortest 4.8¾	
Up to and including 4.11⅞	14
5 ft. and up to 5.0⅞ inclusive	24
5.1 and up to 5.1⅞ inclusive	42
5.2 and 5.2⅛	21
5.2¼ ,, 5.2⅜	15
5.2½ ,, 5.2⅝	26
5.2¾ ,, 5.2⅞	22
5.3 ,, 5.3⅛	25
5.3¼ ,, 5.3⅜	40
5.3½ ,, 5.3⅝	26
5.3¾ ,, 5.3⅞	40
5.4 ,, 5.4⅛	48
5.4¼ ,, 5.4⅜	28
5.4½ ,, 5.4⅝	36
5.4¾ ,, 5.4⅞	37
5.5 ,, 5.5⅛	49
5.5¼ ,, 5.5⅜	46
5.5½ and 5.5⅝	41
5.5¾ ,, 5.5⅞	28
5.6 ,, 5.6⅛	26
5.6¼ ,, 5.6⅜	29
5.6½ ,, 5.6⅝	34
5.6¾ ,, 5.6⅞	23
5.7 ,, 5.7⅛	16
5.7¼ ,, 5.7⅜	24
5.7½ ,, 5.7⅝	19
5.7¾ ,, 5.7⅞	23
5.8 ,, 5.8⅛	19
5.8¼ ,, 5.8⅜	8
5.8½ ,, 5.8⅝	14
5.8¾ ,, 5.8⅞	11
5.9 and over	40
Tallest 6.1¼	
	894

The nation seems to be formed by an admixture of a tall, slim race, presumably coming from the open country to the northward, with the short, thick-set race, which ancient records, dating back as far as the time of the Phœnicians, show to have been the inhabitants of the tropical African forest in past ages: which view the foregoing figures appear to support.

The customs of the Mendes, as far as I can learn from hearsay, do not seem to differ greatly from those of their immediate neighbours, who still remain pagans. The great institution of the country is Poro; an institution similar to which exists among the Vais, their neighbours to the south-east, and I believe also in other adjoining countries. As reference has been made to it, it may be briefly stated that Poro is virtually a system of education. It has been described as a secret society; but there cannot be much secrecy about what has been attended by nearly all the youth of the country. The course of instruction varies with the desire and status of the individual and the fees paid. Dancing, singing, gymnastics, medicine, and mystic rites are amongst the subjects taught, and for some boys the course lasts seven years. Girls also go through a course of instruction suitable for them, which they are not permitted to talk about with the other sex. What is Poro to the men is called 'Sande' or 'Bondo' for the women.

As to the affinities of the Mende language I am unable to say much, having, of the surrounding languages, only been able to examine Vai. Vai is a language of interest from its having a syllabic writing of its own. It has a very considerable number of words in common with Mende, and in many leading particulars the grammar harmonizes. The Vais have a tradition that they themselves came from the north. It is therefore not unlikely that a Mende migration mixing with the already existing coast inhabitants produced the Vai nation. The Mendes call Vais 'Karō,' and the Vais call Mendes 'Huro' or 'Wuro.' Mende must not be confused with Mande, which is the language of the Mandingos. As the structure and grammar of a language are a surer indication of its affinity to other languages than its words, I have in the subjoined table compared Mende with Vai as well as with Hausa. With Hausa, from its distance, it can have no possible connection; but the comparison shows the striking differences in the languages of a relatively small portion of Africa.

COMPARATIVE STATEMENT OF MENDE, VAI, HAUSA.

RULE OF GRAMMAR OR IDIOM.	MENDE.	VAI.	HAUSA.
Foreign words	Not many recognisable.	Many Mende words.	Many Arabic words.
Can build up words from own roots	Yes.	Apparently only to a limited extent.	No.
Whether a written language	No.	Yes.	Yes.
Noun—			
Definite and indefinite forms	Yes.	No.	No.
Several plural forms to each noun	Yes.	No.	Yes.
Plurals on regular lines	Yes.	Yes.	Mixed.
Singular for plural used as an idiom	No.	—	Yes.
Declined	No.	No.	No.
In compound nouns does qualifying noun come before the other?	Before.	Before.	After.
Agent—prefix or suffix	Suffix.	Suffix.	Prefix.
Gender	No gender.	No gender.	Grammatical.
A neuter	No.	No.	No.
Adjective—			
Position with reference to qualified noun	After.	After.	Before and after.
Gender form	No.	No.	Yes.
Comparison, direct or circumlocution	Circumlocution.	Circumlocution.	Circumlocution.
Numerals—18, 19 ; 28, 29, etc.	Added to previous decade.	Added to previous decade.	Taken from succeeding decade.
Basis	Ten.	Ten.	Ten.
Periods used	Scores.	Scores.	Hundreds and thousands.
Pronouns—			
Possessive—position with reference to noun	Before.	Before.	After.
Objective—position with reference to verb	Before.	Before.	After.
Personal—required to complete subject	Yes.	No.	Yes
Relative—number	One.	None.	One.
Gender form	No.	No.	Second and third person singular.

Verb—			
Number of voices	One.	One.	Five.
Same verb used transitively and intransitively	Yes.	Yes.	No.
Moods—special conjugation	No.	No.	No.
a continuous	Yes.	Yes.	Yes.
Tenses—numerous	Yes.	No.	No.
auxiliaries necessary	Yes.	Yes.	No.
singular different from plural	No.	No.	No.
Auxiliaries—numerous	Yes.	No.	No.
gender form	No.	No.	Yes.
Direct object—position if a noun	Before verb.	Before verb.	After verb.
,, ,, pronoun	Before verb.	Before verb.	After verb.
'To have,' how rendered	'Is in the hand.'	—	'Is with.'
Personal pronoun conjugated	Yes.	—	Yes.
Indefinite use of 'one'	'They' with the verb.	—	Passive voice construction.
Adverbs of manner, how formed	Over 150 separate words not derived from adjectives.	Separate words.	Adjective or noun preceded by 'with.'
Prepositions or postpositions	Postpositions, one exception.	Postpositions.	Prepositions.
,, joined to verbs to modify the meaning	Yes, as prefixes mostly.	—	No.
Sundry—			
Negative construction	Very complex.	Simple.	Simple.
Interrogative — reversed pronoun and verb, or intonation	Intonation.	Intonation.	Intonation and a particle.
Elision of syllables	Frequent.	Occasional.	Occasional.
Initial consonantal changes—for euphony	Yes.	No.	No.
for gender	No.	No.	Yes.
In connected propositions—simple co-ordination or subordination	Simple co-ordination mostly.	Simple co-ordination.	Simple co-ordination.

My study of the Mende language has been carried on during my last two tours of service on the Gold Coast. The Mendes that are there to work have come from all parts of their own country, and therefore every form of the language is used. In consequence of this and of their comparatively small number I have not been in a position to strictly confine myself to any one variety of the language. I do not care to use the word 'dialect' in this respect, as the differences seem generally so small as to render the term 'dialect' inapplicable. There are, however, some varieties of Mende spoken on the borders of the country where the people have mixed with their neighbours. There is, for instance, the Kpa Mende on the west. This may possibly be entitled to be called a dialect, but I have not yet had an opportunity of studying it. There is also the Pokpa, on the east, which, I am informed, is a mixture of Mende, Vai, and Gura. In this book I have endeavoured to employ the southern form of speech, following Dr. Schoen, who published a grammar in 1882 and a vocabulary in 1884. The former is out of print, and I believe the latter very nearly so also. Of the stories at the end of the book, Nos. 1 to 7 were dictated to me by a native of Bo, the remainder by a native of Panguma. I have, however, gone through them with a native of Mofwe, as also I have the other portions of the book, and assimilated them in details of pronunciation.

Finally, the scheme I have adopted is one of short sentences of practical use, classified under their proper heads. Whenever possible a sentence is repeated if it can be made to illustrate more than one grammatical rule, and I have endeavoured to avoid the coining of phrases for the sake of furnishing examples of a rule.

F. W. H. MIGEOD.

September, 1907.

CONTENTS

ERRATA AND ADDENDA

Page 18, line 1, for *Mawulu* read *Mawulọ̄*.

Page 20, line 14, for *i na* read *ī na*.

Page 48, line 4 from bottom, for "*With A this practice is rarer*" read "*With A and O this practice is also adopted.*"

Page 49, line 2 from bottom, for *ē* read *e*.

Page 58, after line 13, add—*hindọ̄ and nyaha are used as prefixes, as, hindọ̄ lọ̄i, male child or son; nyaha lọ̄i, female child or daughter.*

Page 67, after line 8, add—*Nwoni saweisia tia mindo? Where are the three birds?*

Page 101, line 8 from bottom, to line—"Ha, to-day, now," add—*until.*

Page 107, line 6 from bottom, add after "same,"—"*and a negative question is answered by Yes, when in English No would be expected.*"

Page 115, line 14, for *jieisia* read *jesia*.

Page 128, line 3 from bottom, for *Bulw* read *Bulu*.

Page 139, line 23, for *Kale, gale* read *to̱lu, to̱lī*.

Page 140, line 7 to read—*tolu or to̱wa, tole or to̱we, bean.*

Page 141, line 13, against Kọ̄bọ̄, for *rubber tree* read *gum copal.*

Page 141, at bottom, add—*njala, njale, indigo.*

Page 143, add new line after "Njahele"—*ngọ̄rọ̄, ngọ̄rī, ape, chimpanzee.*

Page 143, line 8 from bottom, before the word "chimpanzee" insert (*?*).

Page 157, line 7 from bottom, after *gama* insert *Kama.*

Page 203, line 9 from bottom, after *gombui* omit *semicolon.*

Page 203, line 7 from bottom, for *ye* read *ya*.

Page 204, line 15, the words "*they could go awxy*" should be in *brackets.*

Page 214, lines 13 and 21, for *gbwe la* read *gbueila.*

Page 219, line 3 from bottom, after *fu* insert a *fullstop.*

Page 234, line 26, for *go* read *hurry.*

Page 248, footnote, before the word "chimpanzee" insert (*?*).

THE MENDE LANGUAGE

PART I

USEFUL PHRASES

I. One-word Phrases.

Note 1.—o = *o* ; ọ = *aw* ; ọ̄ = *o* approximating to *u*.
Note 2.—When a sentence is sung out to some one at a distance, ' oh ' is usually added.

Note 3.—Accent is on penultimate syllable unless otherwise indicated. See Part II, chap. I, for further remarks on pronunciation.

Bọ̄a.	Salutation on meeting.
Bē !	Here.
Bē-ndo !	Here ! (more emphatic).
Bia !	You !
Dọ̄ !	Stand still, *or* stop ! Stand it up !
Ē !	Yes.
Fe !	Give (me) !
Gbele ? (Gbwele).	What is the matter ?
Gbema ! (Gbwema), *or* Gbelema.	Leave off !
Gbia !	Get out, go out !
Hité !	Lower *or* let down !
Hou, *or* hō, *or* họma !	Catch hold ! Hold tight !
Igbé ?	Which ?
Kaká !	Quickly !
Li !	Go !
Li la, *or* Di la !	Take it away !
Lọ̄ndọ̄ !	Cease !
Mahũguhango ! (pronounced almost *Mā-ngwango*).	It is far !

Mawulu !	Wait !
Mbēka !	This side !
Mbumbu !	Carry ; pick it up ; take it away !
Malewe !	Cut it off !
Mia, *or* Miando !	Yonder !
Miaka !	Yonder side ! Over there !
Mindo ? *or* Mi lo ?	Where is it ?
Nda !	Pull ! *or* lay it down !
Ndakpé ! (Ndakpwé).	Fellow ! (A common form of address for men when no name is used.)
Njē !	Go down, *or* lower !
Nyandengo !	It is fine !
Pã !	Kill it !
Pili !	Throw *or* shoot !
Sao !	No ! (emphatic).
Se ! (*Bi se* is more common).	Thank you !
Te !	Lift it !
Tewe !	Cut it !
Wa !	Come !
Wala !	Bring it !
Yei !	Go down !

II. Two-word Phrases.

A fulo !	Untie it ! (*pl.*)
A kene ? (a = *where*).	Where is master ?
A gbale ? (a = *it*).	Does it hurt ?
A li ! *or* Ali-oh ! (a = *you*, imperative).	Go ! (*pl.*)
A lọ̄ !	Stand (still) ! (*pl.*)
A wa ! *or* A wa-oh !	Come ! (*pl.*)
A yi !	Go down ! (*pl.*)
Bā hama !	You will not die !

(Bā = *you*, singular, imperative, negative.)

Bā lembi !	Do not delay !
Bā lua !	Do not be afraid !
Bā ƥili !	Do not throw, *or* shoot !
Bā yepe !	Do not talk !
Bē gbe ? (bē = you say).	What do you say ?
Bē ka ? (bē = here).	This side ?
Beva be ?	What is the news here ?
Beva na ?	What is the news there ?
Bĭ biyeí ?	What is your name ?
Bĭ gbahã ?	Are you tired ?
Bĭ gboyōa ?	Have you finished ?
Bĭ leí ?	What is your name ?

(Bĭ lei, *or* Bĭ lá, is also used in the sense of *you are called, your name is called.*)

Bĭ mahũgbe.	Be careful.
Bĭ mero ?	Do you hear, *or* understand ?
Bi se ! (*pl.* Wuse).	Thank you ! (also a salutation).
Bi to ?	Do you see it ?
Bia mi ? (Bia mindo ?)	Where are you ?
Bia na ?	How do you do ? (lit. Are you there ?)
Dọ̄ kpe !	Stand still !
Dọ̄ le !	Stand (still) a moment !
Ē gu.	He cannot (do it).
Ē guma.	Ditto.
Ē wa.	He will not come.
Er, er.	No.
Fe be !	Give (it) to me !
Fe mbe !	Ditto.
Gbe mia ? (Gbwe mia ?)	What is it ?
Gbe lo ? (Gbwe lo ?)	Ditto.
Gbi gboyoa (Gbwi gboyoa).	It is all finished.
Gbīa mbu !	Come out from underneath !
Gbo bima ?	What is the matter with you ?
Gele ma !	Stop that !
Gengebra lọ̄li.	Call the labourers.
Gomé mia, *or* Gomé lo.	It is a crow.

Hakeí bumbu.	Take up *or* carry the load.
Hakeí miningo.	The load is heavy.
Hei ndia, *or* ndiei.	Sit in the middle.
Hei panda.	Sit properly.
Hō ngeya.	Catch hold of it.
Ī be-ndo.	It is not here.
I gboyoa.	It is finished.
Ī gboyoai.	It is not finished.
I gua.	It is enough.
Ī guhani.	It is not far.
I la?	Has he placed it?
Ī lini.	He has not gone.
I lọ̄le?	How many?
Ī na.	He is not there.
Ī nyandé.	It is not good.
Ī nyandéni.	Ditto.
I yá.	He has gone.
Igbe le?	Which is it?
Jē gā.	Walk quickly.
Jo lọ̄li.	Call Jo.
Ji bāgbango.	This is dear.
Ke ke!	Master! Father!
Kolĕ igbe?	Which book?
Kolengo le.	It is cold.
Kpandé joso.	Load the gun.
Kpandé ve.	Give (me) the gun.
Kpandingo le.	It is hot.
Kpere gboyoa.	They are all finished.
Kurungo le.	It is agreed, *or* accepted; all right.
La ndia.	Put it in the middle.
Li bu.	Go underneath.
Li gulo.	Go on in front.
Li miaka.	Go yonder side.
Li miando.	Go over there.
Lo̱ lọ̄le?	How many days?
Lo̱ sawa.	Three days.
Lumá mbe.	Answer me.

Mamungo le.	He is foolish.
Maw'u le (= mawulu le).	Wait a little.
Maw'u kru (= mawulu kulo).	Ditto.
Mbomé wote.	Turn the hammock round.
Méndemo angē.	I am a Mende.
Méndemo abië?	Are you a Mende?
Méndemo angië.	He is a Mende.
Mia lo.	It is over there.
Miaka gbē, *or* Mia gbē.	Look over there.
Mi yaka?	Which direction?
Mindo bīna? (= bi li na).	Where have you been?
Na gbē!	Look there!
Na lọ̄le?	How many there?
Nda mahũ.	Put it on top.
Ndakpwe' mbo!	Lit. Fellow! alas! (a note of warning).
Ndaomé gbọ̄.	Shut the window.
Ndaomé lawo.	Open the window.
Ndelingo le.	It is wet.
Ndọ̄mé gbia.	Take off (your) singlet, *or* shirt.
Ndo̱wé lavendá.	Fill the hole.
Ndo̱wé lave.	Ditto.
Ngaleí kọ̄tọ̄.	Roll up the mat.
Ngaleí yei.	Let down the mat.
Ngē dema.	I am not passing.
Ngē luma.	I am not willing.
Ngē wa.	I shall not come.
Ngē pe.	I shall not do it.
Ngĭ gbahã.	I am tired.
Ngī gbahani.	I am not tired.
Ngī gbeni.	I do not care.
Ngī go̱.	I do not know.
Ngĭ gulo.	In front of him.
Ngī hũgo.	I do not understand.
Ngĭ kurua.	I accept (lit. I accepted).
Ngī kuruni.	I do not accept.
Ngĭ menia.	I heard.
Ngī menini.	I did not hear.
Ngĭ tonga.	I have seen.

Ngĭ wiláma.	I am finishing.
Nji dọmeí (nji *for* nje).	Put it on the ground.
Njia gbī.	All right.
Nya le.	It is I.
Nu yira.	One person.
Numu yira.	Ditto.
Nyawo mia, *or* Nyawo le.	It is mine.
Njei susungo.	The water is deep.
Njehũ susungo.	Ditto.
Ngi yakpeí (= ta yakpeí).	He alone.
Njei wōma.	Across the water.
Nya yakpeí.	I alone.
O Jo?	Where is Jo?
Pē bu.	In the house.
Pe ñi, *or* hī.	Do it so.
Pelé nyamungo.	The road is very bad.
Powe mia, *or* lo.	It is a pigeon.
Pu ndọmeí.	Put it on the ground.
Pu ngeleya.	Put it up (aloft).
Pë-ndé gbọ̄.	Shut the door.
Pë-ndé lao.	Open the door.
Pundía.	Put it in the middle.
Ta be.	It is here.
Ta ji?	Is it this?
Ta gulo.	He is in front.
Ta mia.	So it is (a common expression introducing a related subject).
Ta mindo?	Where is he?
Ta kuhama	It is far.
Ta na.	He is there.
Ta pōma.	He is behind.
Ta wama.	He is coming.
Ta yakpeí.	He alone.
Tē wa.	They will not come.
Tei igbe?	Which town?
Telingo le.	It is black.
Tewe botongo.	Cut plenty.
Tī be.	They are not here.
Tī na.	They are not there.

Tī wama.	They are not coming.
Tia na?	Are they there?
Tia wama.	They are coming, *or* Are they coming?
Tia bāgbango.	They are dear.
Tonya mia, *or* le.	It is true, *or* Is it true?
Tukpe kru (=kulo).	Push a little.
Wa be.	Come here (*sing.*).
Wā jore.	Do not make a noise (*pl.*).
Wa káká.	Come quickly (*sing.*).
Wa meheí.	Bring food (*sing.*).
Wa ndia.	Come into the middle (*sing.*).
Wa mbe.	Come to me (*sing.*).
Wā yepe.	Do not talk (*pl.*).
Wala fere.	Bring two (*sing.*).
Wu gbahã?	Are you tired? (*pl.*).
Yē gbe?	What does he say?
Ye mia?	Who is it?
Yē, sao.	He says no.
Yia lele.	Talk slowly.

III. Three-word Phrases.

A mbomé bumbu.	Take up the hammock (*pl.*).
A mbomé wote.	Turn the hammock round (*pl.*).
A mu jēgā (=jia kā).	Let us walk quickly.
A mu li (*or* li-o).	Let us go.
A mu wīme.	Let us run.
A wa kaká.	Come quickly (*pl.*).
A wa nā.	Come now (*pl.*).
A wā (= wa a) mbomé.	Bring the hammock (*pl.*). (lit. Come with the hammock.)
Bā ī gbani.	It is not dear.
Bā li hũguhango (pronounced *'ngwango*).	Do not go far.
Bā li na.	Do not go there.

Bē njiahũ me?	Cannot you hear what is said? (lit. Cannot you eat the word inside?)
Bi bumbúa botongo.	You have taken (lit. took) too much.
Bi hi milo?	Where have you come from?
Bi hiyá mi.	Ditto.
Bi ji hou.	Hold this.
Bĭ līma le.	If you like.
Bī lima le?	Are you not going yet?
Bi li mi?	Where are you going?
Bi lọ̄ mia.	Stand yonder.
Bi ngi wu.	Wake him up.
Bi milo ge?	Where have you been lately?
Bi Mende biyeí?	What is your Mende name?
Bi ndāi milo?	Where did you put it?
Bi ndé gọra!	You lie!
Bi pui milo?	Where did you put it?
Bi nemáhũ lengo.	You are clever.
Bi nemáhũ gbī na.	You have no sense.
Bi yá mi?	Where have you been to?
Bi ye mi?	Where were you?
Bi yepe (*or* yepea) botongo.	You talk too much.
Bī wani káká.	You have not come quickly.
Bi wo le, *or* Bi wo mia.	It is yours.
Bi wo ī le, *or* Bi wo yā na.	It is not yours.
Bia ī le.	It is not you.
Bia lo mi? *or* Bi mi lo?	Where are you?
Bia yese wa.	You come first.
Bia ku mema?	Do you smell anything? (lit. Are you hearing a smell?)
Dē ngĭ ma (see also under *nd*).	Tell him.
De ti ma (see also under *nd*).	Tell them.
Duma nya we.	Answer me.
Fe nya we.	Give it to me.
Ga [1] majiá lo.	I (will) sell it.
Ga meni kru.	I understand a little.

[1] For *Ga* and *Gi* see also under *Nga* and *Ngi*.

Gbe ĭ li.	Let him go.
Gbe ngi wa.	Wait a moment till I come.
Gbe jongo mia?	How much is it?
Gbeva ī loni?	Why did not he want to?
Gbo ba fembe?	What do you give me?
Gbo ba pema?	What are you doing?
Gbo ba pe na?	What are you doing there?
Gbo bi longwola? *or* Gbo bi lǭila?	What do you want?
Gbo bi ma?	What is the matter with you?
Gī ngi loi.	I have not seen him.
Gī lǭi la.	I dislike it.
Gī nwoni loi.	I have not seen the bird.
Gi mboi lo.	I have shot it.
Gi menia hiye.	I heard indeed, *or* I understand perfectly.
Gi ndǭa pebu.	I left it at home.
Gulī mbē ka.	Paddle on this side.
Hou na ma.	Catch hold of it.
Hā gbī na.	Nothing there.
Hāi gbĭ mia?	Is anything there?
Hāi lo mia?	Ditto.
Hiye mu li.	Get up, let us go.
I gula bí.	He fell down with a thump.
Ī hingdei na.	He is not there.
Ī navoi ngeya.	He has no money.
I ndé g̱ora.	He lies.
I lani kpela.	He drew near.
Ī yā gboyoai.	He has not finished.
I ya hũ.	It has gone inside.
Ī yā wele (wīli, *or* wīri).	He has not done it.
I ya miaka.	He has gone yonder.
I ya muama.	He has gone to wash.
I ya poron.	He has gone far.
I yé na? *or* I ye na hoe?	How is it then?
Jo hingdei na?	Is Jo there?
Jo lo mi?	Where is Jo?
Kaka wekeí (*or* yekeí) ma.	On the other side.
Kale lo hũ.	A cartridge is in (the gun).

Kia ji na.[1]	Like this.
Kia na na.	Like that.
Kpele shilli' yira.	All for one shilling.
Koleí nya houa.	Cold has caught me (I have caught cold).
Kpindi jieí nyandengo.	Travelling by night is agreeable.
Kulé ji nyaningo.	This cloth is spoilt.
Li bi mua.	Go and bathe.
Li ngi gama.	Go for him.
Li pe bu.	Go home (*sing.*).
Li, wā golĕ.	Go and fetch the letters.
Lọ̄ ngi gulo.	Stand in front of him.
Lo̱ yeká ma.	Another day.
Lọ̄le mia na?	How many are there there?
Lọ̄ndo a ngepe, *or* njepe.	Cease talking.
Ma gbo we?	What shall we do?
Mā ī guhani.	It is not far.
Ma li lo.	We will go.
Mawulu mu wa.	Wait until we come.
Ma ye pe?	What are we to do?
Mehe gbī na.	No food there.
Mendemo (lo) abie?	Are you a Mende?
Mu soa pu.	We have obtained ten.
Mu ya mbe.	We return.
Mū yā li.	We do not go.
Mū yā wime.	Let us not run.
Mū lo̱voni ha.	We have not been unlucky to-day; we have not returned empty-handed.
Mu yī jiama.	We were travelling all night.
Ndakpwei! jega gurī-oh.	Friend, hurry up with that stick.
Ndē nya ma.	Tell me.
Nga[2] wa lo.	I shall come.
Nga ye pe?	How can I do it?
Ngī bi humani.	I do not cheat you.
Ngi houa kpele.	I take all.
Ngī lọ̄i la.	I do not like him, *or* it.

[1] Any noun in the indefinite form may be substituted for *ji*.
[2] For *Ng-* see also under *g-*.

Ngĩ loni abie.	I do not want you.
Ngĩ lima le.	I am not going yet.
Ngeka gı gula.	I nearly fell.
Ngĭ ya jijiama.	I am going for a walk.
Ngĭ ya yīma.	I am going to sleep.
Ngī ya toni, *or* toi.	I have not seen it.
Ngī ye bia.	I do not talk for you.
Ngileí a nyi.	The dog bites.
Ngileí a gbao.	The dog barks (cries).
Nwoní a gbao.	The bird sings (cries).
Numu gbī na.	There is nobody there.
Njia wulo lo.	It is a small affair (palaver).
Njia gutu lo.	It is a short palaver.
Numu yira dọ̄.	Send one man.
Nyawo le, *or* Nya wo mia.	It is mine.
Nyawo ī le.	It is not mine.
Nyawo yā na.	Ditto.
Pelé ī nyandeni.	The road is not good.
Pelé lo mi?	Where is the road?
Pele nyamu lo.	It is a bad road.
Pewī a gbao.	The bush cat cries.
Pili (piri) njei hũ.	Throw it into the water.
Sina ma to.	To-morrow we shall see.
Ta njī hũ.	He is asleep.
Ta hingdeí na.	He is there.
Ta lo hũ.	It is inside.
Ta mia yira.	That is one, *or* One is there.
Ta ngi gulo.	It is in front of him.
Ta yā na.	It is not that.
Ta yese wa.	He comes first.
Tē mbē yaka.	Pass it over to this side.
Te wumba.	Raise it on your head.
Tī wu pawani?	Have they not paid you?
Ti gbĭ bu.	They are all below.
Ti ya yīma.	They have gone to sleep.
Tia ī le.	It is not they.
Tonya ī le.	It is not true.
Tonya yā na.	That is not the truth.

Train i wa.	The train is coming.
Train lo wama.	Ditto.
Train ta wama.	Ditto.
Wa gboma yira.	Bring one more.
Wā li na.	Do not go there (*pl.*).
Wa mu li, *or* Wa mu li-oh.	Come, let us go.
Wa pelé bu.	Come inside the house.
Wa nga ya (pronounced *wang-gáy-ya*).	Come, I am going.
Yē, bi li.	He says, You go.
Ye bi lọni?	Who sent you?
Yē, gbe na.	He says, Look there.
Ye mia bie?	Who are you?
Ye lo abie?	Ditto.
Yo a bie? Bia bi ye?	Ditto.
Ye gurá lo?	Whose cloth is it?
Ye lo miando?	Who is there?
Ye lo na?	Ditto.
Ye mia miando?	Ditto.
Ye na mbu?	Who is underneath there?
Yo ndē bima?	Who told you?
Yo njiei leni?	Who spoke?

IV. TRAVELLING.

Sina mu li dogbo wai hũ.	To-morrow we go to the bush (*or* up country)
Mi yaka?	Which direction?
Mu li Kumasi.	We go to Kumasi.
Dogbo jiei nyandengo le?	Is bush travelling pleasant?
Nyandengo le, hiye.	It is very nice. (lit. It is nice indeed.)
Wa mu hakeisia hũgbate.	Come, let us pack the loads.
Nya longo a nunga wayakpa hakeisia va.	I want eight men for the loads.
Nunga lọle mia mbomé va?	How many men for the hammock?
Nunga gboma wayakpa mbomé va.	Eight more men for the hammock.

Ti kpele pu mahũ woita.	Sixteen in all. (lit. They all sixteen.)
Mehe navọ̄i lọ nani va.	Subsistence for four days.
Ye lo abië?	Who are you?
Headman ange.	I am the headman.
Bi biyeí?	What is your name? (lit. Your name?)
Bi leí?	Ditto.
Nya la a Bowī.	My name is Bowi.
Nya bijé lo a Bowī (*mia* or *lo* can be inserted after *la* or *bijé*).	Ditto.
Li bi gengeb'ra luli.	Go call the labourers (carriers).
Ti wai lo.	They have come.
Ti gbi ti wai lo.	They have all come.
Ti kpele ti wai lo.	Ditto.
I lọ̄a yira (pronounced *e rua yira*).	There is one left (behind).
Ī ya wai le.	He has not come yet.
Ta wama.	He is coming.
Nga wu go a mehe navoi lo woita va.	I give you subsistence for six days.
Wu meni?	Do you hear?
Mu menia.	We heard, *or* understood.
Bi lei gbo benge bi keni ange?	What name did you give me yesterday?
A li pe bu.	Go home.
Ma li lo a ngenda vọ̄li.	We go at sunrise.
A wa sina ngenda te-te.	Come to-morrow morning early.
A wa wu kome.	Come, collect yourselves.
A fombo.	Fall in.
A hakei wumbu.	Take up your loads.
Bi vala jiei va?	Are you ready for the journey?
Bi hũgbatéa jiei va?	Ditto.
Bi bima gbatéa? (pronounced *batĩa*).	Ditto.
Bi jehũ gbatéa?	Ditto.
Nya longo a numu yira hakéi jima (*or* ji va).	I want one man for this load.
Hakeí ji miningo.	This load is (too) heavy.
Ngī lila miningo le.	I cannot take it, it is too heavy.

Li bi wā ngeyéi mu hakeí ji yilī.	Go and bring rope to tie this load with.
Bi lọ̄ mia (*or* miando).	Stand over there.
Bi lọ̄ na.	Stand there.
Wu fere a li a lenga.	You two go together.
Bia (*or* bi) yesé li.	You go first (*sing.*).
Wā jore.	Do not make a noise (*pl.*).
Bā yepe.	Do not talk (*sing.*).
A londo a ngepe.	Cease talking (*pl.*).
A wa a mbomé.	Bring the hammock (*pl.*).
Kpandé ngili bomé bu (pronounced *ngrī́*).	Tie the gun in the hammock.
Mbomé wote.	Turn the hammock round (*sing.*).
A mbomé wote.	Ditto (*pl.*).
Numui na kutungo bomé va.	The man is short for the hammock.
Li bi peka luli.	Go call another.
Kei a bi lulima.	Master is calling you.
Jo lo mi?	Where is Jo?
O Jo?	Ditto.
Jo, bi la.	Jo, you are called. (lit. Jo, your name.)
Ta be.	He is here.
Ta hingdé na.	He is there. (lit. That place.)
Ye lo na?	Who is there?
Bindi hingdé na.	Bindi is there.
Kpandé lo mi?	Where is the gun?
Ta Wuseni yeya.	Wuseni has it.
Nda mahū̃.	Lay it on top.
A mu li.	Let us go.
A mu li-oh!	Ditto.
A mu jē gā.	Let us walk quickly.
Mu je mavula.	Let us hasten our pace.
A mú te.	Let us raise (it).
A mu bumbu mú te wumba.	Let us take it up and raise it on our heads.
Te bi kpakí ma.	Raise it on your shoulder.
Te bi wumba.	Raise it on your head.
A mu nje gbakíma.	Let us lower it on our shoulders.
A lọ̄!	Stand, *or* stop (*pl.*).
Dọ̄ le!	Stand a moment.
Dọ̄ kpe!	Stand still

Lọ̄ ngi gulo.	Stand in front of him.
Bia wīme kulo (pronounced *kru*).	Run on a little.
A wīme.	Run (*pl.*).
I ya a pīme.	He has run off. (lit. He has gone with running.)
Ye, mu yā wime.	He says we must not run.
Jia panda.	Walk properly, *or* carefully.
Ndakpé, je gā-oh.	Young man, hurry up (*ndakpé* is only used to an equal).
Mu jia lele.	Let us walk slowly.
Ndē dakpalọ̄i ná ma a jē gā.	Tell that young man to hurry.
Bi fukọ̄i lo mi?	Where is your head-pad? (*Kātā* is the Coast-English word for *fukọ̄i.*)
Wa nya fukọ̄i.	Bring my head-pad.
Wa bi nya fukọ̄i la.	Come and place my head-pad.
I la?	Has he placed it?
La ndia.	Put it in the middle.
Gbia mbu.	Come out from under.
Li mbu.	Go underneath.
Gbŏ bĭma?	What is the matter with you?
Ngari nya boa.	A thorn has run into me.
Ngari (lo) nya gowé ma.	There is a thorn in my foot.
Mbowé fe gi gbia.	Give me a knife to get it out.
I gbia?	Is it out?
Ī ya gbiai.	It has not come out.
I gbiai lo.	It has come out.
A gbale?	Does it hurt?
Kotī nya nwonā nya gowé ma.	A stone has wounded my foot.
Peli ī gbekpeni (peli *for* pele).	The road is not good.
Peli nyamungo (le).	The road is bad.
Njeí lo pelíhū̃.	There is water in the road (*i.e.* the road is under water).
Hindé ji ī nyandé.	This place is not good.
Njei na susungo.	That water is deep.
Ga kolo.	I will try it.
Gbe ngi li gi hũgo.	Let me go and try it.
Nga li nga to lo.	I am going to see.

Gbe ngi li ngi to.	Let me go and see.
Ma yepe?	What shall we do? (lit. How can we do?)
Susungo le.	It is deep.
Wa bi nya wōpō.	Come and carry me on your back.
Wa, ga bi wōpō.	Come, I will carry you on my back.
Hei nya gbakima.	Sit on my shoulders.
Ndo̲wé lo.	It is a hole.
Bā lua.	Do not be afraid.
Bā gulā (gurá̄).	Do not fall.
Bā nya gulā.	Do not drop me.
Ngā gulā.	I shall not fall.
Hei panda.	Sit properly.
A mbomé te ngeleya.	Raise up the hammock high.
Bi gbahā̃?	Are you tired?
Gī gbahā̃ni.	I am not tired.
I kpoyoa nā, hité.	It is finished now, let me down.
Kpawū gbī na.	There is no bridge there.
Mu jia ngurī ji ma.	We will walk on this tree.
Tei gbe a ji?	What town is this?
Li bi pēlē gokoli mu va.	Go and find a house for us.
Ngi pēlē doi lo.	I have seen a house.
Nyandengo le?	Is it a good one?
Ī nyande panda.	It is not too good.
Ta lo tei ndia.	It is in the middle of the town.
Ngī loni a pēlē tei ndia.	I do not like a house in the middle of the town.
Li bi pēlē ikelemagéi lo.	Go and look at the last house.
Bi toi lo?	Have you seen it?
Gi toi lo. Nyandengo.	I have seen it. It is fine.
A mu li na.	Let us go there.
Ti wai lo a hakeísia gbi?	Have they brought all the loads?
Haka yira i longa hū̃.	One load is lost.
Ta pōma.	It is behind.
Hakeí igbe lo?	Which load is it?
Mehe kan̉a mia.	It is the 'chop' box (provision box).
Bi ndo̲i lo hū̃.	Your whisky (wine, any strong drink) is inside it.
Bukwé mu pu milo? (kpuko *indef. for* bed).	Where shall we put the bed?
Pu hindé na.	Put it there.

Ngeyé na fulo.	Untie that rope.
Bā tewe.	Do not cut it.
Gbe numu yira i li i ko̱wu ko̱koli.	Let one man go and find wood.
Sandi lo mi?	Where is Sandi?
I ya njehū.	He has gone to the water.
Gbe nu fere ti li ti wā nje.	Let two men go and fetch water.
Li bi nu lo̱lu tuli.	Go and call five men.
Nunga lọ̄le (lūle) bi soa?	How many men have you got?
Li bi ngengé ge atië bi wa.	Go show them their work and come.
Bi ke atië?	Have you shown them?
Ī, ngi ke atië.	Yes, I have shown them.
Mehe navọi i gbo̱yōa.	Subsistence money is finished.
Mehe gbī nya yeya (*or* nī yeya *for short*).	I have no food.
Wa ga bi pawa.	Come, I will pay you.
Tī wu pawani?	Have they not paid you?
Navọi ī nyandéni.	The money was not good, *i.e.* I did not get it correct.
Numu yira i tange huma pelima.	One man stole cassada in the road.
Ngi bijé lo a ye?	What is his name?
Gegbwa mia.	It is Gegbwa.
Ta lo mi?	Where is he?
Ta bē.	He is here.
I nyapọi yahumanga.	He stole from a woman.
Ngi wēhindeí ī nyandé.	His behaviour is not good.
Nga ngi navọi me lo.	I will stop his pay.
Gbēi na mu fonga Sekondi ga ngi gbe lo; *or*,	When we reach Sekondi I will dismiss him.
Gbēi na ma hite Sekondi ga ngi gbe lo.	Ditto.
Bi lemungo le.	I beg pardon.
Ngā yā pī (= pē = wēlē).	I will not do it again.
Ye, bā ngi gbe.	He says, Do not dismiss him.
Nga ye pe ho?	What shall I do then?
Ye, bi ngi dewe.	He says, Beat him.
Kurungo le.	All right.
Headman, li angië pēlē woma bi ngi ndewe pu.	Headman, take him behind the house and give him ten cuts.

I gbọyōa.	It is finished.
Ye bise kā.	He says, Thank you very much.
Pele ji fere ma li a igbo.	There are two roads; which shall we take?
Mu li a peli ji ke ta mia, mu li a ipekéji be ke ta mia.	Whichever we go by it is the same. (lit. We go by this road and it is one, we go by the other and it is one.)
Mu li a ngeyahũ we, nyandengo; mu li a gowohũ we, nyandengo.	If we go to the right it is good, if we go to the left it is good.
Mu yī jiama.	We were travelling all night.
Mu li a pelé na mu waila.	We go (back) by the road we came.
Jī a hije bē a li Chama jia lọ̄le?	How far is it to Chama? (lit. If he gets up here he goes Chama, how much walking?)
Bē ta Chama jia lọ̄le?	How far is it to Chama? (lit. Here and Chama, how much walking?)
Fọ̆ yira jia mia.	One day's journey.
Fọ̆ fere jia mia.	Two days' journey.
Bŏ gulama na? Ga li gi to.	What is the obstacle there? I am going to see.
Pele gbī na.	There is no road there.
Pote ngeja-hũ we.	Turn to the right.
Bi ya bi li a ngejahũ we.	As you go keep to the right.
Peli lagboungo.	The road is shut.
Bi wani pelé ji ngova?	Have you been this road before?
Njei i gula?	Does it rain?
Njei i wa.	The rain comes, *i.e.* is now beginning to fall.
Njei lo wama.	The rain is approaching.
Hũ ya doṅ ha.	There is a calm to-day.
Ligbili hengá ha.	Ditto.

V. Salutations and Kindred Phrases.

Bọ̄a? *Reply*, Bọ̄a.	How do you do?
Wọ̄a?	Ditto (*pl.*).
Bọ̄va.	Ditto.
Biana? *Reply*, Bọ̄a.	Ditto.

Bise.	Thank you. (Used also as a salutation.)
Wuse.	Ditto (*pl.*).
Bevá bi?	What is your news? (The person arriving says this.)
Bevá na?	What is your news? (The person sitting down inquires this of the comer.)
Bevá mbui?	What news down country?
Bevá mahũ?	What news up country?
Bevá piléma?	What news on the road?
Bevá bi weleí bu?	What news in your house?
Gbo wenga miaka?	What news (what has been done) yonder?
Gbo wenga bi wa be?	What has happened that you are here?
Bevá bi hijéma? (*or* hiyéma)	What is the news where you come from?
Hinda gbī dogboi hũ.	Nothing in the bush.
Ī nyamu gbī na.	Nothing bad there.
Hinda gbī na.	Nothing there.
Hinda gbī be.	Nothing here.
Ī nyamu gbī be.	Nothing bad here.
Bi kei lo na, bi njei lo na?	Are your father and mother well?
Tiana.	They are well.
Nya kei nya njei tiă na.	My father and mother are well.
(A)Mu ngenda hoe. (*Pl.* with A in front.)	We say good-bye.
Mu kpọkọ hoe, *or* Mu kpoko. (But the addition of *hoe* is better.)	We say good-night.
I ngenda vei lo mu we ke iya.	He said good-night to us and he went.
I ngenda vei lo mu we ē yā li.	He said good-night to us before he went.
Gi lima sina-oh.	I am going to-morrow.
Gi ya ngi feli tima.	I am going to say good-bye to them.
Gi ya ngi wa.	I go, I come (= I shall bẹ back shortly).
Bi vangíma.	You salute him.

I velia bima ?	Did he say good-bye to you ?
Gi ya mu yei.	I go to my country.
Wa bi gona.	Come, make your report.
Bi wa sina hoe.	Come to-morrow then.
Mu va hoe.	We say good-night.
Gĭ wai !	I have come !

VI. Saying, Talking, etc.

Ndē nya ma.	Tell me.
Dē ti ma.	Tell them.
Yo ndē bi ma ?	Who told you ?
Ye lo i ndeni bi ma ?	Ditto.
Dē ngi ma i wa.	Tell him to come.
I ndei lo ta wama.	He said he was coming.
De ngi ma i li kaka.	Tell him to go quickly.
Bā ndē numu gbī ma.	Do not tell anybody.
Bā lema njiei gi ndē bima.	Do not forget what I tell you.
De ti ma tā sore (*or* sore wē).	Tell them not to make a noise.
Njiéi ji ga ndē, bā gbia nya woma.	Do not repeat what I say.
Bē gbe ?	What do you say ?
Yē gbe ?	What does he say ?
I ye gbe bi ma ?	What did he say to you ?
Ngē sago (*or* sa'o).	I said, No !
Yē sao.	He says, No !
Ngī ye bia.	I am not talking to you.
Ngī yiama bia, *or* Ngī yema bia.	Ditto.
Bia ī le nga ye bima.	Ditto.
Gĭ bi yiama.	I am talking to you.
Ji le, ngā yema (pronounced Jī léngā yema).	I did not say this (= This is the wrong one).
Ngī yema ji.	I did not say this one.
Ngī ye ji ; ngī ye ji.	I did not this ; I did not say this, *i. e.* I said neither of these.
Ji fere le ngā yema.	I said neither of these.
Ngī ye (*or* yema) ji tabao ngī ye (*or* yema) ji.	I said neither this nor that.
Bā yepe.	Do not talk (*sing.*).
Wā yepe.	Do not talk (*pl.*).

Londo a njepe.	Stop talking.
Bi yepe botongo.	You talk too much.
Bi yepé le ngā ye ndōma.	I am not talking your 'palaver.'
Bē yepe nya lenga?	You will not talk with me?
Gbe yepe bi menī?	What talk did you hear?
Bi nde gọra.	You lie.
Ī nde gọlani.	He did not lie.
I ndé yia lénga.	He has lied.
Bia bi lelengo.	You lie.
Bi lele (pronounced almost *ler-le*).	You are wrong.
Bi leni.	You lied.
Bi Mende yiei mero? (= me lo).	Do you understand Mende?
Ga mero kru kru.	I understand a little.
Ba mero?	Do you hear, *or* understand?
Gĭ menia.	I heard.
Ngī menini.	I did not hear.
Bī meni?	Do you not understand?
A Mende yia (*or* yiei) me lo.	He understands Mende.
A Mende yia le lo.	He talks Mende.
Yia lele.	Speak slowly.
Hũge ange panda.	Tell me all about it.
Ti gbia bi woma.	They talk behind your back.
Musa luli i wa.	Call Musa.

VII. Buying and Selling.

Gbe jongo mia?	How much is this?
Gbe jongo lo a ji?	Ditto.
Nyé ji gbwe jongo?	How much is this fish?
Te yalui gbe jongo shili yera va?	How many eggs for one shilling?
Te yalui yira gbe jongo?	How much for one egg?
Penny yira.	One penny.
Kpele shili' yira (va).	All for one shilling.
Tia bā gbango.	They are dear.
Ji bā gbango.	This is dear.
Bā ī gbani.	They are not dear.

Gbwe jongo mia ba nya boya la?	How many will you throw in?
Bī majiai panda.	You cheat me (you did not sell correctly).
Gē bi humani.	I have not cheated you.
Maye, gē ngeyá.	Reduce it, or I do not buy.
Gi mayenga ngeya 3*d*.	I lower it 3*d*.
Gi kurua.	I accept.
Gī kuruni. Gē luma.	I do not accept.
Bise ; Di la ; Ngēngeyama.	Thank you; take it away ; I am not buying.
Kuléji ī nyandeni.	This cloth is not good.
Kuléji nyaningo le ; ngē ngeya.	This cloth is spoilt ; I will not buy it.
Ji kpele ji shili yira.	All these are one shilling.
Navọ̄i kulongo.	The money is short.
Navọ̄i gbotongo le, ji mū lila.	The price is too much, we do not take it.
Ba kula majiá lo?	Do you sell cloth?
Ga majiá lo.	I sell it.
Ngī majiáma.	I am not selling.
Hāi ji ī ngeya.	This thing I have not got.
Li miando ta na.	Go over there, it is there.

VIII. Give (*Fe* and *Go*).

Fembe, *or* Fe'be.	Give (it) to me.
Fe.	Give (me).
Gbe lo wa fembe?	What will you (*pl.*) give me?
Bo ba fembe?	What will you (*sing.*) give me?
Gi fe ngi ye.	I give it to him.
Hani ji bumbu bi fe ngi'e.	Take this thing and give it to him.
Gi fe bē (= bi we).	I give it to you.
I ngi ndei ve.	He gave him his share.
I nde, ye, ti fe ngi we.	He says they must give it to him.
Ti mehe ve lo wu ye?	Have they given you food?
Bi nya kulé fembe.	Give me my cloth.
Kpandé ve.	Give me the gun.
Fe nya we.	Give it to me.
Ta lo nga fe bi we.	That I give you.

I feni mu we.	He gave to us.
Nya go a njei gi gbo̱le.	Give me water to drink.
Nya go a ngurī.	Give me the stick.
Nga wu go a hege.	I give you soap.
Gi bi goi lo.	I have given it you.
Gi bi goi lo a three pensi.	I have given you 3*d*.
I ti goa mehei (= I ti goa a mehei).	He gave them food.
Sina ga bi go lo a hale.	To-morrow I will give you medicine.
Ngi go a kole.	Give him the book.
Sandi go a kole.	Give Sandi the book.
Nya go (a) jihũ.	Give me this.

NOTE.—If 'go' is rendered 'present with' the construction is more easily understood.

IX. GOING.

NOTE.—The verb 'to go' is *li*, past tense *ya*. *Ya* is, however, frequently used with a present meaning.

Bă li ba wa-oh?	Are you coming back?
Ī gu a lila.	He is unable to go.
Ī gu ĭ li.	He cannot go.
Nga gu lo gi li?	I shall be able to go?
Pessima a gu lo i li.	Pessima will be able to go.
Pessima i ya yī ma.	Pessima has gone to sleep.
Pessima i ya ngi yīmi.	Pessima has gone to his sleeping-place.
Nya longo nga (*or* ngi) li.	I want to go.
Migbe (*or* migbe lo) ba li?	When do you go?
Gi ya ngi la.	I am going to lie down.
Gī ko̱ mi e (*for* i) ya nā.	I do not know where he has gone now.
Gī ko̱ mi mia i ya nā.	Ditto.
Mi lo bi li na bengeme?	Where did you go yesterday?
Li bi wa njéi.	Go fetch water.
A mu li pe bu.	Let us go home.
Hiye mu li.	Get up, let us go.
Bia bi liṃa sange?	Are you going just now?
Bī limá le?	You are not going yet?

Ngī limá le.	I am not going yet.
Ngĭ ya yīma.	I am going to sleep.
Li bi wa kolĕ.	Go bring the letters.
Bia bi luma bi li va sange?	Are you willing to go now?
Bā li na.	Do not go there.
Bā li 'ngwango (hũguhango).	Do not go far.
Gī' i la (= Gi li la).	I go away, *or* take it away.
Mu li dogboi hũ.	We go into the bush.
Bi ya mi ge lo fele gē bi lo?	Where have you been these last two days that I have not seen you?
Bi ya ge mi lo fele gē bi lo?	Ditto.
Bī yā li le?	Have you not gone yet?
Gi ya Takwa bengeme.	I went to Tarkwa yesterday.
Ngī yā li na.	I have never been there. (lit. Not been there.)
Gi ya na yira.	I went there once.
I ya hũ (*or* i foa).	It has gone in (as of a nail).
Gi ya jijiama.	I am going for a walk.
Li pe bu.	Go home.
Mu li a pelé na?	Do we go that road?
Mu li a mbēle (= mbe wele).	We go this road.
Dē ngĭ ma i li kaka.	Tell him to go quick.
I yá.	He has gone.
Ī lini.	He has not gone.
Ti gbi ti ya.	They have all gone.
A li-oh.	Go (*pl.*).
Bi lima mi?	Where are you going?
Ba li mi?	Ditto.
Bi li mi?	Where did you go?
Ba li lo, bē li?	Will you go? *or* Will you not go?
Mi lo ti ya nā?	Where have they gone now?
Mi lo ba li na?	Where are you going now?
Wuseni i ya kole gama.	Wuseni has gone for letters.
Gi ya kpande wīme (*for* wilima, indefinite form).	I am going shooting.
I ya kpande wīme.	He has gone shooting.
A mu li mu kpande wili.	Let us go and shoot.

Gī ngi lima gọ.	I do not know where he has gone.
Jī bi male e gbia e li mi lo? (*e* = *i*, he).	When you found (lit. I met) he had gone out, where had he gone?
Ngi male i gbia.	I found he had gone out.
Ti ya yima.	They have gone to sleep.
Ti ya ti yimi.	They have gone to their sleeping-place.
Ye, bi li.	He says, Go.
Li bi wa káká.	Go, and come back quickly.
Ngi ya pebu.	I go home.
Bi ya na yira?	Have you ever been there before?
Bi ya na wo ngova?	Ditto.
A mu li tei hũ.	Let us go home. (lit. Let us go back into the town.)
I ya miaka (we).	He has gone yonder.
I yá poron.	He has gone far away.
I yá muama.	He has gone to bathe.
I yá kpoyeí ya.	It has gone over the sea.
Ti ya tuwo.	They have gone on in front.
Li bi nwoni gama gbe.	Go and look for the bird.
Li mehei gama, bi wala, mu me.	Go for food, bring it, so that we may eat.
Li bi pēlḗ gama gbe.	Go and look at the house.
Li bi wala kia jina.	Go fetch one like this.
Li bi kokoï.	Go and find it.
Li bi na gbe.	Go and look there.
A dē mu li.	Pass on, we are going.
Ngi ya ngi meheí me.	I go to eat.
Nū yera ē li?	Is one man not going?
Sangi mia ti yá.	They have just gone.
Bia wa Wuseni a li mia.	You and Wuseni go yonder.
Wa tieni a li mia.	You and they go yonder.
	(For other similar examples, see under Pronouns.)
Ngi yeto bingi ga li lo dogboi hũ.	I intended yesterday going to the bush.
Mi yaka i ya na?	Which direction has he gone?
Kea bi ya lo?	I suppose you are going now?
Bī ya miando, bi wa, bi ji wē.	Before you go there come and do this.

Li ngi gama.	Go for him.
A mu li gengemi.	Let us go to work.
Mu ya gengeme.	Ditto.
A mu li genge gami.	Ditto.
Gi ya gengeme, *or* gengema.	I am going to work.
Ngia li?	Shall I go?
Bia li, bia bā li?	Do you go, or do you not go?
Lahai i li lo gbĭ gengema?	Did Lahai go to work yesterday?

X. Tewe, Dewe, Lewe, Te, Le = Cut, Surpass. Ndewe, Dewe, Lewe = Beat, etc.

Kọwui dewe.	Cut wood.
Malewe.	Cut off.
Tetewe.	Cut in pieces.
Tētē a ngera ngera.	Cut it in small pieces.
Tewe botongo.	Cut plenty.
I njiei dewēa (*or* dewīa).	He settled the matter.
Mbaké lewe.	Play music.
Ndī lewe.	To be angry.
Ngi lī dewea.	He is angry.
Ngē dema.	I am not passing.
Fọ̄ dewengoi.	Last year.
A de mu li.	Pass on, we are going.
Mu de a ngiyehũ.	Let us pass over the hill.
De a mia we.	Pass round that way.
Dewe kaka wekei ma.	Pass to the other side.
A mu njei dewe.	Let us cross the water.
Pele male.	Cross the road.
I dewia tugo (*or* lugo).	He passed on in front.
Njei i nya madewéa.	The rain detained me.
Ngọ̄i dewe i wa.	Send word for him to come.
Numu yira tewe nya gama.	Send me one man.
Ngi nemahũ lengo.	He is clever.
I dewéa ngi ma ji (*or* a ji).	He surpassed him in this.
I dewéa ngi ma ji hũ.	Ditto.
Kọ̄li ye, nga wime gi lō dopé ma.	The snail said, 'I can run faster than the deer.'
Fọ̄ neni ma mbe le lo.	Next year we will clear here.
Ke mahei na fọ̄ i lewe nani i gbate gboṅ.	And that king for over four years increased in wealth.

I lō i ngi lema.	He left off beating him.
Nde yira.	One cut (with a whip).
Wa ga bi le pu.	Come, I will give you ten cuts.
Gbe a ndewela.	Stop beating.
I yunga lenga a nasia gbele.	He boasted over all of them.

XI. Expressions relating to *Lī* = Heart.

Nya lī gbī hindọi ma.	I do not care for the man; I have no confidence in the man.
Nya lī lo bima.	My heart is with you, *i. e.* I trust you.
Bi lī lo mi?	Where is your heart?
Ngi lī nyania.	His heart is spoiled, *i.e.* broken-hearted.
Nya lī leingo ngi ma.	I am pleased with him.
Ngi lī dewía (dewea).	He is angry.
Ngi lī i lewé nyoko gbī.	He was exceedingly angry.
Bi lī i leli.	Be of good cheer.
Numui na a hinda hou lī ma.	That man is patient.
Ma ngi lī leī lo.	We will soothe him.
Ngi lī heléa.	He was troubled.
Hinga ti lī nyamungo le.	Men whose hearts are evil.
Bi lī yekpengo le?	Is your heart good.
Ngi lī miningo yele kpi.	His heart was very heavy.
Ngi lī lengo wa.	He was very angry.

XII. Gu = Can, Be Able.

Gbe yenge mia ba guma?	What kind of work can you do?
Ī gu a li lá	He is unable to go.
Nga gu lo gi li.	I shall be able to go.
Pessima a gu lo i li.	Pessima will be able to go.
Ba gu bi ji wē?	Can you do this?
Ī gu i li.	He cannot go.
Ba gu bi kakéi ji le?	Can you climb this wall?
Ngē ngi do be.	I cannot see him here.

Bē gu na ma.	Can you not do that.
Ē guma.	He cannot (do it).
Ngi gu nga pe lo.	I can do it.
Ngē gu nga pe.	I cannot do it.
Ngē pē.	Ditto.
Tī guni a njia gbi lela.	They could not say a word.
Ba gu ba yengema?	Can you work?

XIII. Want, Like, etc.

Lọ̄.

Nya longo a mehe.	I want food.
Ngi longo a mehe.	He wants food.
Ngī lọni a hani gbi.	I do not want anything.
Gbo bi longwola (=longola)?	What do you want?
Nya longo a numu yira hakeí ji va.	I want a man for this load.
Nya longo a bië.	I want you, *or* I like you.
Ngī loni a bië.	I do not want you, *or* I do not like you.
Bi longo ange?	Do you like me?
Bi longo a bi navọ̄i?	Do you want your money?
Nya longo a njei ngi bole.	I want water to drink.
Ngī loni á ná.	I do not like that, *or* him.
Ngī loi la.	I do not like it.
Gbo bi lọ̄i la? (Not so common as Gbo bi longwola?)	What do you want?
Gbeva ī loni?	Why did he not want to?
Ngi mbāi ji ta ta ti longoma.	He and his friend were much attached to each other.
Bī lọ̄ni bi li?	Will you not go?
Nya dọ̄longo a bië.	I dislike you.
Ti lọ̄lọ̄ a ngie nu gbate va.	They hated him because he was a rich man.
Nī 'ongwa mehe (is short for *Nya longo a mehe*).	I want food.

Ma = in need of.

Nja gboli māi lo nyama.	I want water to drink.
Hani jisia mani lo wuma.	You covet these things.
Nji mani lo ngima.	He is in want of sleep.

XIV. See, Look, etc. = To, Gbe.

Bi tonga? (pronounced *bit-tonga*).	Have you seen (it)?
Gi tonga.	I have seen (it), *or* found (it).
Ngī toni.	I did not see (it).
Ngī ya toi.	I have not seen (it).
Gī ngi loi.	I have not seen him.
Bi ngi loi lo?	Have you seen him?
Bi Yamba loi lo?	Have you seen Yamba?
Ī ngi doni.	He did not see him.
Wa bi to va.	Come and see.
Bi to?	Do you see it?
Bi toa?	Did you see it?
Sina ma to.	We shall see to-morrow.
Ngē ngi do be.	I cannot see it here.
Na gbē.	Look, then.
Li bi na gbē.	Go and look there.
Li bi pebu gbē.	Go and look in the house.
Li bi pele gama gbē.	Go and look at the house.

XV. To Have.

Kulé lo nya yeya (*nī 'yeya* for short).	I have the cloth.
Ta nī 'yeya.	I have it.
Ta bi yeya, *or* Ta bēya.	You have it.
Ī nī 'yeya.	I have it not.
Mbogbé lo Wuseni yeya.	Wuseni has the cutlass.
Ta lo Wuseni yeya.	Wuseni has it.
Numui na nyaha lo ngi yeya.	That man has a wife.
Ī ngi yeya.	He hasn't it.
Ī navoi ngeya.	He has not the money.
Ha kpande gbī nya yeya.	To-day I have not gun.
Nu lọle mia ti bi yeya?	How many men have you got
Ngi lei fere.	It has two names.
Njia nya ma.	I have a palaver

XVI. Sickness.

Ngi goihũ a lewe (*or* a gbīa).	He has diarrhœa.
Ngi goihũ hōnga.	He is constipated.
Ngi lima lema.	He is retching.
Ngi lī lo gbalema.	His heart hurts.
Ko̱le i nya houa.	I have caught cold.
Kō̱tī nya nwona nya gowé ma.	The stone cut my foot.
Buli lo nyama.	I have a guinea worm (*or* other worm).
Bi wō̱li hũ bondango.	You are deaf.
Nya go̱wé vengo.	My foot is swollen.
Ngi higbéa wokpo.	I have been sick some time.
Nya higbengo le.	I am sick.
Nya higbengo le ge.	I was sick the other day.
Gbwamé na yilī.	Tie up that sore.
Halé na jia lu ma.	Rub that medicine over your body.
Halé ji gbole.	Swallow this medicine.
Bi nei gbīa.	Put out your tongue.
Mi mia a gbale bi ma?	Where does it hurt?
I gbalea gbō̱tongo.	It hurt very much.
Nya mavulango le.	I have fever.
Nya lũi gbandingo.	My body is hot.
Blanketi wē bi ma.	Cover yourself with the blanket.
Fūfū gbandi wē bi gowé ma.	Put a hot poultice on your leg.
Ga mbera (*or* tewe) gi gbīa.	I will cut and pull it out.
Na vōfoeṅ.	Suck it.
Na bono.	Suck it.
Li bi njei gbandi bā yā bi gowé gama wua.	Boil the water before you wash (the wound on) your leg.
Ba bawo lo sina.	You will be better to-morrow.

PART II

GRAMMAR

CHAPTER I

GENERAL REMARKS, PRONUNCIATION, EUPHONY, CHANGES, ETC.

i. Structure of Words.

A noticeable feature of the language is the readiness with which words are built up from simple root forms, (i) by reduplication, (ii) by the addition of other words, or (iii) by the addition of one or more prepositions either as a prefix or suffix.

Example of—

(i) *Mbu*, under; *mbumbu*, carry.
(ii) *Kpande*, gun; *wili*, throw, or shoot; *moi*, suffix of the agent; *kpandewilimoi*, shooter, or hunter.
(iii) *Ma*, on; *hũ*, in; *guhango*, high; *mahũguhango*, pronounced almost *mangwango*, far; *lọ̄*, leave; *hũ*, in; *lọ̄hũ*, lose.

As opposed to this building up is the tendency to cut out, (i) vowels, (ii) syllables, especially *le*, (iii) consonants, especially *l*.

Example of—

(i) *Wā ko̲lé* for *wa a ko̲lé*, bring the book.
(ii) *Wē* for *wēlē*, house.
(iii) *Ngaui* for *ngalui*, month, egg, moon.

ii. Absence of Meaning to Root Forms.

A monosyllabic word expressed by itself rarely conveys a clear meaning. This can only be ascertained from the context; and even a word of two syllables a Mende usually fails to understand if it be put before him without any hint of what it may possibly mean. The only words he is at all likely to recognize are the names of animals, material objects, etc. In every case the word inquired about must, if a substantive, and used without qualification, be put to him in the definite form; and similarly in his reply the definite form will be used. A word is much less distinct in the definite form; and for this reason, and owing to the numerous guises in which words appear, as will be seen later, the language is rendered one of considerable difficulty to Europeans.

iii. Pronunciation—General.

Mende having no literature of its own has been reduced to writing on the basis of the Royal Geographical Society's rules for spelling unwritten languages. The limitations of those rules, however, make an accurate expression of the sound of many words a matter of difficulty; and as, especially with regard to the vowels, a closer approximation than that provided is required, various marks are usually employed to enable words when written to be more readily recognized. The accent is on the penultimate syllable; but when a substantive is put into the definite form singular, it is moved to the last syllable. The very few exceptions are specially marked in this book.

iv. Pronunciation of Consonants.

The consonants call for no special remarks, except that most Mendes when *kp* or *gb* are followed by *i* or *e* insert a *w*, as *gbi* or *gbwi*, all; *kpele* (*kpere*), *kpwele* (*kpwere*), all. The *w* will, however, not be written, except in a few sentences in this book where its insertion will assist the beginner. With *a* this practice is rarer.

ṅ = *ng* is used when the *g* sound is not carried on to the succeeding vowel, as, *káṅa*, box = *kang-a*, not *kan-ga*.

The difference between *l* and *r* is very slight, some words preferring the *l* sound, others the *r* sound. In those words, however, in which *l* is the result of the softening of other consonants as *t*, *d*, *nd*, the distinctive *l* sound is properly retained, as *ndawo*, or *lawo*, to open. Even to this, though, there are exceptions, and the *r* sound is heard, as in *tǭli*, call, which becomes *dǭli*, *lǭli*, *ruri*.

The beginner will often hear what he may take to be a word—*sīati*. This is, however, no word at all, but the last syllable, *sia*, of a noun in the definite form plural, followed by the necessary pronoun *ti*, they. For example, *nwonisia ti ya*, the birds have gone, is pronounced *nwoni siati ya*. Other words are, of course, as in all languages, similarly broken in being spoken.

v. Pronunciation of Vowels.

The pronunciation of the vowels *a*, *i*, *u* call for no special mention.

e has varying values, which are not easily indicated by marks. A general idea of its pronunciation can generally be obtained from its combination with the other letters in the word; but its precise rendering, which is not invariably uniform, can only be obtained by ear.

The *o* sounds are as follows :—

o = the English *o*, either short as in *dog*, or long as in *oh*.

ǫ = *aw*.

ǭ = *o* approximating to *u*.

The difference between *ǫ* and *ǭ* should be very carefully noticed, especially when taking words from a vocabulary, or many errors in speaking may be made. Compare *ndǫmé*, the ground, pronounced *ndawmé*, and *ndǭmé*, the shirt, pronounced *ndoomé*.

Only vowels that it is necessary or important should be long are so marked, but in Part I of this book the short mark has been occasionally placed over vowels in order to draw the beginner's attention to the necessity for their being pronounced short. ˜ denotes a nasal sound.

Modification of vowels is frequent in speaking, but in writing the language it is desirable, if possible, to keep to the proper vowel. *ē* frequently changes into *i* when owing to a syllable being added the accent is moved towards the newly-added

4

syllable. *Malē*, meet, in the past tense is pronounced *malī́a* instead of *malḗa*. Vowels are also very commonly subject to change to fall in with the general run of vowels in the sentence. *i* becomes almost *a* or *o*; *e* becomes *i*, etc. As *dengăma*, tell him, for *de ngĭ ma*. In some parts of the country *u* takes the place of *i* in some words, as *gbua* for *gbia*, pull out.

The diphthongs approximate as written.

All words except some adverbs end in a vowel. The exceptions mentioned end in *ng*.

vi. Contractions.

Contractions and the elimination of consonants and vowels are frequent, and are a contributing cause to the difficulty a European has in understanding what is said.

a,	wā ko̱lé	*for* wa a ko̱lé, bring the book.
i,	tamoi ya	*for* tamoi i ya, the man went.
g,	sao	*for* sago, no.
h,	nyānga	*for* nyahanga, women.
l,	kpāe	*for* kpāle, farm.
	ngau	*for* ngalu, moon, egg.
	pē	*for* pele, house.
	wē	*for* wele, house.
	yakpe	*for* yelakpe, only.
	gbeanga	*for* gbelanga, near.
r,	kā	*for* kara, teach.
w,	dē	*for* dewe, cut.
ya,	bēka	*for* bēyaka, this side.

w and *y* are both frequently dropped when standing between vowels.

vii. Changes of Consonants.

Changes of consonants are a great source of difficulty to foreigners learning Mende. Presented under several forms it is by no means easy to recognize a word, especially a monosyllabic one. The changes are made to suit euphony from the native point of view. The hard sound occurs generally at the beginning of a sentence, but when the second syllable does not admit of softening the first must be softened.

Pronouns, except the first personal pronoun, do not admit of softening. As examples of the difficulty in recognizing words under this process, *sọle* or *jore*, noise, and *tuwo*, *lugo*, before, may be quoted.

Examples.

F into *v*.

Fe, give.	Fembe, give me.
	Kpandé ve, give me the gun.

G into *w*.

Hege *or* hewe, soap.
Tuwo, tugo, luwo, lugo, before.

K into *g*.

Ke, show.	Ke a tië, show them.
	Bi na ge ange, show me that.
Kākā, side.	Kākā wekeí ma, the other side.
	Wa mu gākeí ma, come to our side.

K into *w*.

Kulongo, wulongo, little.

K into *y*.

Kākā, side.	Bē kā, this side.
	Mi yākā? which side?

L into *r*.

Kei a bi lọli ma, master calls you.
Kei a bi ruri ma, ditto.
Mia lo, it is yonder.
Mia ro, ditto.
Bi me lo? did you hear?
Bi me ro? ditto.

The auxiliary, which will always be found written *lo*, is generally pronounced *ro*. An exception is in the idiom *lo a*, where the *l* sound predominates.

Ngenda lo a ji, this is his. (lit. His share is this, nge = ngi.)

P into *w*.

Pīme, run. — Li a pīme! run! (lit. Go with running.)
A mu wīme, let us run.

Pele, house. — Pē bu, in the house.
Massa wē lo a ji, this is master's house.

Pele, do. — Dengima ā pele, tell him not to do it.
Li bi ngenge wili, go and work.

Pēka, other. — Kākā wekeí ma, on the other side.
Wā pēkeí, bring the other.

P into *y*.

Pēka, other. — Kākā yekeí ma, on the other side.

P into *b*, rare.

Pọwé, bọwé, the flower.

S into *j*.

Jole, noise, shout. — Wā jo̱re, do not shout.
Dondo a so̱le, stop that noise.

Joso, plug, load. — Kpandé joso, load the gun.
Ngi sosoi lo, I have loaded it.

S into *y*, rare.

Susungo, jusungo, yusungo, deep.

T into *d*, *l*, *r*.

Tewe, cut, pass, etc. — Tewe! cut it!
Bi dewea? did you cut it?
Ngī leweni, I did not cut it.

Tọ̄li, call. — Li bi ngi tọ̄li, go, call him.
Ke a bi ruri ma (lọ̄lima), master is calling you.
Tugo, tuwo, lugo, in front.

W into *v*.

Tewe, pass. — I dewéa, he passed.
I devīa, ditto.

Wili (pili), throw, shoot. A mu li kpande wīme (wilime, *def. form of* wilima), let us go and shoot.
A mu li kpande vīme, let us go and shoot.

Mb into *b* or *w*.

Mbumbu, lift. Mbumbu, pick it up, *or* take it.
A mu bumbu, let us lift it.
Tī wumbuni, they did not take it.

Nd into *d* or *l*.

Ndē, say. I ndēa nyama, he told me.
Dē ngi ma, tell him.
Gbo ĭ lēa bima? what did he say to you?

Nda, lay. Nda! lay it down.
La ndia, put it in the middle.

Ndia, middle. Hei ndende liei, sit in the middle of the boat.

Ndowe lave, fill the hole.

Ng into *w*.

Only when followed by *o* or *u*.

Ngōva, old. Ngōvango le, it is old.
Iwōvangoi, the old one.

Ng into *y*.

Only when followed by *a*, *e*, or *i*.

Yela, one. Ngera ngera, one by one.
Nu yīra, one person.

Ngalu, egg, month. Ngaui ji, this month.
Te-yalui, fowl's egg.

Ng into *g*.

Ngi, I. Ngī ya li na, I have not been there.
Gī ngi loi, I have not seen it.

Nj into *y*.

Njī, sleep. Ta njī hũ, he is asleep.

Njī, sleep.	Ti ya ti yīmi, they have gone to their sleeping-place, *i. e.* to sleep. *or*, Ti ya yīma, they have gone to sleep.
	Kp into *gb.*
Kpo̱yō, finish.	Ī ya kpo̱yōai, it is not finished. Nu yira gbo̱yongo, one man finished, *i. e.* twenty.
	Kp or *gb* into *b* or *w.*
Kpọ̄tọ, many, much.	Njei lo na bọ̄tongo, there is a lot of water there. Njei wọ̄tọngo, the water is much, *or* deep. Gbọ̄tongo ! plenty ! enough ! Ī yā kpọ̄tọ na, there is not much there.
Kpiti, grass, etc.	Biti gbia, pull up the weeds.
	Kp or *gb* into *y.*
Kpate, make.	A mu ji gbate, let us mend this. I mani yate hũguhango, he made a trap far away.

viii. Changes of Vowels.

The principal change in the vowels is when a substantive is put in the definite form. This is effected by adding *i*, meaning *he*, to the indefinite form. The resulting combination produces a variety of changes difficult to learn. The accent is shifted to the last syllable.

Examples.

Indefinite termination.	Combination.	Definite termination. How pronounced and written.	
ă,	ăi,	é,	Goma, gomé, crow.
{ ă,	ăi,	eí,	Nyaha, nyaheí, woman.
{ ā,	āi,	(as in *hay*)	Kākā, kākeí, side.
ā,	āi,	ā́i, (as in *why*)	Wā, wā́i, big.

Indefinite termination.	Combination.	Definite termination. How pronounced and written.	
ĕ,	ĕi,	é,	Pene, pené, ringworm.
ĕ,	ĕi,	eí, (as in *hay*)	Ke, keí, father.
ē,	ēi,	ḗ,	Pēlē, pēlḗ, house.
ĭ,	ii,	ī́, (as in *bee*)	Lọ̄li, lọ̄lī́, dance.
ī,	ii,	ī́,	Ngalī, ngalī́, thorn.
ŏ,	oi,	é *or* í,	Go̱lo, golé (golī́), book.
ō,	oi,	ṓï,	Méndemo, Méndemṓï, Mendeman.
o̱,	o̱i,	o̱í, (as in *boy*)	Dogbo, dogboí, bush.
ọ̄,	ọ̄i,	ī́,	Fọ̄lọ̄, fọ̄lī́, sun.
ọ̄,	ọ̄i,	uí, (almost *wī*)	Nyapọ̄, nyapuí, girl.
ọ̄,	ọ̄i,	ọ̄ï,	Sasalọ̄, sasalọ̄ï, a partridge
ŭ,	ŭi,	ŭï,	Ngalu, ngalŭï, egg, moon.
u,	ui,	ī,	Ko̱tu, ko̱tí, stone.
ū,	ūi,	úi, (almost *wī*)	Tutu, tutuí, a swamp bird, a messenger.

ix. Words Much Alike.

The following list includes a few nouns that in their definite form are much alike, as well as some other similar words.

ngarī́,	thorn.
ngaré,	a coarse grass.
ngalé,	mat.
kulé, gulé,	cloth.
ko̱lé, go̱lé,	book.
go̱lī́,	scissors.
ko̱lī́,	iron.
ko̱lé, go̱lé,	cold, clean.
golé,	weeping.
gọ̄lé,	buy a wife.
ko̱lí,	search.
ko̱lé, go̱lé,	divide.
ko̱lé,	barrel.
ko̱lī́,	leopard.

kulī́,	small.
kọ̄lī́,	snail.
kọ̄lī,	lizard.
gulī́,	tree.
kené,	elderly person.
kenī́,	bamboo.
wulī́,	tree.
wulī́,	oil.
wulī́,	small.
ndọ̄pé,	deer.
ndọ̄puí,	child.
ndọ̄ndé,	pig.
ndo̱ndoí,	millipede.
ndọ̄ndī́,	silence.

Also :

lo,	be.
lo,	see.
lọ̄,	send.
lọ̄,	like (*verb*).
lọ̄,	leave.
lo̱,	day.
lo̱i,	day, rum.
lọ̄i,	son.
lo̱é,	country.
lọ̄li,	call.
lọ̄le ?	how many ?
ngera,	one.
ngera,	sweep.
nyī,	bite.
yī,	sleep.
la,	lay.
la,	name.

And many others.

CHAPTER II

SUBSTANTIVES

i. Definite and Indefinite Forms.

There is no definite or indefinite article in Mende. Its place is taken by *i*, he, which is added to the indefinite form of the word. The pronunciation of the resulting combination of vowels has already been explained, see Chapter I, viii.

The indefinite form is used—

(i) When an indefinite meaning is clearly indicated, as *kia gombu na*, like fire.

(ii) In negative sentences, as *numu gbī na*, nobody is there; *Gī numu loi*, I saw nobody.

(iii) When followed by an adjective. The adjective then takes the definite form. *Hindọ̄ wōvei*, the old man.

(iv) When followed by a numeral adjective, as *tamo yira*, one man, or a certain man; *numu lo̱lu*, or *nu lo̱lu*, five persons.

(v) Vocative case, as *Ngewo!* God!

The definite form is used—

(i) When in English the article *the* is used, as *ngeyeī lo mi?* where is the rope?

(ii) When the word is used independently as in answer to a question, as *Gbo bi longola? Mbogbé*. What do you want? The cutlass.

(iii) After a possessive pronoun, as *nya kulé*, my cloth.

(iv) When followed by a demonstrative pronoun, as *dakpalọ̄i ji*, this young man.

(v) Vocative case, as *ndakpeī!* young man! It will be seen that for the vocative case both indefinite and definite forms are used.

There are a few words which are not invariably put into the definite form, the reason for using the indefinite form being probably euphony. *Kaña*, box, is usually heard only in the one form; and substantives having *hū* as an affix may remain unchanged, or the *i* indicating the definite may be added to the first component word, or be put at the end, as *gohũ, goihũ, gohui*, belly. Sometimes it is immaterial whether the indefinite or the definite form be used, as *hei ndia*, or *hei ndiei*, sit in the middle. Occasionally the indefinite is used when the definite is clearly indicated, or *vice versâ*. The reason may be euphony or carelessness.

ii. Gender.

There is no gender to nouns, adjectives, or any other part of speech.

For human beings different words are used to express the sex, as—

hindọi (*def.*), man. nyaheí (*def.*), woman.

For further examples see Vocabulary of Relationships, etc., Part III, vii.

To the names of animals the words *hina, hinei*, male ; *ha, hei*, female, are added, as—

nika hinei (*def.*), bull. te hinei (*def.*), cock.
nika hei (*def.*), cow. te hei (*def.*), hen.
nika ha wãí (*def.*), the big cow.

iii. Number.

The indefinite plural is formed by adding *nga*, *a* or *ni* to the indefinite form singular.

The definite plural is formed by adding *sia* to the definite form singular, and also more rarely by adding *sia* to the indefinite form plural, *nga*, the *a* being modified under the rules for using the definite.

Examples.

Singular.		Plural.		English
Indefinite.	Definite.	Indefinite.	Definite.	
Maha	maheí	mahaa *or* mahā	maheísia	king.
		mahanga *or* mānga	mahangéisia	

Singular.		Plural.		English.
Indefinite.	Definite.	Indefinite.	Definite.	
Nyaha	nyaheí	nyahaa	nyaheísia	woman.
		nyahanga	nyahangeísia	
		or		
		nyānga		
Nwoni	ṅwonī́	nwonīa	ṅwonísia	bird.
		ṅwoninga	nwoningeísia	
Pupu	pupuí	pupua	pupuísia	ant.
		pupunga	pupungeísia	
		Irregular.		
Mendemo	Mendemoí	Mendébela (b'ra)	Mendebeleísia	Mende-man.
		Mendinga		
Ngengemo	ngengemoi	ngengeb'ra (this form is often used for the definite)	ngengebeleísia	labourer.
Numu *or* nu	numúi	nunga	nungeísia	person.
Higbemo	higbemoí	higbebera	higbebeleisia	sickman.
		higbenga	higbengeisia	
	ihigbengói		ihigbe'goisia	the sick one.
Hindo	hindọi	hinga	hingeisia	man.

The termination *ni* added to the indefinite singular seems to be employed to give a collective sense. Some Mendes do not appear to know it.

iv. Case.

There are no case inflections. The nominative, vocative and accusative cases are the simple word with no adjunct. The dative and ablative are rendered by the aid of prepositions, the various uses of which are given in their proper place. After verbs of motion, though, the name of the place is stated without a preposition, as *i ya Bonth*, he has gone to Bonthe.

The genitive case is expressed by placing the possessing noun first, both being in the definite form, as *mahei pelei*, the king's house; or by inserting a possessive pronoun between the two nouns, as *mahei ngi pelei*, the king his house.

v. Compound Nouns.

Compound nouns are formed by placing the qualifying noun first in the indefinite form.

Examples.

Indefinite.	Definite.	English.
Pelenda	pelendeí	doorway.
Ngelegohũ	ngelegohũ	heaven.
Njala	njalei	landing-place.
Fuhaninga (hani, thing)	fuhanīsia	insects.
Wehinda	wehindei	conduct.
	Diminutives.	
Nika lọ̄	nika lọ̄i	calf.
Te lọ̄	te lọ̄i	chicken.

vi. Substantives formed by Addition of Suffixes to other Parts of Speech.

Numerous substantives are formed by the addition of prefixes or suffixes to other parts of speech.

Prefix i.
Suffixes ge, hũ, la, ma, mo, nyo, ya.

All suffixes are added to the indefinite form.

Uses.

i. This prefix is added to adjectives in the definite form, and forms a substantive which only appears in the definite form.

It is also added to abstract nouns, serving to emphasize their meaning, and forming a sort of superlative.

Examples.

(i) ifelegei, the second; *from* fele, two.
ipekeisia, the others; *from* peka, other.
ihigbengoi, the sick one; *from* higbe, sick.

(ii) ikelemei, the end; *from* kelema, kelemei, end (*verb*, kele).
itātomei, the beginning; *from* tātoma, tātomei, beginning (*verb*, tato).
imahui, the top; *from* mahũ, top (*prep.* mahũ).
ingui, the head; *from* ngũ, ngũi, head.

Ge or *gi*, a rare suffix to form abstract nouns.

mamage, foolishness; *from* mamu, foolish.
nyandegi, beauty; *from* nyande, fine.

Added to numerals, and with the prefix *i*, it forms a series of ordinal words, as

isawagei, the third; *from* sawa, three.
ikelemagei, the last; *from* kelema, end.

This must not be confused with *ga*, definite *gei*, meaning husk, etc.; as

nwoni gei, oyster-shell. *kali gei*, empty snake-skin.

Hũ, literally *inside*, is used to emphasize words, chiefly those of one syllable, as *ta*, *tahũ*, town (but *teí hũ*, in the town); *nja* or *nje*, *njehũ*, water (but *njeí hũ*, in the water). The indefinite form only is used.

La is added to the simple form of the verb to form a verbal noun. It becomes *lei* in the definite form. See under Verbs.

Ma is added to the simple form of the verb to indicate place, as

njī, sleep; *njīma*, *njīmeí*, sleeping-place.
la, lie down; *lama*, *lameí*, lying down or sleeping-place.
kele, end; *kelema*, *kelemeí*, end.

Mo is added to adjectives or verbs to indicate agent, as

ngenge, work; *ngengemo*, *ngengemoi*, worker.
kowu yale, split wood; *kowuyalemoi*, wood-cutter.
Mende, Mende; *Mendemoi*, Mendeman.
Pu, European; *Pūmoi*, European.

Nyo denotes companion. Its uses are few.

hei, sit; *heinyo*, *heinyoi*, neighbour.
ko, war; *konyọ*, *konyọi*, enemy.
jia, journey; *jianyọ*, *jianyoi*, travelling companion.
Sandi, an institution for women; *Sandi nyọ*, *Sandi nyọi*, companion in the Sandi bush.

Ya denotes quality, condition. It forms abstract nouns.

Ngōva, old; *ngōvaya*, *ngōvayei*, old age.
mba, friend; *mbaya*, *mbayei*, friendship.

CHAPTER III

ADJECTIVES

i. Inflection.

Adjectives are inflected like nouns. They follow the same rules as to hard and soft consonants, and they have their indefinite and definite forms, singular and plural.

Singular.		Plural.		
Indefinite.	Definite.	Indefinite.	Definite.	
Míni	miní	minia mininga	minesia	heavy.
Miningo	miningoi	miningoa	miningoisia	heavy.
Yekpe	yekpeí	yekpea	yekpeisia	good.
Yekpengo	yekpengoi	yekpengoa	yekpengoisia	good.

ii. Syntax.

The adjective follows the noun it qualifies. The rule of qualification is as follows :—

The noun remains (i) in the indefinite form,
(ii) in the singular number.

The adjective may be either in the indefinite or definite form, singular or plural, according to the meaning required.

Examples.

Haka (*indef.*), hakeí (*def.*).	Load.
Haka mini.	A heavy load.
Haka miní.	The heavy load.
Haka mininga.	Heavy loads (*indef.*).
Haka minísia.	The heavy loads (*def.*).
Nya haka mini.	My heavy load.

(My load *is* nya hakei).

If a demonstrative pronoun be added the rule is as follows:—

The noun is (i) in the indefinite form,
(ii) in the singular number,

the adjective is (i) in the definite form,
(ii) in the singular number,

and the demonstrative pronoun is in the singular or plural as necessary.

Examples.

Haka miní ji.	This heavy load.
Haka miní nasia.	Those heavy loads.
Hindo woveí ji.	This old man.

Exceptions.

There are a few exceptions to the rule.

(i) The first concerns a few plural nouns which may be considered as collective nouns, as *nunga*, persons; *ndenga*, children; *nunga gbĭ*, all persons.

(ii) The word *yakpe*, meaning *the same* or *only*, seems to follow the noun either in indefinite or definite form—

Ngi lọï yakpei.	Her only child.
Fōlī yakpei na ma.	On that same day.
I njia yakpei lē.	He spoke the same word.

(iii) A further exception is when an adjective joins with *mo*, the suffix meaning *person*, to form a compound noun. The adjective is then treated as if it were a qualifying noun, and comes first, as—

Kpatemo (*indef.*), kpatemoï (*def.*), rich man.
Yekpemo (*indef.*), yekpemoï (*def.*), good man, but nū yekpei, the good man, *or* the good person.

The difference is, that *yekpemoi* is a complete noun in itself, independent of any question of qualification, whereas *nu yekpei* states the fact, which is the purpose of an adjective, that the man is good.

Further examples.

Haka gbī hindei na.	No load is in that place.
Hakei gbĭ.	Every load.
Haka yira.	One load.
Haka fere.	Two loads.
Haka fere jisia.	These two loads.
Nya yakpei.	I alone.
Ngi yakpei.	He alone.
Ngi lọï yakpei.	Her only child.
I njia yakpeí le.	He said the same word.
Numu gbī.	Nobody.
Numui gbĭ.	Everybody.
Nunga gbi.	All persons.
Hani gbi.	Everything.
Numu tenga.	Somebody.
Hindei gbi.	Every place, wherever.
Ji nyandengo le genge gbi va.	This is useful for every kind of work.
Bi wa na gbi.	Bring all of them.

iii. Adjectives ending in *ngo.*

There is a class of adjective formed from other adjectives by the suffix *ngo*, as *nyande*, fine ; *nyandengo*.

The *ngo* form is generally used in the predicative sense, and *le* (to be) may be added or not.

Adjectives in *ngo* are also formed from verbs. When the verb stem has this termination a past participial sense is created, and the word so formed can be treated as an adjective.

Examples.

Kula nyande.	A fine cloth.
Kura nyandeí.	The fine cloth.
Kuré nyandengo, *or* Kulé nyandengo le.	The cloth is fine.
Numu higbengo.	A sick man.
Numui na higbengo le.	That man is sick.
Ti sawango (ti jāngó).	They are three.

This adjectival form is inflected for definite and plural.

iv. Comparison.

There are no inflections to indicate comparison, but as in many, if not most, African languages, an indirect method has to be made use of.

Comparative.

(i) *Tēwē, dēwē, tēwē, dē*, meaning to cut, pass, etc.

Nya halei ĭ lēwē na ma.	My medicine is better than that.
Hani ji i dēni jima.	This thing is better or bigger than this one; *or*, has some better quality whatever it may be.

(ii) *Ma.* = to *or* on, with a word representing size, etc.

Numui na wōvango bima.	That person is older than you, *i.e.* is old to you.
Numui na ndọ̄pọ̄ bima.	That person is younger than you, *i.e.* is a boy to you.
Ndamba ngi gbayango hũanga gbọ̄to ma.	The crocodile is stronger than all animals.

(iii) A simple adjective, with the *ngo* termination, frequently expresses a comparative when used absolutely.

Bi yepe gbọ̄tongo.	You talk too much (lit. plenty).
Mahũguhango (pronounced mahũngwango).	Too far.

(iv) The phrase *I fīsa*, it is better.

I fisa bi ji wili.	It is better you do this.

Superlative.

Tewe with 'all,' or other similar word added, forms the superlative.

Ngileí ji wongo le, i dēwē ipekeisia ma.	This dog is the biggest.

The definite state of the adjective is often sufficiently emphatic to express a superlative.

Nya longo a ikulongoi. } I want the smallest one.
Nya longo a ikulọ̄i.

v. Numeral Adjectives.

(i) Cardinal Numerals.

1 yẹ̄la *or* yira (ngera). 'Ita' is used only in counting.
2 fele.
3 sawa.
4 nani.
5 lo̱lu.
6 wo̱ita.
7 wo̱fela.
8 wayakpa.
9 tau.
10 pu.
11 pu mahũ yira.
12 pu mahũ fere.
18 pu mahũ wayakpa.
19 pu mahũ tau.
20 nu (*or* numu) yira gboyongo.
21 nu yira gboyongo mahũ yira.
29 nu yira gboyongo mahũ tau.
30 nu yira gboyongo mahũ pu.
31 nu yira gboyongo mahũ pu mahũ yira.
40 nu fere gboyongo.
70 nu sawa gboyongo mahũ pu.
100 nu lo̱lu gboyongo, *or* usually hondo, a corruption of the English.
200 hondo fele.

A hundred is the Mende's limit. Anything beyond that is 'many'; and for all practical purposes this is sufficient, seeing that there are no accounts to keep, nor matters requiring mathematics, and that precision in West Africa is unimportant from the native point of view.

The cardinal numerals come after the noun, which retains the indefinite form either singular or plural.

Examples.

I ndọ̄i le fere.	She bore two children.
Nwoni sawa.	Three birds.
Wa gboma yira.	Bring one more.
I hũei wã pu a ngendé na.	He killed ten beasts on that morning.
Yira be ī na.	There is not even one there.
Jia sawa bi dọ̄.	Walk three paces and stop.

(ii) Ordinal Numerals.

The prefix *i* and suffix *ge* are added to the cardinal to form the ordinal numerals.

First, *ihalageí.* This is an exception.
Second, *ifelegeí.*
Third, *isawageí.*
And so on. Any great extension of these forms does not seem to be in practical use. The cardinals are fallen back on.

Yese also means *first* adverbially. See under Adverbs.

Some other words seem to acquire an ordinal use, as—
ikpakolageí and *ikelemageí*, the last ; *ikākāmageí* the side part.

Examples.

Pēlē ihalageí.	The first house.
Bia yese wa.	You come first.
Ta yese wa.	He comes first.
Ji yese wani bima.	This one came before you.
Pēlē ikpakolageí.	The last house.
Pēlē ikelemageí.	Ditto.

(iii) Distributive Numerals.

The distributive numerals are formed by reduplication of the cardinal numerals, as—

Bi ti la ngera, ngera.	Lay them one by one.
I ti dewe a fefele (*or* felefele).	He sent them two by two.

(iv) Multiplicative Numerals.

Hũ yela, once.
Hũ fele, twice.
Hũ pa, ten times.
Hũ gbotongo, plenty of times.

The *hũ* is often omitted, as—

Massa ye i bi lahĩnga yira.	Master says he has already warned you, *or* warned you once.
(Hani) pu pu na sawa.	Three times ten.
(Hani) nani nani (*or* na nani) na sawa lōle mia?	How many are three times four?

(*Hani*, thing, may be used or not used.)

Bi ya na yira?	Have you ever been there?

Ma is substituted for *hũ*, as—

Ngi pe hĩ ma pu.	I have done it ten times.

(v) Predicative Form.

Ti jāngo.	They are three.
Ti sawango.	Ditto.
Ti felengo.	They are two.
Bi yāngo ī le (yāngo = yelango).	You are not the only one.

CHAPTER IV

PRONOUNS

i. Personal Pronouns.

The personal pronouns are the following—

a.	*b.*	*c.*	*d.*	*e.*	*f.*	*g.*	*h.*	*i.*	*j.*
ngi	–	nga	–	ngia	ngi	nya	nya	ngē	(a)ngē
bi	bi	ba	{bia / bië}	bia	bia	bia	bi	bē	(a)bië
i	–	a	ta	ta	ta	ta	ngi	ē	(a)ngië
mu	–	ma	{ma / mueni}	mua	mua	mua	mu	mē	(a)muë
wu	a	wa	{wa / wueni}	wua	wua	wua	wu	wē	(a)wuë
ti	–	ta	{ta, tia / tieni}	tia	tia	tia	ti	tē	(a)tië

Ngi and *nga* (first person) are sometimes softened to *gi* and *ga*.

Explanation.

a. The simple form as used with the aorist and past tenses. With the vowel lengthened the negative is implied.

b. The form used with the imperative mood.

c. The form used with the present and the future tenses. With the vowel lengthened the negative is implied.

d. The form used in combining persons. Its use is further explained below.

e. A lengthened or emphatic form. It is made more emphatic by a repetition of the simple personal pronoun, as, *ngia, ngi, bia, bi,* etc.

f. This form followed by *be* makes a compound personal pronoun, as *ngi be*, even I.

g. The form used with the continuous mood, as, *nya lo wama*, I am coming. It is also used when the pronoun is repeated for emphasis. It is then sometimes followed by *lo*, to be. *Mua lo mu* . . . we it is, we . . .

h. The objective form. It stands before the verb it is governed by.

Also the possessive form. It precedes the noun, which is in the definite form. It is used to form the compound personal pronouns, *nya vuli*, myself; *nya nda* and *nya wo*, my own, *or* mine.

It is, further, the form used in conjugating verbs when they take the *ngo* termination. See Chapter VI, iii. Tenses.

i. The negative conditional form.

j. An independent form of the personal pronoun. It has a special use, as—

Méndemo (lo) abiĕ?	Are you a Mende?
Méndemo angē.	I am a Mende.

Gender.—There is no gender to any of the personal pronouns. This is only ascertained by the context.

Syntactical observations.

(i) A personal pronoun is required between a noun and a verb.

(ii) The only form of pronoun the use of which requires special illustration is that under *d*. In English two personal pronouns can be joined by the simple copulative *and*, and the following verb stands in the plural. In Mende the construction is different. The first pronoun, of whatever person, is put in the plural, and the second pronoun immediately follows it, the verb being in the plural and preceded by its proper pronoun. Hence *I and you* becomes *we you, we*; *he and she* becomes *they he, they*.

The lengthening of the vowel is possibly caused by the preposition 'a,' with, being merged into the pronoun.

The combination is as follows—

Mā bia, *or* ma biĕ.	I and you (*sing*.).
Mā ta.	I and he.

Mā wueni.	I and you (*pl.*).
Mā tieni.	I and they.
Wā ta.	You and he.
Wā tieni.	You and they.
Tā ta.	He and she.
Tā tieni.	He and they.

Examples.

Wā ta a li.	You and she shall go.
Wā ta lo wa li.	Ditto.
Wā ta mia wa li.	Ditto.
Ke tā ta ti ya.	And he and she went.
Ye mia wā ta wu lima? A mu kei.	Who are you going with? With our master.
Wā teni a li mia.	You and they go yonder.
Tā tieni ti li.	He and they have gone.
Mu gbi a hei.	Let us all sit down.
Mā tieni mu li.	I and they go.
Mā ta (mia) ma li.	I and he will go.
Hindei gbi bi li na mā bia ma li.	Wherever you go we both go.
Ti ye lo na tā tieni a fọlī na.	They were both there, he and they on that day.

(iii) A similar construction occurs when a noun is combined with a pronoun, as—

Bia wa Wuseni (lo) a li mia.	You and Wuseni go there.

(iv) Another idiom of the language is seen in the following examples, the plural appearing where the singular is used in English.

Mua nya lọi mu longa.	I see my child at last (what a mother says after her child's long absence).
Gi ya mu yē.	I go to my own country.
Mu nya lenga gbele mu goi ve.	I will fill all my children's and my own belly.
Ye, mu hei na mbē.	He said, Stay here with us.
I ya ti yē.	He went to his country.

(v) *Same*, or *self*, is rendered by *yakpe*.

Nya yakpei.	I myself, *or* I alone.
Bi yakpei ma.	You yourself.
Bi yakpei bima.	Ditto.
Ngi yakpei, *or* ta yakpei.	He himself.
Ti gbi ti yakpei.	They are all the same.

The Mende does not say *it is the same*, but *they are the same*.

(vi) There is a negative use of the pronoun in *j* as follows—

Mabia muë yā hei hinda yira.	You and I will not sit down in one place.
Bē, muë sese.	You said, Let us not slice it.

ii. Demonstrative Pronouns.

There are two demonstrative pronouns.

Ji, this.	Plural, *jisia*, *jia*.
Na, that.	Plural, *nasia*, *naa*, or *nā*.

Na is sometimes best translated *the*. The demonstrative pronoun follows the noun, which stands in the definite form singular. If it follow noun and adjective, the noun is in the indefinite form singular and the adjective in the definite form singular. The demonstrative pronoun alone takes the plural form, with one or two exceptions. Both *ji* and *na* can be used substantively, taking also the forms *ijí*, *iná*, *inai*.

Examples.

Kulé ji ī nyandeni.	This cloth is not good.
Bindi hiñdei na.	Is Bindi there. (lit. That place.)
Naa ti gula?	Have they fallen?
Naa ti na.	Those there.
Bi ji lǫnga.	You left this.
Ngī loni á ná.	I do not like that.
Kea ji na.	Like this.
Kea na na.	Like that.
Li bi wā na mia.	Go bring that (thing) over there.
Ta yā ji; ta lo a ji.	It is not this; it is this.
Ji ta yā na.	It is not that.
Ga na hũgo lo.	I will attempt it.

Ijí mia.	It is this one.
Ji nyandengo le genge gbi va.	This is useful for everything.
Ji nyandengo bọ va?	Is this of any use?
Ye, mba wai na.	He says that man is the senior.
Na gbĭ bi waila.	Bring either.
Bi wa na gbi.	Bring all of those.

NOTE.—*Na*, that, must not be confused with *nā*, now, or *na*, there.

iii. RELATIVE PRONOUN.

Na, that, plural *nasia* or *nā*, is the only one. It is, however, rather the demonstrative pronoun than a true relative pronoun.

Numui na a wa nya ye. The person who comes to me.

A sentence in which a relative would occur in English is usually broken up into two simple co-ordinate sentences.

iv. INTERROGATIVE PRONOUNS.

Ye, who. *Gbe*, what.

Ye, who, whose. Plural, *yea*, *yeni*.

It is followed in all forms by *lo*, is, are. *Ye lo* is frequently shortened to *yo*.

Ye also means how. For this meaning see Chapter VII, v.

Examples.

Ye lo a bie? Yo a bie?	Who are you?
Ye mia bie?	Ditto.
Bia bi ye? (unusual).	Ditto.
Ye lo na?	Who is there?
Ye ndē bima? *or* Yo ndē bima?	Who told you?
Ye lo indē bima?	Ditto.
Ye lo bi mbai le?	Who is your friend?
Yeni lo ta wa be?	Who come here?
Yea lo ta wa be?	Ditto.
A ye bijei lo wu ji weni?	With whose name did you do this?
Ye gurá lo?	Whose cloth is it?
Yo ngi wọ a kulé ji?	Ditto.
Ye mia?	Who is it?
Ye lo miando?	Who is over there?
Bi bi yo va?	For whom are you here?

Also—

Ngi gbiayeí lo a ye?	What is he (ít) like?
Ngi bijéi lo a ye?	What is his name?

Gbe, what; *igbe*, which; plural, *igbea*, *igbeni*, *igbo*, *gbo*.
Gbe lo = *Gbo*.

Gbo ba pe na?	What are you doing there?
Gbe hani lo a ji?	What thing is this?
Gbe lo a ji?	What is this?
Gbo i weni a hakei ji?	What has he done with that load?
Gbo bi longwola?	What do you want?
Gbo ba pema?	What are you doing?
Gbe yenge mia bá guma?	What kind of work can you do?
Gbŏ bima?	What is the matter with you?
Bo ba fembe?	What are you going to give me?
Gbe lo? *or* Gbe mia?	What is it?
Gbe le?	What is the matter?
Bē gbe? *or* Gbo ba nde?	What do you say?
Yē gbe?	What does he say?
Ma gbo we?	What shall we do?
Igbé? *or* i gbe le?	Which?
Kole igbe?	Which book?
Gbe hakeísia mia mia?	What are those loads there?
Gbe mia pa pena?	What are you going to do then?
Bi lei gbo benge bi keni ange?	What name did you give (lit. show) me yesterday?
Bo bi wa kama?	What do you come for?
Gbe kulá lo?	What cloth is this?
Gī ko gbo i wenga.	I do not know what has become of him.
Gbo bi waila?	What have you brought?
Gī ko gbwe mia.	I do not know what it is.
Gī ko gbwe mia aji.	I do not know what this is.
Numui igbé? *or* igbé le?	Which person?

Other ways of rendering *what.*

Bi biyéi?	What is your name?
Bi Mende biyei?	What is your Mende name?
Bi le biyei?	What is your birth name?
Ngi bijéi lo a ye?	What is his name?
Ngi gbiayéi a gbo? *or*	What is its appearance?
Ngi gbiayéi lo a ye?	Ditto.

CHAPTER V

THE VERB *TO BE*

THERE are many forms of the verb *to be*, as—*lo*, *mia*, *le*, *ye*, *yele*, *ya*.

i. *Lo*.

The usages of the *lo* form of the verb *to be* may be classified as (i) Substantival, and (ii) Auxiliary.

Lo, substantival.

1. It is used impersonally.
2. It can follow a noun without an intermediate pronoun.
3. It can stand between a noun and an adverb.
4. It cannot be used as a copulative between two nouns.
5. It cannot be used as a copulative between a noun and adjective, but follows the adjective.
6. It does not appear in a negative sentence, being a distinction of the positive.
7. It usually follows words like *ye?* who? *gbe?* what? *migbe?* when? *mi?* where?

Examples.

Mia lo. (1)	It is yonder.
Ta lo na. (3)	It is there.
Nya yenge lo be. (3)	My work is here.
Ye lo abie? (7)	Who are you?
Ye lo na? (3 and 7)	Who is there?
Ye kulé lo? (2)	Whose cloth is it?

Njia wulo lo. (5)	It is a small affair.
Kpō lo nyama. (2)	I am busy.
Migbele lo bi wa be? (7)	When did you come here?
Migbe lo bi wa be? (7)	Ditto.
Ye lo i ndeni bima? (7)	Who told you?
Gbe lo?	What is it?
Powe lo.	It is a dove.
Bia wa Wuseni lo a li mia.	You and Wuseni go yonder.
Bia lo i lọ̄a.	You are left.
Gbe lo ma pe abiẽ?	What shall we do with you?
Nya lo ngi kali wani.	It was I who killed the snake.
Bia lo mi?	Where are you?
Bi mi lo?	Ditto.
Bi pui mi lo?	Where did you put it?
Nya lo.	It is I.
Nwoni lo?	Is it a bird?
Jo lo mi?	Where is Jo?
Pele nyamu lo.	The road is bad.
Nje gbotongo lo be.	There is much water here.
Bi bia bi bi lo?	Are you here for yourself?
Numu lo na?	Is anybody there?

Lo, auxiliary.

As an auxiliary *lo* is used to emphasize the positive form of some of the past and future tenses, as—

I wai lo.	He has come.
A wa lo.	He will come.
Ta lo mba mema.	He is eating rice.

Lo a.

When it is required to express existence irrespective of time the form *lo a* is used. It is used when an attribute is required to complete the sense.

Gbe hani lo a ji?	What thing is this?
Ye lo a biẽ?	Who are you?
Ta lo a ji?	Is this it?
Mendemo lo abiẽ?	Are you a Mende?
Bia bi Mendemo lo abiẽ?	Ditto.
Ngi bijei lo a Bindi.	His name is Bindi.
Gbe jongo lo a ji?	How much is this?
Kpele lo a ji.	It is all these.
Nyanda lo a ji (*or* nyandéi).	It is mine.

Conjugation of Lo.

Lo, as a substantival verb, is only conjugated in the present tense.

Nya lo.
Bi *and* bia lo.
Ngi, i, *and* ta lo.
Mu *and* mua lo.
Wu *and* wua lo.
Ti *and* tia lo.

Also—

Lo ange.
Lo abiē.
Lo angiē.
Lo amuē.
Lo awuē.
Lo a tiē.

(The negative of *lo ange* is *yā angē*. See under *Yā*.)

ii. *Mia*.

This is an impersonal form, positive only. It is not conjugated and is only used in the present tense. It must not be confused with *mia*, yonder. *Mia* and *lo* (substantival) are usually interchangeable.

Examples.

Kēmei mia ?	Is that the end ?
Tamo mia wo.	There was once a man.
Nya wo mia.	It is mine.
Ye mia bie ?	Who are you ?
Ta mia.	Therefore.
Tā mia ?	Is he there ?
Tonya mia.	It is true, *or* Is it true ?
Gbe mia ba pe na ?	What are you doing there ?
Hā gbi mia ? (Ha = hani).	Is it anything ?
Nya mia.	It is I.
Gbe jongo mia ?	How much is it ?
Gome mia.	It is a crow.
Ye mia ?	Who is it ?
Ta mia yira.	That is one.
Soja mia nā angie.	He is a soldier now.

Nya mia Jo.	I am Jo.
Ngi yeto Jo mia.	I thought it was Jo.
Mā ta mia ma li.	I and he will go.
Gī ko gbwe mia.	I do not know what it is.
Gī ko gbwe mia aji.	I do not know what this is.
Ta mia a ji?	Is it this?
Nya bije mia a Jo.	My name is Jo.

iii. *Le.*

Le is a substantival verb representing a statement of fact without any attribute, unlike *lo a*, which requires an attribute. It is unconjugated. It is used with adjectives and verbs ending in *ngo*. It seems occasionally to be changed with *lo* for euphony.

One of its most important uses is to form the negative phrase *ī le*, it is not, which is used to transform what would otherwise be a positive statement into a negative one. This is dealt with later in Chapter VI, vi. on negative construction.

NOTE.—It must not be confused with *le*, yet.

Examples.

Nya le.	It is I.
Mua le.	It is we.
Bi wo le.	It is yours.
Gbo le i lọ̄a?	What is left?
Komo wa a le.	He is a great warrior.
Kurungo le.	All right, *or* It is accepted.
Tonya le.	It is true.
Kpandingo le.	It is hot.
Bi wo ī le.	It is not yours.
Bia ī le ga bi dọ̄li.	It is not you I call.
Tia ī le.	It is not they.
Tonya ī le.	It is not true.
Ngi lahīngo le.	He {is / has been} warned.
Mi le? (rarely used).	Where is it?
Nya le Jo le.	I am Jo.
Hakeí gboma le?	Is it another guinea-fowl?

iv. *Ye.*

Ye is a past form of the verb *to be.* It does not stand at the end of a sentence as the last word, but requires a complement. It is the only form of the verb *to be* that is somewhat fully conjugated.

	Present.	Past.
Sing.	Ngi ye.	Ngi ye lo.
	Bi ye.	Bi ye lo.
	I ye.	I ye lo.
Pl.	Mu ye.	Mu ye lo.
	Wu ye.	Wu ye lo.
	Ti ye.	Ti ye lo.

	Future.	Future continuous.
Sing.	Nga ye lo.	Nga yema.
	Ba ye lo.	Ba yema.
	A ye lo.	A yema.
Pl.	Ma ye lo.	Ma yema.
	Wa ye lo.	Wa yema.
	Ta ye lo.	Ta yema.

For the negative of the above the vowel of the pronoun is lengthened, the Past and Future losing the *lo*.

The *lo* is occasionally transferred to the end of the sentence.

As an auxiliary it is used in the pluperfect tense, and in the continuous mood with the past tense.

Examples.

Ngi ye lo na.	I was there.
Ī ye na.	He was not there.
Ti ye nu woita gboyongo.	They were 120 persons.
Bi ndēi a ye lo be sina.	Your brother will be here to-morrow.
Ke tōpōmamo yela lo i ye Damasku.	And there was a disciple at Damascus.
Kina le i ye na, bi wo ī yele?	Whilst it was there, was it not thine own?
Ī ye gbengeme be.	He was not here yesterday.
I ye gbengi be lo.	He was here yesterday.

Bi ye mi gbĭ?	Where were you yesterday?
I ye gbĭ bi (be)?	Was he here yesterday?
I, i mbe gbĭ.	Yes, he was here yesterday.
Ti ye nu yira gboyongo.	They were twenty.

v. *Yele.*

Yele is a form that is chiefly used with adjectival and verbal forms in *ngo.* It is also a past form which can be used without an attribute.

Examples.

Ngi lahĩngo yele.	He was warned.
Ngi lahĩngo a yele.	He will be warned.
Ngi gbakisia tewengo yele.	His wings were cut.
Kia le i ye na, bi wo ī yele?	Whilst it was there, was it not yours?

vi. *Ya.*

Ya is unconjugated. It is not of common use in its positive form. In its negative form, *i. e.* with the lengthened vowel *yā*, it stands as a negative to *lo* in its combination *lo a.*

Note.—There are words *ya* = go and *ya* = not.

Yā a-ngē.
Yā a-biĕ.
Yā a-ngiĕ.
Yā a-muĕ.
Yā a-wuĕ.
Yā a-tiĕ.

Examples.

Maha yā a biĕ.	You are not a chief.
Tonya yā na.	That is not true.
Powo yā na.	That is not a pigeon.
Kpele yā ji.	It is not all these.
Ta yāna.	It is not this.
Nu weka gbī yā na.	There is no one else there.

vii. *To be* omitted.

Where in English the verb *to be* is expressed, in Mende it is often left out.

Examples.

Ta be.	He is here.
Ī bendo.	He is not here.
Ī na.	He is not there.
Mëndemo abië?	Are you a Mende?
Bia mi?	Where are you?
Hindé ji ī ya nyande.	This place is not good.
Njiei kulọ̄ngo.	The matter is a small one.
Peleí nyamungo.	The road is bad.
Peleí ī kpekpeni.	The road is not good.
Ta mindo?	Where is he?
Ta hindeí na.	He is there.
Yambasu hindeí na?	Is Yambasu there?
Ngau nani i Sandi hũ.	She was four months in the Sandi bush.
Ti a be? Tī be.	Are they here? They are not here.
Yira be ī na.	There is not even one there.
Kalé ji ta nwonisia va.	This cartridge is for birds.
Ti nu gboyongo.	They were twenty.
Nya la a Jo.	My name is Jo.
Ngi lọ̄i i nyālọ̄i.	Her child was a girl.
Bondé nyapọ̄i wēlē wōma.	The okra tree was behind the woman's house.
Ta ji?	Is it this?
Nu wa angie.	He is a big person.

CHAPTER VI

THE VERB

i. Division. Voices.

Separate forms do not exist for transitive, intransitive, active or passive. The exact meaning can only be judged by the context. For instance, *hei*, intransitive, means *to sit;* transitive, *to set. Pele, pe,* to do, means also *to become* or *to be done. Gula* means either *to fall down* or *to throw down.*

The passive may, however, be rendered by the use of *they* with an active verb; as, *he has been beaten* may be translated *they beat him,* ti ngi ndeweí lo.

A passive sense may also be obtained by the addition of the suffix *ngo* to transitive verbs, as *ngi dewengo yele,* he was beaten. This suffix makes a past participial meaning when added to transitive verbs, and verbs can also be formed from adjectives by means of the same. The conjugation is the same in both cases.

ii. Moods.

With the exception of the continuous mood there is no inflection of the verb form for mood.

IMPERATIVE MOOD.

The imperative, strictly speaking, consists of only the second person singular and plural.

Examples.

	Singular.	Plural.
Intransitive.	Li, go!	A li, go!
Transitive.	Pã, kill it!	A pã, kill it!
	Bi ngi hou.	A wu ngi hou, catch him.
	Ngi go a kole.	Give him the book.

INFINITIVE MOOD.

Three suffixes are used to indicate the infinitive mood, *ma*, *la*, *va*.

Ma is used after verbs of motion, as—

I ya muama	He has gone to bathe.

Such sentences may, however, be rendered—

Gi ya ngi mua.	I go, I wash.

La is used when the infinitive depends on certain other verbs, as *can*, *begin*, *finish*, *show*, etc. This form is preceded by *a*, a preposition meaning *with*, and is thus clearly shown to be a verbal noun. As such it is capable of taking all the inflections of a noun.

Ī guni a lila.	He could not go.

This may also be rendered—

Ī guni i li.	He could not go.

Va is used whenever *ma* or *la* are not strictly applicable as—

Kpoyeí ī kpekpe gboli va.	The sea is not good to drink.
Mu ya me va.	We go to eat.

Examples of sentences in which the infinitive is avoided—

Ngi yeto bingi ga li lo dogboi hũ.	I intended yesterday going to the bush.
Bi fembe ngi me.	Give it to me to eat.
Dē ngi ma ā na wiri.	Tell him not to do that.

INDICATIVE AND SUBJUNCTIVE MOODS.

The indicative mood calls for no remarks. The subjunctive mood is the indicative in a subordinate position, preceded by a particle or having the particle understood.

CONTINUOUS MOOD.

The continuous mood is formed by adding *ma* to the verb-stem. It is conjugated throughout by the aid of auxiliaries. It presents the *-ing* termination in English, as *I am going*, nya lo lima.

iii. Tenses.

The pronoun is inflected as well as the verb, and with the aid of auxiliaries a great variety of tenses is produced.

The complete conjugation of the verb is as follows—

AORIST.

Positive.	Negative.
Ngi tewe, I cut.	Ngī tewe, I do *or* did not cut.
Bi tewe.	Bī tewe.
I tewe.	Ī tewe.
Mu tewe.	Mū tewe.
Wu tewe.	Wū tewe.
Ti tewe.	Tī tewe.

(Sometimes, but rarely, *lo* is added to the positive to render the form quite past time.)

PRESENT.

Nga tewe, I cut.	Ngā tewe, I do not cut.
Ba tewe.	Bā tewe.
A tewe.	Ā tewe.
Ma tewe.	Mā tewe.
Wa tewe	Wā tewe.
Ta tewe.	Tā tewe.

PAST, I.

Ngi tewea, I cut.	None.
Bi tewea.	
I tewea.	
Mu tewea.	
Wu tewea.	
Ti tewea.	

PAST, II.

Positive.	Negative.
Ngi teweni, I cut.	Ngī teweni, I did not cut.
Bi teweni.	Bī teweni.
I teweni.	Ī teweni.
Mu teweni.	Mū teweni.
Wu teweni.	Wū teweni.
Ti teweni.	Tī teweni.

Lo may be added to the positive to emphasize it.

PAST, III.

Positive	Negative
Ngi dewenga, I have cut.	None.
Bi dewenga.	
I dewenga.	
Mu dewenga.	
Wu dewenga.	
Ti dewenga.	

PERFECT.

Positive	Negative
Ngi teweí lo, I have cut.	Ngī teweí, I have not cut.
Bi teweí lo.	Bī teweí.
I teweí lo.	Ī teweí.
Mu teweí lo.	Mū teweí.
Wu teweí lo.	Wū teweí.
Ti teweí lo.	Tī teweí.

PLUPERFECT.

Positive	Negative
Ngi ye { tewenga, I had cut. / teweí lo. / teweni. }	Ngī ye teweni, I had not cut it.
Bi ye { tewenga. / teweí lo. / teweni. }	Bī ye teweni.
I ye { tewenga. / teweí lo. / teweni. }	Ī ye teweni.
Mu ye { tewenga. / teweí lo. / teweni. }	Mū ye teweni.
Wu ye { tewenga. / teweí lo. / teweni. }	Wū ye teweni.
Ti ye { tewenga. / teweí lo. / teweni. }	Tī ye teweni.

FUTURE.

Positive.	Negative.
Nga dewé lo, I shall cut.	Ngā tewe, I shall not cut.
Ba dewé lo.	Bā tewe.
A dewé lo.	Ā tewe.
Ma dewé lo.	Mā tewe.
Wa dewé lo.	Wā tewe.
Ta dewé lo.	Tā tewe.

FUTURE AND CONDITIONAL NEGATIVE.

	Ngē tewe, I shall not cut, *or* I may not cut.
	Bē tewe.
	Ē tewe.
	Mē tewe.
	Wē tewe.
	Te tewe.

FUTURE PERFECT.

(Kina) ngi tewea lo, (When) I shall have cut.	Ngī tewea, I shall not have cut.
Bi tewea lo.	Bī tewea.
I tewea lo.	Ī tewea.
Mu tewea lo.	Mū tewea.
Wu tewea lo.	Wū tewea.
Ti tewea lo.	Tī tewea.

The emphatic form of the above tenses consists in the repetition of the personal pronoun either with or without *lo*, as *nya nga tewe*, or *nya lo nga tewe*. For the form of personal pronoun used, see Chapter IV, i, *g*.

IMPERATIVE

Gbe ngi lewe, let me cut.	—
Tewe, cut.	Bā tewe, do not cut.
Gbe i tewe, let him cut.	A (or Ē) tewe, he must not cut.
Gbe mu tewe, *or* A mu tewe, let us cut.	—
	—
A tewe, cut.	Wā tewe, do not cut.
Gbe ti tewe, let them cut.	Tā (or Tē) tewe, they must not cut.

CONTINUOUS MOOD

NOTE.—The accent is on the first syllable of 'tewema' throughout.

AORIST.

Positive.	Negative.
Ngi tewema (lo), I am, *or* was, cutting.	Ngī tewema, I am not, *or* I was not, cutting.
Bi tewema (lo).	Bī tewema.
I tewema (lo).	Ī tewema.
Mu tewema (lo).	Mū tewema.
Wu tewema (lo).	Wū tewema.
Ti tewema (lo).	Tī tewema.

PRESENT.

Nya lo tewema, I am cutting.	None.
Bia lo tewema.	
Ta (lo) tewema.	
Mua (lo) tewema.	
Wua (lo) tewema.	
Tia (lo) tewema.	

PAST.

Ngi ye tewema, I was cutting.	Ngī ye tewema, I was not cutting.
Bi ye tewema.	Bī ye tewema.
I ye tewema.	Ī ye tewema.
Mu ye tewema.	Mū ye tewema.
Wu ye tewema.	Wū ye tewema
Ti ye tewema.	Tī ye tewema.

FUTURE, I.

Nga ye tewema, I shall be cutting.	Ngā ye tewema, I shall not be cutting.
Ba ye tewema.	Bā ye tewema.
A ye tewema.	Ā ye tewema.
Ma ye tewema.	Mā ye tewema.
Wa ye tewema.	Wā ye tewema.
Ta ye tewema.	Tā ye tewema.

FUTURE, II.

Positive.	Negative.
Nga tewema, I am about to cut.	Ngā *or* ngē tewema, I am not cutting, *or* shall not cut.
Ba tewema.	Bā *or* bē tewema.
A tewema.	? ē tewema.
Ma tewema.	? mē.
Wa tewema.	? wē.
Ta tewema.	? tē.

(The deficient persons I have not found.)

NOTE.—It is a matter of great difficulty to find a verb that can be accurately conjugated throughout. *Tewe* may of course become *dewe*, *lewe*, *te*, *de* or *le*, to suit the euphony of the sentence.

INFLECTION OF THE *NGO* FORM

PRESENT.

Nya lahingo le, I am warned.
Bi lahingo le.
Ngi lahingo le.
Mu lahingo le.
Wu lahingo le.
Ti lahingo le.

PAST.

Nya lahingo yele.
Bi lahingo yele.
Ngi lahingo yele.
Mu lahingo yele.
Wu lahingo yele.
Ti lahingo yele.

FUTURE.

Nya lahingo a yele.
Bi lahingo a yele.
Ngi lahingo a yele.
Mu lahingo a yele.
Wu lahingo a yele.
Ti lahingo a yele.

The negative of the above may be rendered—

Tī nya lahīni, They did not warn me, etc.

iv. Examples of the Uses of the Various Tenses.

AORIST.

Largely used in narration and for subordinate sentences without a conjunction.

Ye, ti li ti ngi yenge wili.	He said they should go and work for him.
Ke ti yama ti yetahũ.	And they return, *or* returned, to their home town.
Tamoi i ya wo̱ i nyahei jo.	A man went once upon a time to get a wife.
A mu li mu yenge wē.	Let us go and work.
Bī ya li le?	Have you not gone yet?
Gī hũgo.	I do not understand.

PRESENT.

Ye, nga hũei ji fe bi ye.	He said, I give you this meat.
A ngi wili ngombui ya.	He throws him on the fire.

PAST, I.

Mu waa be bengeme.	We came here yesterday.
Ke ti ya ke ti hitia mbei ma do̱le tima.	And they went, and they reached the rice hungry.
Bi bumbúa botongo.	You took too much.
Gi menia, hiye.	I heard all right.

PAST, II.

This is the form mostly used in negative sentences.

Ye bi tọ̄ni?	You sent you?
Ngī gbeni.	I don't care.
Yo njiei leni?	Who spoke?
Ī ya lini.	He has not gone.

PAST, III.

This form is often used to express a conditional sentence.

Sange mia gi ngi longa.	I have just seen him.
Gi kpo̱yōnga.	I am just finishing.
Ke i ngi mbāi lulinga.	And he called his friend.
Bi penga lo, ba ha lo fe.	If you do it, you will surely die.

PERFECT.

Ngi wai lo angië.	I have brought him.
Gbeva bī wai kaka?	Why did you not come quickly?
Gī toi, *or* gī ngi toi.	I have not seen it.
Ī kpande wuai.	He has not cleaned the gun.
Mu yamai! (*lo* is omitted).	We are back!
Gbo bi waila? (*Note verb form.*)	What have you brought?
Bi hití lo na so?	Did you go all the way?
Fọlī i gbiai lo ke nwonīsia ti wa.	If the sun came out the birds would come.
Ngī numu loi.	I saw nobody.
Ngi mbọ̄i lo.	I have hit it (*of shooting*).
I ngi hakei lọ̄ilohū. (*Note verb form.*)	He has lost his load.

PLUPERFECT.

Kina ti ye welani.	When they had finished.
Iye pei lo kina bi ye na?	Had he done it when you were there?

FUTURE.

Ngē wọ, ga bi bawo lo.	I said the other day, I will cure you.
Ngā yā na wiri gboma.	I shall not do that again.
De ngi ma ā pele.	Tell him he must not do it.
Sina ma to (*lo* omitted).	To-morrow we shall see.
A ti dō lo.	He will send them.

FUTURE PERFECT.

Kina bi ngi doa lo, bi ngi wa.	When you shall have found (lit. seen) him, bring him.

Doi (the perfect tense) can be used instead of *doa*.

IMPERATIVE.

Wā li na.	Do not go there.
A wā mbomé.	Bring the hammock.
Wa mbe.	Come to me.
Tā li.	They must not go, or shall not go.

CONTINUOUS MOOD

AORIST.

Ngi wiláma.	I am finishing.
Ye, mu lima lo.	He said we are going.
Ye, nya be, ye, ngi hama.	She said, I too, she said, I shall die.

PRESENT.

Ta lo nye gbema.	He is catching fish.
Ye ke mua wama.	And he said we are coming.
Train ta wama.	The train is coming.
Train lo wama.	Ditto.
Train i wa.	Ditto.
Mua jiama.	We are moving (*i.e.* in a boat or train).
Ta wama.	He is coming.

PAST.

Kina mu ye jiama.	Whilst we were travelling.
I ye kine guláma.	It was nearly falling.

FUTURE, I.

Bi kenye a ye wama a kpokovọi ji?	Will your uncle be coming this afternoon?

FUTURE, II.

Bā hama.	You will not die.
Ngā tema. Ngē dema.	I am not passing (*i.e.* I do not want you to make way for me).
Nga wama.	I am (just) coming.
Ē tōtōma.	He is not going to begin.

NGO TERMINATION

PRESENT.

Kurungo le.	It is accepted; all right.
Ngi kpakisia tewengo yele	Its wings were cut.
Ngi gahũ hango yele.	He was very tired.

v. A Special Form of Conjugation is used for *I say*, etc.

Ngē, I say, or said.
Bē, you say.
Yē, he says.
Mē, we say.
Wē, you say.
Tē, they say.

It is used alone, as—

Ngē, bi wa a londemi imumui.	I said, Bring the small nails.

If it follows *ndē, say*, it is best rendered *saying*, as—

I ndea, ye, bā li na.	He said saying, Do not go there.
Ye, ngē wọ ga bi bawo lo.	He said, I said before I will cure you.
Tē,mu mbei yilia gengebra we.	They said, We cooked rice for the labourers.

vi. Negative Construction.

The expression of the negative is one of the greatest difficulties in the Mende language. The addition of a single word the equivalent of *not* to a positive statement, for the purpose of rendering it negative, does not occur.

The following methods are adopţed.

(i) The one invariable indication of a negative is the engthening of the vowel in the pronoun attached to the verb.

Ngĭ li, I go; *Ngī li*, I do not go.

(ii) The auxiliary *lo*, which is an indication of a positive statement, disappears when the sentence becomes negative.

Ngă li lo, I shall go; *Ngā li*, I shall not go.

(iii) The negation may be rendered more emphatic by the addition of *yā*, not (sometimes *lā*), between the pronoun and the verb.

Ngĭ toi lo, I have seen him; *Ngī yā toi*, I have not seen (him).

(iv) The phrase *ī le*, it is not, is sometimes added to the end of a positive sentence to render it negative.

Ji nyandengo ī le, this is not good.

(v) When the verb *to be* is negatived, the lengthened pronoun stands alone before the complement.

Tĭ gbǭtǫngo, Tī gbǭtǭ, they are not many.

(vi) If the verb or adjective in the positive sentence has the *ngo* termination, the negative may be rendered by the addition of *ī le*, or by dropping the *ngo* and substituting *ni*, which is a past tense termination.

Mahëungo ī le. Tī mahëuni. Ma-ī-hëuni	They are not equal.

(vii) *Gbī*, none (positive *gbĭ*, all), following a noun in the indefinite form will also put a sentence into the negative.

Kayei lo ti ma.	They are to blame.
Kaye gbī ti ma.	They are not to blame.
Hā gbī na.	Nothing there.

(viii) For the second persons of the imperative mood the future tense is used.

(*Bi*) *li*, go ; *Bā li*, do not go.
A li, go ; *Wā li*, do not go (*pl.*).

(ix) *Yā* is the negative of *lo a*.

Mahei lo abie.	You are the chief.
Mahei yā abie.	You are not the chief.

Further Examples of Negative Sentences.

Hindei na ī kuhama.	That (*or* the) place is not far.
Ī nyandé.	It is not good.
Nu gbǭtǭ ī wai.	Not many persons came.
Nunga gbǭtǭ tī wai.	Ditto.
Nunga gbǭtǭa tī wai.	Ditto.
Nunga tī gbǭtǫni tī wani.	Not many people came.
Nga li lo, ngē lembi.	I will go, I will not delay.
Gī yā li na.	I have not been there.

Bī yā li lē?	Have you not gone yet?
Ngē la pe gboma.	I will not do it again.
Ngī lila, miningo le.	I cannot take it, it is heavy.
Ngī ya toi.	I have not seen it.
Ngī la hindeí ji we.	I did not do this thing.
Ī yā wele.	He did not do it.
Ye, mū yā wime.	He says we must not run.
Ī yā gbo̱yōai.	It is not finished.
Ī yā magbo̱yōai.	He has not finished.
Tī yā lini le.	They have not gone yet.
Ī lini.	He did not go.
Ī guni a ngi bawola.	He could not cure him.
Ī gbō̱tọni.	Not much.
Tī ngi go̱ni.	They did not know him.
Ngī lọni a hale.	I do not want medicine.
Pele ī nyandeni.	The road is not good.
Hindei na ma-ī-guhani.	The place is not far.
Wē pe.	You must not do it. Cannot you do it?
Nya laguli guhango ī le.	My beak is not long.
Gbayango ī le.	There was no strength in him.
Bia ī le.	It is not you.
Bia ī le ga bi dọli.	I do not call you.
Tonya ī le.	It is not true.
Bi wo ī le.	It is not yours.
Numu gbī na.	There is nobody there.
Bā nde numu gbī ma.	Do not tell anybody.
Nya gbwe gbī na.	I have no business there.
Nya lima gbī njiei hū̃.	I have no heart in the matter.
Ye, numu gbī e soro.	She said, Nobody shall marry her.
Navo gbī mu yeya.	We have no money.
Ī navọi ngeya.	He has not the money.
Ke ī nu gbī loni.	And he saw nobody.
Bi nemáhū̃ gbī na.	You have no sense.
Ye, bi nduwinga lo, mbe gbī na bi me.	He said, If you clear the ground you will have no rice from it to eat.
Bā lua.	Do not be afraid.
Wā li na.	Do not go there.
Ba li lo? Bē li?	Will you go, or not?

Tonya yā na.	That is not true.
Nu gbọ̄tọ ī na.	There are not many persons there.
Yira be ī na.	There is not even one there.
Ī ya gbọ̄tọ na.	Not much there.
Mabia muë yā hei hinda yira.	You and I will not sit down in one place.
Bē, muë sese.	You said, Let us not slice it.
Ye, mu yā li.	He says, We must not go.
Ī pēlḗbu mbe.	He is not in the house here.
Gbeva bī bere wuai?	Why have you not washed your trousers?
Bā li hũguhango (ngwango).	Do not go far.
Gī ko.	I do not know.
Ī bēndo.	He is not here.
Ngē wa.	I shall not come.
Ha kpande gbī nya yeya.	To-day I have no gun.
Ma-ī-guhani.	It is not far.
Ta yā na.	It is not this.
Kowe yāna.	It is not an eagle.
Li bi njei gbandi bā yā bi gowé gama wua.	Boil the water before you wash (the wound on) your leg.
Dē ngi ma ā na wiri.	Tell him not to do that.

CHAPTER VII

ADVERBS

There are adverbs of place, time, manner, and of affirmation and negation; also many adverbial phrases of the same nature.

I. Adverbs of Place.

The number of words used solely as adverbs of place is very small. They are supplemented by other parts of speech used as such. There are, further, many words which can be used either as adverbs or prepositions.

(1) The following are pure adverbs of place—

Bē, here.
Bē-ndo, here.
Mbē, here.
Na, there.
Mia, yonder.
Miando, yonder.
Mi ? where ?
Mindo ? where ?
A or O ? where ?
Polon, far.

(2) The following are used also as prepositions—

Mbu, beneath.
Bu, beneath.
Ma, on, above.
Mahũ, on the top, above.
Hũ, inside.
Kpela, near.
Gbea, near.
Gbeanga, near.
Lugo, Luwo, *or* Tuwo, *or* tugo, in front.
Gulo, in front.
Pōma, behind.
Wōma, behind.
Ndia, middle.
Gama, towards.
Nga, on top.

(3) The following adverbial expressions occur—

Kūha (*adj.*), far (in various inflections).
Hindé ji, here.
Hindé na, there.
Domeí, on the ground.
Ngitíya, outside.
Ngeléya, aloft.
Kaka, side.
Kakeí ji, this side.
Kakeí na, that side.

Examples of the uses of the foregoing.

Bē, here (not to be confused with *be*, even, also). *Bē-ndo* is a strengthened form.

Wa be.	Come here.
Nya yenge lo be.	My work is here.
Ta be.	He is here.
Ī be-ndo, *or* Ī be.	He is not here.
Massa ye wu yama be.	Master says come back here.

Mbē, here, to me, with me, etc.

Mu yama mbe?	Shall we return to where we came from?
Ngi yama mbe-oh!	I am going back home!
Wa mbe.	Come to me.
Mbe ka.	This side.
Lọle mia mbe?	How many are there here?
I ye gbĭ bi (be)? Ī, i mbe gbĭ.	Was he here yesterday? Yes, he was here yesterday.
Nū ji mbe i ndea bima.	This person here told you.
Gbeva bī luma mbe?	Why don't you answer me?

Na, there (not to be confused with *nā*, now).

Ta na.	He is there.
Mi lo bi li na gbengeme?	Where did you go yesterday
Ī na.	He is not there.
Ngi ya ngi na gbwē.	I am going to look there.'
Mi lo gbĭ Yamba i yenge na?	Where did Yamba work yesterday?
Mu yá na.	We went there.

Mia, yonder. *Miando* is a strengthened form.

Mu yama miando.	We return yonder.

7

Mi, where; also *mindo, mi lo, lo mi.*

Jo lo mi?	Where is Jo?
Bi pe lo mi?	Where is your house?
Bi ye lo a mi?	Where is your home *or* country?
Bi were lo mindo?	Where is your house?
Wu ndewe ta mindo?	Where is your brother?
Bia mi?	Where are you?
Bi mi lo?	Ditto.
Bia lo mi?	Ditto.
Ta mindo?	Where is he?
Ta lo mi?	Ditto.
Ta mi lo?	Ditto.
Bi mbai lo mi?	Where is your friend?
Bi hiya mi?	Where have you come from?
Bi hi mi lo?	Ditto.
Bi pui mi lo?	Where did you put it?
Bi nda mi lo?	Ditto.
Bi li mi lo lo̱ fele ji hũ gī bi loni?	Where have you been these last two days that I have not seen you?
Bi mi lo ge?	Where have you been?
Kole jī hī mi lo?	Where is this letter from?
Ma li mi lo?	Where shall we go?
Mi lo ti ya na?	Where have they gone?
Mi yaka.	Which direction?
Bi ye mi? *or* Bi ye mi lo?	Where were you?
Mindo bi yi lo gbuë?	Where did you sleep last night?
Gī ko̱ mi mia i ya na.	I do not know where he has gone.
Gī ko̱ mi i ya na.	Ditto.
Gī ko̱ mi lo i ya na.	Ditto.
Gī ko̱ mi le i ya na.	Ditto.
Bi ya gbĭ mi lo?	Where did you go yesterday?
Mi lo gbĭ Yamba i yenge na?	Where did Yamba work yesterday?

A or *O*.

A bi kei?	Where is your master?
O Jo?	Where is Jo?

Polon or *poron*, far.

I ya miando poron.	It has gone far away.
I ya poron.	Ditto.
Numui na gī toni; i ya poron.	I did not see the man; he has gone far.

Mbu or *bu*, underneath.

Li bu.	Go underneath.
Gbia mbu.	Come out from under.
Yo na mbu?	Who is under there?

Ma, on.

Gbelé ma.	Leave off, let go.
Hō ma.	Catch hold.
Hani gbī ma.	There is nothing on it.
Ngi pe hī ma pu.	I have done so ten times.

Mahũ, on the top.

Nda mahũ.	Lay it on the top.
Te mahũ.	Raise it up.

Hũ, inside.

Mbawé lo hũ.	It is full of soap.
Kalé lo hũ.	The cartridge is inside.
Ta lo hũ kru.	There is a little inside.
Ngalui i la hũ yia nani.	The moon is four days old.
I kpia hũ.	She takes it out.

Kpela, *gbea*, *gbeanga*, near.

Bā pu gb'rá.	Do not put it near.
Bā dọ̄ kpela.	Do not stand too near.

Lugo, in front, *luwo*, *tuwo*, *tugo*.

I dewea lugo.	He passed in front.
Ti ya tuwo.	They have gone on in front.
Tia tuwo.	They are on ahead.

Gulo, in front.

Li gulo.	Go in front.
Ta gulo, Tia kulo (but *ngi gulo* = in front of him, see Prepositions).	He is ahead, they are ahead.
Lǭ kulo.	Stand in front.
Li kulo bi wime ngi to.	Run on and look for him.

Pōma, wōma, behind.

Ta pōma.	He is behind.
Na wōma.	Afterwards.

Ndia, lia, middle.

La ndia.	Lay it in the middle.
Pu ndia.	Put it in the middle.
Ngīrī ndia.	Tie it in the middle.
Gurī yiri ndia, *or* Gurī yiri ndia we.	Tie the stick in the middle.
Hei ndia, *or* Hei ndiei	Sit in the middle.
Wa ndia.	Come into the middle.

Gama, towards.

Wala gama.	Bring it to me, *or* forward.
Gbo bi wa kama.	What do you come for?

Nga, on top.

Pu nga.	Put it on top.

Kuha, far. This is properly an adjective meaning *high*.

Ta kuhama.	It is far.
Mahũguhango (pronounced *Mah'ngwango*).	Ditto.
Ma ī guhani.	It is not far.
Ī guhani.	Ditto.
Ī kuhama.	Ditto.
Numui na gī toni i ya kuhama.	I don't see that man, he has gone far.
Numui na gī toni i ya mahuguhango poron.	Ditto.
Bia kuhama loma poron?	Can you see far (from where you are)?

Hindé ji, hindé na, here, there (slight variations in pronunciation).

Hindé ji.	This place.
Hindeí na.	That place.
Ta hingdeí na?	Is he there?
Vandi hindeí na?	Is Vandi there?
Ī hindeí ji.	He is not here.

Ndo̱meí, on the ground. *Ndo̱me* is a noun meaning *ground.*

Pu ndo̱meí.	Put it on the ground, *or* floor.

Ngitiya, outside, in the yard, etc.

Pili ngitiya.	Throw it outside.
Jia lọ̄i i lēma ngitiya.	A small child was passing in front.

Ngeleya, aloft.

I le ngeleya.	He climbs aloft.

Kaka, side; *kakeí ji, kakeí na*, this side, that side.

Kaka wekei (*or* yekei) ma.	The other side.
Mi yaka?	Which direction?
Bē ka.	This side.
Li bi pu miaka (= mia yaka).	Put it on the far side.
Mi aka (= mi-yaka) i ya na?	Which direction has he gone now?

ii. Adverbs of Time.

(1) They are as follows—

Nā	Now.
Sange.	Just now.
Tētē.	Early.
Ha.	To-day; *often simply* now.
Sina.	To-morrow.
Gbenge, gbengeme, *or* gbĭ.	Yesterday.
Sina ndambai, *or* Sina ndambuai.	The day after to-morrow.
Gbenge ndamb(u)ai.	The day before yesterday.
Gbue, *or* kpindiji.	Last night.
Ge, gege, *or* ho̱we.	Some time ago; a few days ago; recently.

Wo̱.	Formerly.
Wo̱gba, wo̱kpo̱.	Ditto.
Wo̱ polon.	Ditto.
Ke yakpe.	At once.
Peṅ, *or* pei.	First.
Yese.	Ditto.
Pēpē.	Often.
Kunafọ̄.	In future.
Kunaka.	Ditto.
Le.	Yet, still.
No Mende word.	Soon (for examples see under 4).
Ngōva, gba, etc. (also by subjunctive sentence).	Before.
Kina.	When (is also a conjunction).
Kina gba.	Since. (For examples of *kina* see under conjunctions).

(2) The following are nouns which are used as adverbial expressions of time in various combinations—

Kpēle, kpē, gbē (*migbe lo* = when).	Time.
Kpoko vọ̄lọ̄.	Evening.
Kpindi.	Night.
Ngenda.	Morning.
Ku, fọ̄lọ̄, lo̱.	Day.
Fọ̄.	Year.
Ngalu, ngau.	Month.

There is no word for *week.* It is translated *seven days.*

Examples.

Nā, now.

A wa nā.	Come now (*pl.*).
Ye nā mu hei na.	He says now we are to sit down here.

Sange, just now.

Bi lima sange ?	Are you going just now ?
Sange mia gi ngi longa.	I saw him just now.
Sangi mia ti yá.	They have just gone

Tētē, early, coupled with *ngenda*.

Sina ngenda tētē mu li.	We go to-morrow very early.

Ha, to-day, sometimes means simply *now*.

Mū lo̱voni ha.	We have not been unsuccessful to-day.
A wa lo ha?	Will he come to-day?

Sina, to-morrow.

Sina ndamb(u)ai.	The day after to-morrow.
Sina mu li dogbo wāi hũ.	To-morrow we go 'bush,' *or* up-country.
Sina ma to.	To-morrow we shall see.
Sina ndambuai a wa lo.	He will come the day after to-morrow.

Gbengeme, gbenge, gbĭ, yesterday.

Bengeme ndamb(u)ai.	The day before yesterday.
John Bull i li lo gbĭ gengema?	Did John Bull go to work yesterday?
I ye gbĭ be?	Was he here yesterday?

Gbuë, last night; also *guë*.

Ti yi gbuë.	They slept the night.
Mindo bi yi lo gbuë?	Where did you sleep last night?
Bi ndo̱ gboli lo gbuë?	Did you drink spirits last night?
Bi na gbo̱yōa guë?	Did you finish that last night?

Ge, recently, or *gege*.

Bi ya mi ge lo̱ fele gē bi lo?	Where have you been recently?
Bi ya ge mi lo̱ fele gē bi lo?	Ditto.
Bi mi lo ge?	Where have you been lately?
I ye lo be ge.	He was here just now.

Howe, recently.

I ye lo be howe.	He was here a short time since.

Wọ, wọgba, wọkpọ wọ poron, formerly.

Tamo yira mia wọ,	There was once a man.
Ngi higbea wọkpọ.	I have been sick a long time.
Ji wọ bi wa bi hea be?	How long have you been sitting here?
Kea wọgba mū wai be.	It is a long time since we came here.
Bia wọ na welema?	Have you done that before?
Ji wọ gi ndea, nge, ba dogboi luwi.	I told you before not to clear the bush.
Gĭ hani longa wọ poron.	I saw the thing long ago.
Gĭ hani longa wọ hũgu-hango.	Ditto.

Ke yakpe, at once.

Bi ji wiri keyakpe.	Do this at once.

Peṅ, pei, or *pẽ* first.

Ji wiri pẽ.	Do this first.
Mu hei peṅ fọlī gbia.	We sit here until sunrise.
Mawulu peṅ njei i wa.	Wait until the rain comes.

Yese, first.

Ta yese wa.	He comes first.
Bia yese wa.	You come first.
Ji yesé wẽ.	Do this first.
Ji yesé wili peṅ.	Do this first.
Ji yesé wani bima.	This one came before you.

Pēpē, often.

Bi wama be pēpē.	Do you often come here?

Kunafọ̄, kunaka, in future.

Kunafọ̄ ba ji wiri.	In future you will do this.
Kunaká ba ji wiri.	Ditto.
Kunafọ̄ bā pe hẽ.	In future do not do so.

Le, yet.

Bī yā li le?	Have you not gone yet?

(3) *Before*, *formerly*, etc.

Before is expressed in a variety of ways, as illustrated below. See also *peǹ*, *wo̱*, *yese*.

Bi numui na go̱lo ngōva ?	Did you know that person before?
Gĭ ngi go̱lo ngōva.	I knew him before.
Gī ngi go̱ ngōva gbī.	I did not know him before.
I ngenda ve lo mu we ī yā li.	He said good-bye to us before he left.
Ji wili peǹ bī yā li offici hũ.	Do this before you go to the office.
Bi ji wī gba ngī yā li.	Do this before I go.
Ji lo ba pe bī yā li gengemi.	Do this before you go to work.
Bi wani pele ji ngōva ?	Have you come this road before?
Bi na doilo ngova, *or* ngōva-ma ?	Have seen that before ?
Ji yese wani bima.	This one came before you.
Bī ya miando bi wa bi ji we.	Before you go there come and do so.
Ma li lo peǹ ngelei ī yā wa.	We will go before daylight.
Ji wo̱ ngi ndea, ngē, bā dogboi luwi.	I told you before not to clear the bush.
Bia wo̱ na welema ?	Have you done that before ?
Bi ya na wo̱ ngova ?	Have you been there before ?
Bi ya na yira ?	Have you ever been there ?

(4) Miscellaneous expressions relating to time.

Be gbele.	Just now.
Ku yeká ma.	Another day, another time.
Lo̱ yeká ma.	Ditto.
Ngau lọ̄le mia a wa ?	In how many months will he come ?
Bi lima yengema ngau woita va.	You are going to work for six months.
Fọ̄ lọ̄le ?	How many years ?
Fọ̄lọ̄ yira.	One day, *i.e.* period of daylight.
Fọ̄ yira.	One year.
Lo̱ lọ̄le ?	How many days ?
Ku fere, *or* Lo̱ fere.	Two days.
Fọ̄lī ji hũ.	To-day (a more emphatic form than *ha*).

Fọlī ji kpeṅ.	All this day.
Fọlọ ngundiei.	Midday.
Ku gbi ma.	Everyday.
Ye, ikpemé i leinga.	He says the time is late.
Ke i hueí wā pu a ngendé na.	And he killed ten animals that morning.
Migbele lo bi wā be?	When did you come here?
Ye, bi ngi mawulu kru.	He says, Wait for him a little.
Ngau nani i Sandi hũ.	She was four months in the Sandi bush.
Ke i ya hũ-i-yi fele.	And he went away for two days.
Fọ̄ yira so̲i gī bi loi.	I have not seen you for a whole year.
Fọ̄ yira i dogboi hũ.	He was one year in the bush.
A kpindi.	To-night.
Kpindi ji.	Last night.
Fọ̄ dewengoi.	Last year.
Fọ̄ neni ma mbe le lo.	Next year we will cut (the bush) here.
Bi li mi lo lo̲ fele ji hũ gī bi loni?	Where have you been these last two days?
Ngalui i la hũ yia nani.	The moon is four days old.
Ma li lo a ngenda vọlī.	We will go at sunrise.
Nga yi pu mahũ lo̲lu nya wama.	I will come in a fortnight.
Nga yi woita iwofelema nya (lo) wama.	I will come in a week.
Lo̲ wo̲fera nya wama.	Ditto.
Kpindi ji pi ngī yīni.	I did not sleep all night.
Ti me a kpindi na.	They ate that night.
Folī gbīa ke mu ya.	At sunrise we go.
Ngi yeto bingi ga li lo dogboi hũ.	I intended yesterday going to the bush.
Gī ko; be (*i. e.* gbe) ngewo.	I don't know; wait till daylight.
A wa lo kaká.	He will soon come.
Tato kaká.	Begin soon.
Yeka a gbowu nyama ji va.	I shall soon be tired of this.
Bi gbahã pei ji va.	You will soon be tired of this.

Bi na wei lo bi wa sange.	As soon as you have done that come.
Bi luva gbĭ mi lo ?	Where did you spend the day yesterday ?
I tewea poma kpeṅ.	He spent all the day cutting.
Kina gba ngi wani ngī bi loī be.	Since I came I have not seen you here.
Ti yī na sawa.	They spent three days there.
Kia ha wu wani migbe mia i lini ?	How long is it since he went away ?
Kina ha gba wu wani gbe yenge lo wu peni ?	Since you came here what work have you been doing ?
Kpindī wa.	Night comes.
Kpindī welea.	Ditto.
Ngelewo sina mu li na.	We will go there at daybreak to-morrow.
Lo̱ wo̱ita i bumbu ndo̱me.	After six days he picked himself up.
Mahei na fọ̄ i lewe nani i gbate gboṅ.	That king for over four years increased in wealth.
Ngau lọ̄le mia mu kei a wa ?	In how many months will master come ?

iii. Adverbs of Affirmation and Negation.

Ī *or* Ē.	Yes.
Er er.	No.
Sao, sago.	No (emphatic).
Hiye.	Certainly.
Kere ?	Is it not so ?
Yā, lā, mā.	Not.

A question is often answered in a few words similar to those used in asking the same.

iv. Adverbs of Manner, Intensitives, etc.

Adverbs of manner follow the verb they modify. They are numerous, numbering in all some hundred and fifty. A large proportion of them seem to have a very limited use, and are possibly only employed to modify certain verbs to which they specially belong. In their etymology they seem to have no connection with any other part of speech. In English, adverbs are largely formed from adjectives by the addition of the suffix *ly*, other European languages having a corresponding suffix. But Mende, though richer than some other African languages in adjectives, does not adopt any similar formation. An approach to it may, however, be considered as made in the use of the preposition *a*, *with*, with a noun, as *a pime*, with running, *a kaso*, with cunning, *a tonya*, with truth. Some adjectives also, as *gboto*, many, are used as adverbs.

Examples.

I ya a pime.	He ran off.
I penga a mamagé.	He acted foolishly.
Tewe gbotongo.	Cut plenty.
Tewe gboto.	Ditto.
I mea gbi.	He ate all.
I pei lo a nguwumage.	He did it of his own accord.
I ndọi le gboto.	She bore plenty of children.
I ndenga le gboto.	Ditto.

The following *adverbs of manner, etc.*, are in common use—

Gbama.	To no purpose, for nothing,
Gboma.	Again.
Gboṅ.	Very much.
Kā.	Very much.
Káká.	Quickly.
Lele.	Slowly.
Le.	A little.
Lome-lome.	Cautiously.
Lenga.	Together.
Tenga.	Perhaps.
Ni, *or* hĩ.	So, thus.
Panda.	Properly.
Tē (much drawn out in speaking).	Continuously.
Wā.	Very (is the adj. *great*).
Yeka, yeke, kine.	Nearly.

Examples.

Kpekpengo le gbama.	It is good for nothing.
I fei lo nya we gbama.	He gave it to me for nothing.
Wa gboma yira.	Bring one more.
Wa fere gboma.	Bring two more.
Wa gboma fere.	Ditto.
Hokeí gboma le?	Is it another guinea-fowl?
Bise, kā, kā.	Thank you very much indeed.
Ndakpei! je gā ngurī-oh.	Friend! hurry up with the stick.
I lembinga kā.	He delayed very much.
I pọ, kā kā.	He cut hard.
Wa káká.	Come quickly.
Pe káká.	Do it quickly.
Jia lele.	Walk slowly.
Jia lome-lome.	Walk cautiously.
Maw'u (mawulu) le.	Wait a little.
Tato le, *or* Tato gboma.	Begin again.
Wu fere a li a lenga.	You two go together.
Pe ṅi.	Do it so.
Pe panda.	Do it properly.
Bā dọ̄la sowi.	Do not stand too near.
Bi wolonga tē, bē gbē?	You have cried a long time, will you not stop now?
I ye jiama tē, ke i numu gbī loni.	He was walking continuously, and he saw nobody.
Bā nyoko we gboma.[1]	Do not do so again.
Bā yā na wī gboma.	Ditto.
Tenga mu li dogboi hũ sīna.	Perhaps we shall go into the bush to-morrow.
Kunafo bā pe hī.	Do not do it so in future.
Kunafo bā na nyọko wili.[1]	Ditto.
Njei yeka i wa.	The rain will soon be here. (lit: The rain has nearly come.)
I ye kine gulāma.	It was nearly falling.
Yeka i ha.	He is nearly dead.

[1] *Nyọko* is a noun, meaning 'manner.'

v. How?

The English *how* is expressed in many different ways as the following show—

Fọ̄ lọ̄le bi kenye ji hũ?	How many years have you been in this country?
Lọ̄le mia á ná?	How many are there there?
Nunga lọ̄le bi soa?	How many men have you obtained?
Nu lọ̄le mia ti bi yeya?	How many men have you?
Gbe jongo lo a ji?	How much is this?
I ye na ho?	How is it then?
Ta mia ga ye pe?	How am I to do it? What am I to do?
Tē, ma ye pe mu mbei ji me?	They said, How are we to eat this rice?
Ke angie ga ye pe.	Show him how to do it (how I do it).
Fọ̄ lọ̄le? lo̱ lọ̄le?	How many years? how many days?
Nwoni na ba ye tọ̄li?	How do you call that bird?
Ji wo bi wa bi hea be?	How long have you been sitting here?
Lo̱ lọ̄le bi ji weni?	How often have you done this?
Ji a hije be a li Mo̱fwe jia lọ̄le?	How far is it to Mo̱fwe?
Be ta Mo̱fwe jia lọ̄le?	Ditto.
Ba ye ji luli?	How do you call this?
Nga tuli a . . .	I call it . . .
Ta, *or* ti, tuli a . . .	They call it . . .
Kia ha wu wani migbe mia i lini?	How long is it since he went?
Ngau lọ̄le (mia) mu kei a wa?	In how many months will master come?

CHAPTER VIII

PREPOSITIONS

There is only one preposition properly so called in the Mende language, viz. *a*, with. The others are all postpositions. As, however, the word preposition is a recognized grammatical term it is more convenient to adhere to it. The reason for the idiom is not far to seek. A large number of the words used as prepositions are actually nouns, and the others, of which the derivation is not immediately apparent, are probably so by origin. Taking, therefore, the phrase *Ta pelei woma*, he is behind the house, it is seen at once that it can be translated, 'He is (at) the house's back,' *woma* being a noun meaning *back*, and the qualifying or possessing noun coming first in Mende as it also does in English. The noun, therefore, which is employed as a preposition is placed last.

There are no words for *from*, *without* and *out*. Prepositions representing *in* or *at*, etc., are used coupled with verbs whose sense is *exit*. Examples are given below.

List of Words used as Prepositions.

(1) Preposition preceding the noun—*a*, with

(2) Prepositions following the noun.

We *or* ye (according to euphony)	To.
Ma.	To.
Gama.	To, towards.
Va.	Of, for, and also the *to* in the infinitive mood.
Mahũ.	Upon.
Gulo, lugo.	In front.
Tenga.	Together with.

Of the above, *ma, gama, mahũ, gulo, tenga* are used also as adverbs ; *va* (as *fa*) is used as a conjunction. *A* and *we* therefore are the only ones that can be classified under prepositions, and under no other part of speech.

(3) Nouns used as prepositions. They follow the noun they govern.

Ngama (yama) (lit. eye or a face).	Before.
Labu (mouth—under).	Ditto.
Wōma.	Behind.
Kākā.	Side.
Kpela.	Near.
Ngeya (lit. hand).	With.
Ndia.	Middle.
Mba.	On top.
Ya (lit. edge).	Ditto.
Mbu.	Under.
Hũ.	In.
Gohũ.	Inside.

Examples.

a, with, etc.

Following the verb *gbate*, make, construct.

Ti hege gbate a gulī ji.	They make soap of this tree.

Following the verb *gili*, think.

Ye, bā gili á ná.	He said, Do not worry about it.

Following the verb *go*, give, or present with.

I ti go̱a a mehe.	He gave them food.
Sina ga bi go̱ lo a hale.	To-morrow I will give you medicine.

Following the verb *gū*, can.

Ī gu a lila.	He cannot go.

Following the verb *henga*, dream.

Ke nyapui be i hengá a pumoi.	And the girl dreamt of the white man.

Following the verb *jā*, touch.

Bā jā a tië.	Do not touch them.

Following the verb *ke*, show.

Ke angië ga ye pe.	Show him how to do it (how I do it).
Ke i hũgenga a ngi hiní.	And she told everything to her husband.
I ngi mayia ge a ngi kei.	She complained to her father.

Following the verb *li*, go.

Mu li a pelé na mu waila.	We go the road we came.
Li a ngië.	Take him away.

Following the verb *lọ̄*, want, like.

Nya longo a mehe.	I want food.
Gī loni á ná.	I do not like that.

Following the verb *dọ̄lọ̄*, dislike.

Ti lọ̄lọ̄ a ngië nu gbate va.	They disliked him because he was rich.

Following the verb *ndondo*, cease.

Ndondo a sore !	Stop that noise !

Following the verb *tọ̄tọ̄* or *tatọ̄*, begin.

I tọ̄tọ̄ a wo̱la.	She began to weep.
I tọ̄tọ̄ a nyandela.	It is beginning to improve.

Following the verb *wa*, come.

Bi wai lo a njiei ?	Have you brought a complaint ?
Bī wai lo a ngië ?	Have you brought him ?
Wā ko̱lé = wa a ko̱le.	Bring the paper or book.

Following the verb *yọ̄nga lewe*, boast.

Ke i yọ̄nga lenga a nasia gbele.	And he boasted over all of them.

Following the verb *pe* or *we*, do.

Gbo ba pe a gurī na.	What are you doing with that stick.

Other verbs sometimes admit of the same construction.

I ti dewe a fefele.	He sent them two by two.

We or *ye*, to, for.

Wala nya ye.	Bring them to me.
Tē, ngi wala bi ye.	I was told to bring them to you. (lit. They said, I bring to you.)
Ye lo bi wani a gọlé ji ngi ye?	Who have you brought this book for?
Ye lo i kọlé fe bi ye?	Who gave you the book?
Tē, mā kulu ngi ye.	They said, We do not agree to him.
Ji lọ̄ nya we.	Lift this for me.
Gbele, bē luma nya we?	What is the matter that you do not answer me?
I ya miaka (we).	He has gone in that direction.
I yala a pīme ngi lenga we.	He ran off with it to his children.
Ta pe yakama we.	It is somewhere round about the house.
Wā yenge silọï we.	Do not work for the spider.
Mu mbeí yilinga gengeb'ra we.	We have cooked rice for the labourers.
I ya ngi yei ye.	He has gone to his own country.

Ma, to.

Dē ngĭ ma.	Tell him.
Wa kakéi ji ma.	Come to this side.
Wa bi gbo nya ma.	Come and help me.
Hou na ma.	Catch hold of that.
Mbowé yakpa kọtī ji ma.	Sharpen the knife on this stone.
Njia nya ma.	I have a complaint.
Ke ti hitía mbei ma.	And they reached the rice.
A gbe sọré ma.	Leave off making that noise.
Ndọle ti ma.	They were hungry.
Bē gu na ma.	Cannot you do that.
Lọ yeká ma.	Another day.

Ko̱tī nya nwo̱na nya gowé ma.	A stone has cut my foot.
Hũei ji i ndowī boa ndo̱lé ma.	This animal dug the hole in the ground.
Ba ngi lo lo pelé ma.	You will see it in the road.
I ndọ̄mé gbia ngi ma.	He took off his shirt.
Nda table ma.	Lay it on the table.
Njī bi gbakima.	Lower it on your shoulder.
Ke i ngi lokoi lọ̄a dọ̄méma.	And he pointed his hand to his shirt.
I nye gbia njeí hũ, i pua ngiyé ma.	He took the fish out of the water and put it on the bank.
Gbonda ngi ma i wa.	Compel him to come.
Mu li jieisia ma ke mu wai.	We have been for a walk and we have come (back).
Nga na ma ko̱lo.	I shall try that.
I hite peli wāi ma.	He reached the road.
I gombui dọ̄a kpāléma.	He put fire to the farm.
Ke ti punga ndo̱lema.	And they planted it in the ground.
I tọ̄nga ti ma pelihũ.	He followed them into the road.
Mu gbi mu hite mu yeí ma.	Let us all go and meet our mother.
Nya gbãi lo bima.	You are indebted to me.
Nya gbãi bia.	Ditto.
Ngi gbãi lo nyama.	I am indebted to him.
Jo ngi gbãi lo Wuseni ma pun yira.	Wuseni owes Jo one pound.
Ta ngi banga ti gboni hini yira ma.	She and her friends shared one husband.
Gele na ma, *or* gele ma.	Stop that.

Ma is generally used after the verb *to go* when a place is not specified. When the place is mentioned by name no preposition is necessary. When another verb stands subordinate to the verb *to go*, the subordinate verb is treated as a pure infinitive, as *ti ya yīma*, they have gone to sleep; or as a verbal noun having the suffix *ma*, which takes all the inflections of a noun, as *ti ya ti yīmé* (indef. *yīma*), they have gone to their sleeping-place.

Mu li Sekondi.	We are going to Sekondi.
A mu li nya kpãi.	Let us go to my farm.
I ya gbōma.	He has gone to the w.c.
I ya ngọ̄li bọ̄ma.	He has gone to piss.
Mu ya yengemé.	We go to work.
Ke i ya jejiamé dogboi hũ.	And he went for a walk in the bush.
Li bi yengemé.	Go to your work.
Gī ngi lima gọ.	I do not know where he has gone.
Ke ti ya mehe go'eme.	And they went to find food.
Gbo bi wa pema nya gbeanga?	What are you coming to do with me? (lit. Near me.)
I ya nye gbeme njei hũ.	She went to catch fish in the water.

Gama, towards, at, etc.

Li bi nwoni gama gbe.	Go look for that bird.
Li mehé gama bi wala mu me.	Go and bring our food.
Kolé ji wumbu bi kei gama.	Take this letter to your master.
Wala gama.	Bring him forward.
Ti wa nja yela gama.	They came to some water.
Fomemoi i hei lo selé gama.	A man with a whip sat at the banana tree.
Numu yira lo nya gama.	One person is with me.
Numu yira dọ̄ nya gama.	Send one man to me.
Numu yira tewe nya gama.	Ditto.
Wuseni i ya kọle gama.	Wuseni has gone for letters.
Li bi pelei gama gbe.	Go and have a look at the house.
I hei lo sele gama.	He sat at the banana tree.
Wuseni lo Sandi gama.	Wuseni is with Sandi.
Li ngi gama.	Go for him.

Va, for, of.

Gboyei ī gbekpe gboliva.	Salt water is not good to drink.
Hale wu pundisia va.	Medicine for your mosquito (bites).

Mu ya me va.	We are going for food.
Kale ji ta nwonisia va.	This cartridge is for birds.
Ti lọlọ a ngie nu gbate va.	They disliked him because he was a rich person.
Ke nya va navo gbī nya yeya.	And as for me I have no money.
Bia lo nya va.	You belong to me.
Bī nya va	You are not here for me.
Bi be yo va? Ngi be bia va.	For whom are you here? I am here for you.
Ke i ya dogboi hũ nduwi va.	And he went into the bush to clear a farm.
Hani ji ī kpekpeni hani gbī va.	This thing is good for nothing.
Ji nyandengo bo̱ va?	Is this good for anything?
Ye, ngi wala bi va.	He said I was to bring it for you.

Mahũ, upon.

Pu kaṅa mahũ.	Put it on the box.
Nda table mahũ.	Put it above the table, *i. e.* on something on the table (on the table is *ma*).

Gulo, before.

Lọ ngi gulo.	Stand in front of him.
Ta pē gulo.	He is in front of the house.
Li bi hei ngi gulo.	Go sit down in the way for him.
Ta ngi gulo.	It is in front of him.

Tenga, along with, towards.

Bē yepe nya lenga?	Will you not talk with me?
Moremo a ti lenga.	Some of them were More men.

Yama, *ngama*, before.

Kpã ngi yama.	Count it in front of him.

Labu, before.

Ta (lo) pe labu.	It is in front of the house, *i.e.* just at the door.
Gulá ngi labu.	Throw it down in front of him.

Luwo, tuwo, lugo, tugo, before.

Ti tenga ta jia ngi lugo, ipe-keisia ngi woma.	Some walk in front of him, some behind.
Ta pē lugo.	He is in front of the house.
Pu ngi lugo.	Put it before him.

Wōma, behind.

Ta njei wōma.	He is across the water.
Ta lo nya wōma.	He is behind me.
Ku sawa wōma.	After three days.
Na wōma.	After that.
Li pelei wōma.	Go behind the house.
Njiei ji ga nde ba gbia nya wōma.	Do not repeat what I say.
A mu li njei wōma.	Let us cross the water.
Numu yira pē gohũ numu yira lo pe wōma.	One person is inside the house one is outside.
Ta pelei wōma.	He is outside the house.

Kaka, side.

Ta pe yaka ma we.	It is somewhere round the house.

Gbela, gbeanga, near.

Bā lọ̄ gbĭ ngombui gb'ra.	Do not stand too near the fire.
Bā pu gb'ra.	Do not put it near.
A mu jia njei gbeanga.	Let us walk close to the water.
Tia mu gbeanga.	They are near us.
Ti la mu gbela.	They approach us.
Gbo bi wa pema nya gbeanga ?	What are you coming to do at my place ?
I kpâle la tei gbela.	He laid out a farm near the town.

Ngeya, with.

Mbogbweí lo Wuseni yeya.	The cutlass is with Wuseni. (lit. The cutlass is in Wuseni's hand.)
Ta bi yeya.	It is with you.
Ī ngi yeya.	It is not with him.

Lia, middle.

Hei ndéndeí lia.	Sit in the middle of the boat.

Mba, upon.

Te wumba, *or* Te bi wumba.	Raise it on your head.
Ngulu wumba.	On the tree-top.
Ke i gbo̱lé gbia wumba.	And he took off his hat from his head.
Ti punga ngi wumba.	They put it on his head.
Bi bo̱ré wē bumba (= bi wumba).	Put on your hat.

Ya or *nga*, upon.

Pu ngombui ya.	Put it on the fire.
Hele fọ̄lī ya.	Hang it in the sun.
Ngulī ya.	On the tree.
Ko̱wī pu kọ̄lī ya.	Put wood in the fireplace.
I ya kpoyei ya.	It has gone over the sea.
Ke i bumbui welenga nga.	And he set the fish-trap on top.
Ngelewo i wa kale ya.	At daybreak he came to the fish-weir.
Ke i mbọ̄mbui gbia kalé ya.	And he took the trap off the weir.

Mbu, under.

Pē bu.	Indoors.
I gbia pebu.	He comes out of the house.
Yo na mbu?	Who is under that?
Li bi pebu gbe.	Go look inside the house.
Gi ya pebu.	I go home.

Hũ, in, inside.

NOTE.—*Hũ* is used as an affix to emphasize nouns which are material objects. It is attached to the indefinite form, as *nja*, *njăhũ*, water; but *njei hũ*, in the water. *Ta, tahũ*, the town; but *tei hũ*, in the town.

Nya gurī hũ.	I am in the tree.
I hitia ngulī hũ.	He came down the tree.
Pīli njei hũ.	Throw it into the water.
Pu njei hũ.	Put it in the water.
Kolé ji pu kaṅa hũ.	Put this paper in the box.
Ta njī hũ.	He is asleep.
Mu de ngiyeíhũ.	Let us cross the hill.
A mu li tei hũ.	Let us return home, *or* Go into the town.
Gbeva bi lembi hũ?	Why are you late?
Bi li milo lọ fele ji hũ gī bi loni?	Where have you been these last two days?
Njei lo pele hũ.	The road is under water.
I de ngeleya ngulī hũ.	He climbs the tree.
Fọlī ji hũ.	To-day.
Ba gbia fofu (*or* fofui) hũ.	Do not expose it.
Wa pe gohũ.	Come inside the house.

FROM, OUT, WITHOUT, ABOUT.

There are no separate prepositions for *from, out, without* and other similar words which have a sort of negative sense. They are expressed by words signifying positive position coupled with a verb of motion from.

Examples of *From*.

Bi na kpia ngi yeya.	Take that from him.
Bi na bumbu ngi yeya.	Ditto.
Nga nyahei gbia lo bi yeya.	I will take the woman away from you.
I nya yahumanga (to steal is *huma*).	He stole from me.
Sumba geya (= ngi yeya).	Snatch it from him.
Hō ngeya.	Ditto.
I hijéa ndọme.	He got up from the ground.

Out.

I gbiai lo pebu.	He has gone out of the house.
Gbia ndendeí hũ.	Get out of the boat.

Ta pelei woma.	He is outside the house.
I gbia dogboí hũ.	He came out of the bush.
I nye gbia njei hũ.	He pulled the fish out of the water.

Without.

Bere gbĩ ngi ma.	Without trousers.

About.

De nya ma kina ti ye ha jiani.	Tell me about their palaver.
Wu ye ha jiani ?	What was the discussion about to-day ?
Hũge angẽ panda.	Tell me all about it.
Ndapi ti koni nda lọ̃ni gbo ma ?	What did you fight about ?
Ndapi nda hije gbo ma ?	What did the fight arise about ?
Gbo̱ wani a ndapi ?	Ditto.
Njiei na lo navo va.	The affair was about money.

CHAPTER IX

CONJUNCTIONS

CONJUNCTIONS in the Mende language are few in number. A sequence of short direct sentences is made use of, each preceded by 'Ke, and'; or, if the subject is getting out of control, 'tamia, also, further' is put in to keep up the connection. Disjunctive conjunctions proper do not exist. The contrast of a positive sentence with a following negative sentence, or *vice versâ*, either with or without the assistance of a conjunctive conjunction, supplies the necessary distinction.

Some of the words in the following list of conjunctions might equally well be treated as adverbs.

Ta, *and;* only joins nouns, not sentences.
Ke, *and;* it can also be translated *but.* It is, however, not an emphatic *but,* which does not occur.
Be, *even, also, too.*
Jibe, kebe, *although.*
Ina, *if, supposing.*
Kina, kea, kia, *when, while, like.*
Ji, *when, if.*
Ko, *so that.*
Ngiye, *except.*
O, *or,* or *nor.*
Tabao, *neither.*
Tamia, *also, further.*

Therefore = Jiva, tamia, famia, fa le, ta ji, ta va.
But. No word. See examples.

And, ta, ke.

Hindọ̄i ta nyahei.	The man and the woman.
Ji ta ji le.	It is this and this.
Ke i ya.	And he went away.
Nyahei na ke ngi lọ̄i ti ya dogboi hũ.	That woman and her child went into the bush.
Fọ̄lī gbia ke mu ya.	At sunrise we go.
Ji ta ji ti mahë-u lo.	This and this are equal.

Pronouns joined together have a special construction, which see under 'Pronouns.' A similar construction prevails when pronouns are joined with nouns.

Ke ta ta ti ya.	And he and she they went.
Mā Wuseni mu ya.	I and Wuseni we went.
Hindei gbi bi lina, mā bia ma li na.	Wherever you go, you and I will go together there.
Bia wa Wuseni a li mia.	You and Wuseni go there.
Ke ta ngi kei ti gome.	And he and his father met.
Mu li ma nya ndewe.	Let us go, I and my brother.

Be, *even*, *also*, *too*, Ji be, ke be, *although*.

Be never occurs as the first word in the sentence. It follows *ji* and *ke*, and the meaning of the combination is *although*. *Be* may be regarded as an adverb, but it is more convenient to treat it with conjunctions. It must not be confused with *be* here.

Nya be gē bi go.	I will certainly not give you any.
Ndakpalọ̄i be ī pe lọ̄i koti-ma.	And the young man did not build the house on the rock.
Ke bawé be i gbale la.	And the 'maggot' also laid out a farm.
Yira be ī na.	Not even one is there.
Ke be nyawo ī le gbe i wa i ji wiri.	Although (=and indeed) he is not mine (one of my men), let him come and do this.

If = ina, etc.

If is rendered in a variety of ways. The conjunction *ina* may be employed, or a leading conditional sentence, in the perfect tense, etc.

Ina ga wa lo nga nde lo bima.	If I come I will tell you.
Nga ye wama nga nde lo bima.	Ditto.
Ina ngē wa nga nde lo bima.	If I do not come I will tell you.
Fọ̄lī gbiai lo ke nwoṅisia ti wa.	If the sun came out the birds would come.
Bi nduwenga lo, bē mbei me.	If you clear the ground you will not eat the food.
Bi penga lo, ba ha lo fe.	If you do it you will surely die.
Ye, bia bi lini siḷoi yengeme, bē mehe nene me.	He said, If you go and work for the spider, you will not eat nice food.

Kina, kea, when, as, etc., etc.

Kia ji na ; kia na na.	Like this ; like that.
Kia ngombu na.	Like fire.
Li bi wala kia ji na.	Go bring one like this.
Kea wogba mū wai be.	It is a long time since we came here.
Kina i ngi vogba kasiloi i gbenda.	When it beat him the spider snatched the fruit.
Kea bi nya gbe gē bi go.	If you drive me away I will not give you any.
Kina gba ngi wani ngī bi loi bē.	Since I came I have not seen you here.
Kia wo̱ bi nya njei gbeni nga bi wā lo.	Since you drove my mother out in former times I will kill you.
Kia nā mabie mu longa.	Since now we see each other.
Kea bi ya lo.	I suppose you are going.
Kia ha wu wani migbe mia i lini?	How long is it since he went?

So that, in order that, ko, or usually only consecutive sentences.

Ji gbate gi ko̱[1] lo.	Do this so that I may know.
Gbate kea gi ji we la.	Do this so that I can do it myself.
Ko̱ i ngi go̱le.	So that he might try him.

[1] *Ko̱* here means 'know.'

Therefore, ji va, fale, famia, ta ji, ta va, tamia.

Ta ji bi hanga.	Therefore you have died.
Ta va, ye, mu lima na.	Therefore he said, Let us go there.
Ngi yengé ī nyandeni tamia (*or* famia) ngi ngi gbeni.	His work was not good, so I dismissed him.

Tamia, further.

Ngē, ā nya la ge; tamia ā nya hinda hũge a ngi wongeisia.	I said, She must not mention my name; further, that she must not talk about my affairs to her relations.
Tamia ga ye pe?	So how am I to do it?

Except.

Numu gbī nya lọ̄i jolo ke a pe lọ̄ kotima.	Nobody shall marry my daughter except he build a house on the rock.

Neither, *nor*; *either*, *or*, tabao, o.

Ngī ye (*or* yema) ji tabao gī ye (*or* yema) ji.	I said, Neither this nor that.
Ndakpalọ̄i be ī pe lọ̄i kotīma, nyapọ̄i be ī ngi loko wuai mbei bu.	The young man neither built his house on the rock nor did the woman put her hand under the rice.
Ji fere le ngā yema.	I said neither of these.
Gī ye ji, gī ye ji.	Ditto.
O kea iji be na?	Or one like this?

Ji, when.

Ji wo ngi ndea nge, bā dogboi luwi.	I told you before not to clear the bush.
Ji wo bi wa bi hea be?	How long have you been sitting here?

But.

The contrast of positive and negative sentences supplies the equivalent.

Ye, Bi ji wī, tamia ye, bā na wī.	He said do this, but not that (lit. further he said, do not do that).

CHAPTER X

INTERJECTIONS

The following are the most common—

Oh, suffix, added especially when calling out in a loud voice to add emphasis, as—A mu li-oh, *let us go.*

E is also used in this sense as—Sandi-e, *i. e.* calling Sandi's name.

O, *O;* O Ngewo, *O God.*

K̲o̲ ! *ah !* an exclamation of surprise.

Ă ! *ah !* ditto.

Ombo ! *don't !* ndakwé' mbo ! *friend, don't !* an exclamation of warning.

Sio̲, *a curse = don't care.*

Ŭhŭ (er-hér), an exclamation of pleasure on grasping a fact.

Hoe ? An interrogative particle, equivalent to—shall we ?

PART III

VOCABULARIES

NOTE.—The accent in the definite is on the last syllable.

I. FURNITURE, UTENSILS, ETC.

Indefinite.	Definite.	English.
The English word.		table.
Kpakali.	kpakali.	arm-chair
Hewuru.	hewuri.	seat, stool (lit. sit-wood).
Kpuko.	kpukọi.	bed.
The English word.		pillow.
Tenti.	tenti.	mosquito-net.
Kańa.	kańa.	box, chest.
Kpangba.	kpangbe.	broom.
Ndīvale.	ndīvale.	broom or fly-brush.
Fe	fei.	pot.
Mita.	mite.	spoon.
The English word.		fork.
Mbowa.	mbowe.	knife.
Sani.	sani.	bottle.
The English word.		glass.
Mbọ̄la.	mbọ̄le.	cup.
Peleti.	peleti.	plate.
Kalu.	kalui.	basin.
Mbọ̄li.	mbọ̄li.	ditto
Meme.	meme.	looking-glass.
Faji.	faji.	(brass) kettle.
Washi = watch.		clock.
Kpegbe.	kpegbe.	comb.

No Mende word. Mori word is *Fayafŏnĭ*, pen.
No Mende word. Mori word is *Luave*, ink.

Parts of a pot.

Indefinite.	Definite.	English.
Fei dagbola.	fei dagbole.	stopper.
Fei mbọ̄lọ̄.	fei mboli.	neck.
Fei kohũ.	fei kohu.	body.
Fei togbula.	fei togbule.	bottom.
Samba.	sambe.	broad, open basket.
Tekpe.	tekpe.	closed basket.
Kāhã.	kāhei.	basket.
Kọ̄nda.	kọ̄nde.	mortar.
Ngala.	ngale.	mat.

II. Implements, etc.

Mbowa.	mbowe.	knife.
Mbogba.	mbogbwe.	cutlass.
Kpogbo.	kpogbwe.	hammer.
Hipo.	hipoi.	heavy hammer.
Kpakpa.	—	to hammer.
Kpato.	kpatoi.	cutlass.
Konu.	koni.	axe.
Gbānya.	gbānye.	pincers.
Buma.	bume.	gimlet.
Kegbwi.	kegbwi.	awl.
Kali.	kali.	hoe.
So̱wi.	so̱wi.	saw.
Geṅe.	geṅe.	saw (Not known by all Mendes).
Go̱li.	go̱li.	scissors.
Londema.	londeme.	nail.
Londema mumu.	londema mumui.	small nail.
Ndo̱li.	ndo̱li.	hook.

III. Colours—Adjectives.

Teli.	dedeli, telingo.	black.
Kole.	gogole, golengo.	white.
Kpou.	kpogbou, gboungo.	red, brown.
Bulw.	bulungo.	blue.
Pune.	punengo.	green.
Ngahũpu.	ngahũpungo.	variegated.

IV. Metals.

Indefinite.	Definite.	English.
Kani gbolo.	kani gboli.	gold.
Kani gọ̄le.	kani gọ̄li.	silver.
Tongo bolo.	tongoboli.	copper.
Tongo.	tongoi (tongwe).	brass.
Ko̱lu.	ko̱lī.	iron.
Sumbu.	sumbui.	lead.

V. Parts of the Body.

Note.—In addressing any question to a Mende about the following, the beginner is recommended to prefix *ngi*, his, to each word. The softened form of the initial consonant must then be used, also the definite form.

Indefinite.	Definite.	English.
Ngu.	nguï (wuï).	head.
Tāwa.	tawe (dawe).	forehead.
Ngama.	ngame (yame).	face, eye.
Hokpa.	hokpe.	nose.
La.	lei.	mouth.
Ne.	nei.	tongue.
Laguru.	laguri.	lip.
Ngongolu.	ngongoli (yongoli).	tooth.
Yele-yongolu.	yele-yongoli.	front-teeth.
Bato.	batoï.	back-teeth.
Kpo̱no.	kpo̱ne (gbo̱ne).	brain.
Kpokpo.	kpokpoï.	chin.
Ngọ̄li.	ngọ̄li (wọ̄li).	ear.
Ngonge (?).	ngonge (gonge).	back of head just above the neck.
Mbọ̄lọ̄.	mbọ̄li.	neck in front.
Mbọ̄ gohū.	mbọ̄ gohúi.	throat itself.
Mbọ̄ woma.	mbọ̄ womei.	back of the neck.
Mbọ̄li gọ̄tu.	mbọ̄li gọ̄tī.	apple in the throat.
Ngama bweka.	ngama bweké (yamabweke).	eyebrow, *or* eyelash.
Kpele.	kpele.	beard.
Ngundia.	ngundiei (wundiei).	hair of the head.
Njọ̄mbọ̄.	njọ̄mbọ̄i (yọ̄mbọ̄i).	hair of the body, plumage of birds.
Ndega.	ndege.	hair round the private parts.

Indefinite.	Definite.	English.
Ko̱lo.	ko̱le (go̱le).	skin.
Ndīma.	ndīmei (līmei).	chest.
Kọ̄.	kọ̄ï.	belly.
Kohũ.	kohui (gohui) *or* koihũ.	belly.
Gombu.	gombui.	lower part of the belly.
Hama.	hame.	waist.
Pōma.	pōmei (wōmei).	back.
Kaka.	kakei (gakei).	side.
Ngọ̄to.	ngọ̄tui.	backside.
Ngowo.	ngowi.	back below the waist.
Hokpo.	hokpoi.	navel.
Yōvota.	yo̱votei.	testicles.
Mbulo.	mbule.	penis.
Ngoli.	ngolī (wolī).	tail.
Nini.	ninī.	breasts.
Toko.	tokoi (lokoi).	hand, lower arm.
Yeja loko, *or* yejama loko.	yeja lokoi.	right hand.
Kowo loko, *or* kowoma loko.	kowo lokoi.	left hand.
Kpaki.	kpaki (gbaki).	shoulder, upper arm.
Kpambu.	kpambui (bwambui).	arm-pit.
Nŏko.	nŏkoi.	elbow.
Lokoyuo.	lokoyuī.	finger.
Ngengalu.	ngengalui.	finger-nail.
Loko hina.	loko hinei.	thumb.
Loko vele.	loko vele.	palm of hand.
Kowo.	kowe (gowe).	foot, leg generally.
Lowe.	lowe.	hip.
To̱hũ.	to̱hui.	hip.
Kpala.	kpale.	thigh.
Ngombi.	ngombi (gombi).	knee.
Haka.	hakai.	lower leg, calf.
Gbowo.	gbowi.	ankle.
Ko̱wola.	ko̱wolei.	ankle.
Go̱woyuo.	go̱woyui.	toe.

Indefinite.	Definite.	English.
Gowo hina (short for *gowo yuo hinéi*).	gowo hinei.	big toe.
Kowo digbe, *or* digba.	kowo digbi.	heel.
Kaka.	kakei (gakei yakei).	rib.
Ndata.	ndate (late).	vein *or* tendon.
Gowo-woma-lata.	gowo-woma-late.	tendon at back of ankle.
Kale.	kale (gale).	bone.
Līhũ gale.	līhũ gale.	backbone.
Nyene.	nyene.	liver.

VI. Diseases.

Indefinite.	Definite.	English.
Kohũgbia.	kohũgbiei.	diarrhœa.
Kpūkpula.	kpūkpule.	ditto.
Sondo higbe.	sondo higbe.	dysentery.
Legeli.	legelī.	ulcer.
Kpama.	kpame.	sore.
Geli.	gelī.	sore.
Kanya.	kanye.	gonorrhœa.
Kegeri.	kegeri.	yaws.
Bombo.	bombui.	small-pox.
Nyenye.	nyenye.	chicken-pox.
Pene.	pene.	ringworm.
Noho.	nohoi.	craw-craw.
Sugbu.	sugbui.	a wasting skin disease.
Kpokpolu.	kpokpolui.	leprosy.
Pupu.	pupui.	freckles.
Ndivo.	ndivōï.	small boil.
Fehani.	fehanī.	tumour.
Bweli.	bwelī.	bad boil.
Kala.	kale *or* kãe.	a boil that travels.
Bọlo.	bọlī.	a worm of any kind, tapeworm, guinea-worm.
Kporo, kporongo (adj.).		lame.
Gbale (verb).	—	to pain.
Bālī (verb).	—	to vomit.
Kāle higbe.	kale higbei.	rheumatism.

Indefinite.	Definite.	English.
Njī higbe.	nji higbei.	sleeping sickness.
Pǫpǭle.	pǫpǭlei.	a skin disease leaving white patches on the (black) skin.

VII. Relationships, Titles, etc.

Hiñdǫ.	hindǭi.	man.
Tamo.	tamoi.	man.
Kena *or* kene.	kene.	elderly man.
	kene !	sir !
Kena wova.	kena wovei.	old man.
Ndakpalǫ.	ndakpalǭi.	young man.
	ndakpwe !	young man ! Used by men to each other when no name is expressed
Hini.	hini.	husband.
Bo̱ilǭpǫ.	bo̱ilǭpǭi.	servant.
Ndǭpǫ.	ndǭpǭi.	boy.
Nu dogbe.	nu dogbe.	young man.
Ke.	kei.	father, master.
	keke !	my father ! sir !
	nya kei	my father ! my master !
Mbā	mbāi.	friend or companion of the same sex.
	mbā ! / mbǭi !	friend ! used by women to each other.
Nyaha.	nyahei.	woman, wife.
Nyapǫ.	nyapui.	girl, young woman.
	ngi nyahei.	his wife.
	ngi nyapui.	his concubine.
Nyālǫ.	nyalǭi.	girl as opposed to boy.
Nje.	njī.	mother.
	Ye !	mother ! madame !
Mama.	mamé.	an elder person of either sex.

Indefinite.	Definite.	English.
	mamé !	mother ! A title of any old woman.
	mamé na.	that old woman.
	mama wovei.	the old woman.
	mama !	mamma. Used by an infant to its mother.
Kpawọ̄.	kpawọ̄i.	widow.
Njamo.	njamoi.	friend. Used by men or women.
	njamo !	friend.
Ndiamo.	ndiamoi.	friend.
Kombi.	kombi (same as *ndiamoi*).	friend.
	nya njamoi.	my friend.
Lēmo.	lēmoi.	natural father.
	pappa.	what an infant calls its father.
Ke.	kei.	not necessarily the natural father—rather master.
	keisia.	ancestors.
Ndewe, nde.	ngi ndiwi, *or* ngi ndĭ.	his brother.
	ngi nde wāi.	his big brother.
	ngi nde wulī, *or* wu'i.	his little brother.
Nde nyalọ̄.	nde nyalọ̄i.	sister.
	ngi nde nyalọ̄i.	his sister.
Lọ̄.	lọ̄i.	son, daughter.
Njī wulọ̄.	njī wulī.	aunt.
Kenya.	kenye.	uncle.
Mama.	mama.	grandfather or grandmother.
Mbela.	mbile (mbiri).	brother-in-law or father-in-law.
Njīmo.	njīmoi.	mother-in-law
	ngi yemoi.	his mother-in-law.
	ndengesia.	children, also followers.
Maha.	mahei.	chief.

Indefinite.	Definite.	English.
Sama.	same.	wealthy person or distinguished person.
Felanga.	felangesia.	twins.
Mba wa.	mba wai.	elder brother or senior; applied to things also.
Kpia lọ̄.	kpia lọ̄i.	first-born.
Jia lọ̄.	jia lọ̄i.	a child that can just walk.
Pọ̄ndọ̄.	pọ̄ndọ̄i.	orphan.

VIII. Seasons, Times, etc.

Indefinite.	Definite.	English.
Hawa.	hawa.	hour.
Ku.	kuï.	day.
Lo̱.	lo̱ï.	day.
Fọ̄lọ̄.	fọ̄lī.	day *or* sun.
Ngalu, ngau.	ngaluï, yaluï.	month.
Fọ̄.	fọ̄ï.	year
	(No word for week.)	
Hāma.	hame.	wet season.
Ngọ̄vọ̄.	ngọ̄vọ̄ï (ngēvọ̄).	dry season.
Kpēle.	kpēlei.	season.
Kpē.	kpei.	season.
Kpelema.	kpelemei.	time.
	ngēlēwo, ngewo, ngewa.	at daybreak.
Ngenda vọ̄lọ̄.	ngenda vọ̄lī.	morning sun.
Ngenda.	ngende.	morning.
	fọ̄lī gbīa.	at sunrise.

(Fọ̄lọ̄ hijengoi, the risen sun, but this is apparently not used as a mark of time.)

Indefinite.	Definite.	English.
Fọ̄lọ̄ ngundia.	fọ̄lọ̄ ngundiei.	noon.
Kpoko vọ̄lọ̄.	kpoko vọ̄lī. / kpoko vọ̄'i.	afternoon and evening.
	fọ̄li gula.	at sunset.
Kpindi.	kpindi.	night.
Kpindi lia.	kpindi liei.	midnight.

Months.

Definite.	English (roughly).
Pegbe.	January.
Vuī.	February.
Nyaha wo̱li.	March.
Burui.	April.
Goli.	May.
Cheje.	June.
Nanoi.	July.
Dawi.	August.
Sāi.	September.
Galui.	October.
Lubuyalui (pron. almost *lubwiale*).	November.
Pọ̄ndọ̄i.	December.

Rice Seasons.

Po kpwele.	Bush cutting time.
Moto kpwele.	Burning time.
Duwe kpwele.	Clearing time for small bush.
Dọ̄kwaiambwehũ.	Clearing time for bigger bush. (lit. Big clearing in the rice.)
Mbawu kpwele.	Rice planting time.
Wugbia kpwele.	Weeding time.
Mbale kpwele.	Rice cutting time.
Kova kpwele.	Slack or fallow time.

IX. House, and its Parts.

Indefinite.	Definite.	English.
Pēlē, wēle, pē, wē.	pēléi, wēléi.	house.
Kongọ̄.	kungọ̄i.	annex, outhouse, room.
Kundọ̄.	kunde.	corner, recess.
Kundéhũ.	kundéhũ.	corner, recess for a bed.
Sokuihũ.	sokuihũ.	corner, etc. Sometimes used for *kundehũ*.
Pēlē la, *or* pēlē nda.	pele ndei.	doorway.
Nete.	nete.	door itself.
Ndaoma.	ndaome.	window.

Indefinite.	Definite.	English.
Pē yasehũ (pr. pīásihũ).	pē yasehũ.	verandah.
Pe gohũ.	pe gohũ.	the inside of the house.
Kulahũ.	kulahũ.	ridge-beam.
Ndia wulu.	ndia wulī.	ditto.
Kpekpahũ.	kpekpahũ.	ditto.
Dingbo.	dingboï.	long posts of a house.
Po̱junge.	po̱junge.	rafter.
Nde kpenge.	ndekpenge.	cross-beam.
Sema.	seme.	bamboo. Used in construction.
Keni.	keni.	
Kọ̄nu.	kọ̄nī.	'nduvu' palm branch used in construction.
Njasa.	njase, yase.	thatch, generally.
Tọ̄wa.	tọ̄we.	side posts, whether forked or not.
Ndo̱mē.	ndo̱me.	floor.
Ndo̱wa.	ndo̱we.	hole.
Pewumba.	pewumba.	house-top.
Pewunga.	pewunga.	
Kăta.	kate.	fence.
Kātéhũ.	kātéhũ.	garden, compound.
Kātė la.	kāté lei.	gate.
Ngoré la.	ngoré lei.	ditto.

Ngitiya.	Outside.
Pē wọ̄ma.	Behind the house.
Pē bu.	Indoors.
Ta pē lugo.	It is in front of the house.
Ta pē labu.	It is at the door.
Ta pē tawe.	It is just beyond the doorway.
Ta pē gulo.	It is in front of the house.
Ta pe lamei.	It is just inside the entrance.

X. Games, Dances, Music, etc.

Dọ̄li.	dọ̄lī.	dance, play.
Dọ̄limo.	dọ̄limoi.	dancer.

Indefinite.	Definite.	English.
	ngeya lǭli.	a skipping dance.
	kogba lǭli.	somersault.
	mbembe lǭli.	two persons swinging round on a rope until one falls.
	kpala lǭli.	a dance on stilts in costume.
	sohina lǭli.	a dance with a string tied to the big toe.
	wundai.	a dance round the fire.
	jeke lǭli.	dance with rattles.
	kǭsi lǭli, *or* ndǭsǭ lǭli	a conjuring play.
	ko lǭli	war dance.
	kangbumbu lǭli	a play of cutting wood and narrowly escaping cutting the hand.
Sangba.	sangbai.	drum.
Segbula.	segbule.	a rattle made of a calabash with beads.
Mbiri.	mbiri.	a big drum.
Fanga.	fange.	drum with strings on the side to press on.
Bulu.	bului.	trumpet.
Mbaka.	mbake.	music; any stringed instrument.
Ba.	bāï.	a musical instrument with notes which are tapped.
Ndapi.	ndapi.	wrestling.
Ngule.	ngule.	song, *or* to sing.
Tēgǭkǭ.	tēgǭkǭi.	board for playing the game of *ti*, a game played with pebbles on a board of a dozen holes.

XI. Trees, Plants, etc.

General.

Nguru.	ngurī.	tree.
Kpiti.	kpiti.	plant, weed, grass.
Kowu.	kowī.	wood, fallen tree.
Nguru bǭwa.	nguru bǭwe.	flower.
Ndā, lā.	lāi.	leaf.

Indefinite.	Definite.	English.
Tifa.	tife.	leaf, twig.
Kale.	kale.	seed.
Mbeke.	mbeke.	branch.

Grasses and Grains.

Indefinite.	Definite.	English.
Fo̱ni.	fo̱nī.	grass.
Yāni.	yānī.	a spreading grass.
Ngara.	ngare.	a very tall coarse grass.
Potē.	potē.	a grass the seeds of which are eaten.
Nyọ̄.	nyọ̄i (newee).	maize.
Nyoko.	nyokoī.	sugar-cane.
Gbēlinyọ̄.	gbēlinyọ̄i.	millet.
Keti.	ketī.	guinea-corn.
Mba.	mbei.	rice.

Descriptions of Rice.

Indefinite.	Definite.	English.
Kokovaia.	kokovaia, *or* kokovaiye.	slow growth; several heads to one stalk; grows anywhere.
Bongo.	bongoë.	short thick grain; planted in mud.
Manika.	manikei.	long grain.
Jo̱bo.	jo̱bo̱i.	long grain, sweet flavour.
(?) Vubata.	vubatei.	the same rice, plentiful grain in ears.
(?) Bagiba.	bagibei.	(ditto, bracketed with above)
Sangenya.	sanganya.	ripens slowly.
Wuja wuru.	wuja wurī.	small grain, black, grows quickly.
Pava.	pave.	tasteless, grows slowly.
Fase.	fase.	ditto.
Sandi.	sandi.	ditto.
Tupu bongo.	tupu bongoi.	striped.
Gorofeli.	gorofeli.	long haired.
Gete.	gete.	short grained.
Pende.	pende.	early rice, short.
Pendege.	pendege.	ditto.
Yake.	yake.	American rice, grows in water.
Gobe.	gobe.	
Yele.	yele.	requires cutting quickly after ripening.
Mbawu.	mbawuï.	ear of rice.

Palms.

Indefinite.	Definite.	English.
Tokpo.	tokpoi.	oil palm.
Kewe.	kewe.	fan palm.
Nduvu.	nduvuī.	rafia vinifera.
Keri. Madrá.	keri. madrá.	sharp-leafed palm; grows on edge of brackish water; used for making mats. Neither are pure Mende words.
Sema (?), *also* semi.	seme, *or* semi.	bamboo.
Keni.	keni.	ditto.
Kavū.	kavuï.	palm with very slender leaves and stem.
Pamba.	pambe.	screw palm.
Kpura.	kpuré, kpurāi.	rattan.
Ngavu.	ngavui.	inferior date palm.
Pulo̲lu, *or* pudo̲lu.	pulo̲lī.	cocoanut palm.

Products of Palms.

Tọ̄wu.	tọ̄wī.	oil palm nut.
Tewu.	tewī.	ditto.
Kale.	gale.	kernel.
Kaje.	kaje.	piassaba—fibre of the *nduvu*.
Kenji.	kenji.	seed of the *nduvu*.
Nini, *or* niniha.	nini, *or* ninihe.	flower of the oil palm.
Tokpo lo̲.	tokpo lo̲i.	palm wine.
Ngulo gbou.	ngulo gbouï.	palm oil.
Konu.	konī.	branch of the *nduvu*.
Dāngulo.	dāngule.	palm kernel oil.

Foods.

Mana.	mane.	plantain.
Sele.	sele.	banana.
Saro.	saroï.	orange.
Dumbele.	dumbele.	lime, *or* orange.
Dumbele nyenye.	dumbele nyenye.	lime.
Fakali.	fakali.	pawpaw.

Indefinite.	Definite.	English.
Nesi.	nesi.	pineapple.
Belu.	beluï.	pineapple (not so much used).
Bondo.	bonde.	okro.
Kojo.	kojī.	garden egg.
Gbŏla.	gbole.	garden egg, different variety.
Tola.	tole.	bean.
Tọ̄wa.	tọ̄we.	pumpkin.
Puje.	puje.	pepper.
Tọ̄lọ̄.	tọ̄lī.	kola.
Ngengele.	ngengele.	crincre.
Yawa.	yawe.	onion.
Ngawū.	ngawī.	yam.
Mbōle.	mbōle.	yam.
Njọ̄wī.	njọ̄wī.	sweet potato, *or* any potato.
Tanga.	tange.	cassada.
Nikili.	nikili.	ground nut.

Trees.

Indefinite.	Definite.	English.
Tingo.	tingi.	mangrove.
Nja wulu.	nja wulī.	soap tree, *or* sea apple.
Hege gulu.	hege gulī.	ditto.
Yowulu.	yowulī.	ditto.
Kata wulu.	kata wulī.	tree used for hedges. Sierra Leone English, 'pig nuts.'
Nguwo.	nguwe.	silk cotton tree.
Bọ wulu.	bọ wulī.	baobab.
Hendō.	hendōi, *or* hende.	a red hardwood tree.
Tijo.	tijoï.	a hardwood tree with fibrous bark.
Mbele.	mbele.	a hardwood tree with buttresses.
Sema.	seme.	a big forest tree.
Kpatọ̄.	kpatọ̄i.	? a kind of wild walnut.
Mambo.	mambui.	a tree with soft nuts with velvety shell; edible.
Timipofo.	timipofoi.	(ditto, bracketed with above)
Gbọ̄ji.	gbọ̄jī.	a tree with a yellow plum-like fruit with pleasant taste.
Bōnī.	bōnī.	a sap tree with large fleshy leaves. The juice is said to cure toothache.

Indefinite.	Definite.	English.
Yōgbū yambe.	yōgbū yambe.	a tree with red fruit size of an apple, rough skin, red inside.
Bondo.	bonde.	tree with flowers like apple blossom. The red seeds from pods, which grow in clusters, make an orange dye.
Guava.	guava.	guava.

Rubbers.

Indefinite.	Definite.	English.
Bobo.	boboë.	funtumia.
Kobo.	koboë.	a rubber tree.
Jenje.	jenje.	a rubber vine.
Gomo.	gomoë.	a rubber tree, also another tree from which gum exudes.
Jiawa.	jiawāi.	a rubber tree inferior to *bobōë*; ? the kickxia.
Hǫle.	hǫle.	a tree with a juice used for catching birds.

Plants, Flowers, etc.

Indefinite.	Definite.	English.
Tāwa.	tawe.	tobacco.
Tāwa vuka.	tāwa vuke, *or* tāvuke.	snuff.
Vo̱nde.	vo̱nde.	a plant used for tobacco; the juice is drawn up into the nostrils for snuff.
Manga.	mange.	a parasitic plant on fan palms; has sharp cones at base.
Dawu.	dawui.	a vine; the leaves crushed put into a pool kill the fish.
Kama.	kame.	a plant with coarse leaves which are used for sand-paper.
Fale.	fale.	mushroom, *or* fungus.
Pŏni.	pŏnī.	a plant for making baskets; the red pod at the root is eaten.

Indefinite.	Definite.	English.
Kpŭlă.	kpŭle.	a large gourd.
Fore.	fore.	canna lily.
Nengbe.	nengbe.	a water lily with long leaves.
Pupende.	pupende.	a water lily with round leaves.
Nyọ̄mba (?)	nyọ̄mbe.	a shrub with small red seeds having black heads.
Njọ̄we.	njọ̄wī.	a large poisonous bean.
Fande wulu.	fandé wulī.	the cotton plant.
Mbalu.	mbalui.	a creeper used to make a loop to climb palm trees.

XII. Animals.

Indefinite.	Definite.	English.
Hũa.	hũei.	animal.
Ndopa.	ndope.	antelope, *or* deer.
Nika.	nike.	cow (generally).
Nika ha.	nika hei.	cow.
Nika hine.	nika hinei.	bull.
Mbala.	mbale.	sheep.
Nje.	njei.	goat.
Ndọ̄nde.	ndọ̄nde.	pig.
Ko̱li.	ko̱lī.	leopard.
Kọ̄wi.	kọ̄wī.	? jackal.
Nguahī.	nguahī.	a small animal that eats roots; same size guinea-pig.
Pekulọ̄.	pekuli.	small animal with a sharp nose and mouth set underneath.
Kewulọ̄.	kewuli.	different dialectic names for same kind of animal, a big spotted bush cat, hair rather than fur, loose ridge of skin down its back.
Ko̱wulọ̄.	ko̱wuli.	
Subu.	subuï.	hyæna.
Njala.	njale.	lion.
Kaikulọ̄.	kaikuli.	a ground squirrel.
Ndandakulọ̄.	ndandakuli.	? mongoose.
Pewi.	pewī.	bush cat, long tail; paradoxus.
Nyamgbe.	nyamgbe.	bush cat, soft fur, spotted.
Go̱ne.	go̱ne.	cat.

Indefinite.	Definite.	English.
Lọ̄lọ̄.	lọ̄lī.	cat.
Kānye.	kānye.	ant-eater.
Tọ̄wa wulọ̄.	tọ̄wa wulī.	bush goat; ? gazelle, very small horns.
Ngo̱to.	ngotī.	water-buck.
Heke.	heke.	bush cow.
Tewu.	tewī.	bush cow, a buffalo.
Nguli.	ngulī.	? hartebeest.
Hagbewulo̱.	hagbewuli.	small brown animal.
Hāgbe.	hagbei.	ditto; ? weasel.
Ngila.	ngile.	dog.
Nyine.	nyine.	rat.
Kiwulọ̄.	kiwuli.	ground pig.
Kuwulō.	kuwuli.	ditto.
Fọ̄lọ̄gbetē.	fọ̄lọ̄gbete.	striped rat.
Lendé.	lende.	mouse.
Piwi.	piwi.	porcupine.
Sewulo.	sewulī.	guinea-pig.
Sese.	sesei.	a squirrel.
Bovi.	bovī.	something like a *sese*, but larger.
Seje.	sejei.	small animal with quills on its tail like a porcupine.
Dava.	dave.	bat, small.
Taja.	taje.	bat, medium.
To̱ka.	toke.	bat, large.
Bamọ̄.	bamọ̄ï.	baboon.
Gbūlō.	gbūlī.	a tree bear; calls at night as it climbs a tree.
Kwa.	kwāi.	monkey.
Tọ̄wa.	tọ̄we.	big black monkey, long tail.
Dogbo yusu.	dogbo yusui.	chimpanzee; regarded as a half-man.
Kŏnjō.	kŏnjō.	gorilla.
Hele.	hele.	elephant.
Njahele.	njahele.	hippopotamus.

XIII. Birds.

Ko̱wo.	ko̱we.	a large black and white eagle.
Kokogbia.	kokogbie.	a brown eagle.

Indefinite.	Definite.	English.
Bombo.	bomboï.	same as *kokogbie.* Different dialect.
Gere.	geri.	brown fish hawk. Different names.
Kuanja.	kuanje.	
Hewe.	hewe.	same as *geri.*
Dogbo gere.	dogbo geri.	bush *geri.* Larger than *geri.* Similar appearance. Lives in the bush.
Sekpende.	sekpende.	grey hawk.
Sekulo.	sekuli.	small speckled hawk. Chases small birds. Sits on a tree very upright.
Yība.	yibe.	vulture.
Jība.	jibe.	same as *yibe.* Different dialect.
Goma.	gome.	black and white crow.
Pǭwǭ.	pǭwī *or* pǭwe.	big brown dove. General name given to any dove or pigeon.
Bǭmǭkulǭ.	bǭmǭkulĕ.	small brown ground dove.
Povǭvǭ.	povǭvui.	green pigeon.
Hǭkē.	hǭkēi.	guinea-fowl.
Kokoye.	kokoye.	bush-fowl.
Sāsālo.	sāsālōï.	red-legged partridge.
Fǭk(u)lǭ.	fǭk(u)lǭï.	small brown partridge the size of a quail.
Kokolowe; ?also kowedǭwe.	kokolowe.	like the *sāsālōï.* Calls at night.
Gǭwa.	gǭwāi.	clock-bird. Green. Crested.
Piangbia.	piangbiĕ.	hornbill. Black mostly. All feathers.
Gula.	gule.	? toucan. A reputed two-headed bird from a growth on top of its head. Size of a crow. Black, with long tail.
Ndulu.	ndulī.	brown bird with white breast and mournful cry. Said to kill snakes. Size of a grey parrot.

Indefinite.	Definite.	English.
Bovonwoni.	bovonwoni.	small yellow bird.
Goronwoni.	goronwóni.	blackbird larger than a sparrow. Live in parties.
Mbaku.	mbakui.	weaver-bird. Black with red. Size of a sparrow.
Sele.	selei.	weaver-bird. Blue and green. Size of a sparrow.
Dea.	deai.	weaver-bird. Like *mbaku* in appearance.
Ndābọ.	ndābọ̄ï.	a small bird that weaves a nest in the grass.
Sokulimanja.	sokulimanje.	black and white bird. Male has a tail nearly a foot long. Smaller than a sparrow.
Pangbambalu.	pangbambalui.	black bird with yellow slash. Size of a sparrow.
Kpā-ndēvē, *or* bādēvē.	kpā-ndēvē, *or* bādēvē.	swallow.
Jeme.	jeme.	greenish bird with long curved beak. Smaller than a sparrow.
Membọ.	membui.	brown bird with red breast and neck. Smaller than a sparrow.
Kpopomanja.	kpopomanje.	woodpecker.
Dogbobaku.	dogbobakui.	canary.
Sọ̄kele.	sọ̄kele.	tiny bird. Many live together.
Yegbe.	yegbe.	? night-jar. Mottled brown bird. Size of a pigeon. Flies at dusk. Different dialects.
Jowi, *or* Yowi.	jowī, *or* yowī.	(ditto, bracketed with Yegbe)
Gbegbe.	gbegbī.	parrot.
Fabọ.	fabuī.	ditto.
Fawugbekpe.	fawugbekpei.	grey parrot. The combination seems dialectic.
Kakibo.	kakibōï.	greenish bird. Size of a sparrow.
Sanga.	sange.	kingfisher. Many coloured.

Indefinite.	Definite.	English.
Kakibo.	kakiboï.	kingfisher. Some black and white; some all colours rainbow.
Tē	tēi.	fowl.
Tē hina.	tē hine.	cock.
Tē ha.	tē hei.	hen.
Tē lọ̄.	te lọ̄ï.	chicken.
Do̱wi.	do̱wī.	duck.
Tolotolọ̄.	tolotolọ̄ï.	turkey.
Tọ̄lọ̄ngenge.	tọ̄lọ̄ngengé.	water-wagtail.
Mbū.	mbūï.	owl.
Yọ̄vo.	yọ̄vui.	pepper-bird. A bird something like a sparrow, but larger. Eats peppers.
Kegewe.	kegewe.	witch-bird. As big as a parrot. Calls at evening. Children are said to be changed into it.
Tutu.	tutui.	small wading bird. Body brown; throat white; beak $\frac{3}{4}$ in. and bluish; blue patch on top of head; legs grey.
Kingi.	kingi.	grey wading bird. Same size as *tutui*. Beak yellow with black on top.
Hoho	hohoi	? cormorant. Body like a duck's. Breast white with thick plumage; back greenish; throat brown; feet webbed and black; beak short, hooked, yellow, with black end. Size big pigeon. Also the black cormorant.
Kekele.	kekele.	snippet.
Jakoku.	jakokui.	grey water-bird. Larger than a pigeon.
Nyagbesuli.	nyagbesuli.	small greyish-green heron.
Solōwa.	solōwai.	Ditto. Different dialect.
Yọ̄nembe.	yọ̄nembe.	egret. Body white, beak yellow.

Indefinite.	Definite.	English.
Banī.	banī.	white wading bird. Smaller than *yọnembē*.
Tevenwoni.	tevenwonī.	big black wading bird. Four feet wing to wing. Long beak black with red; white neck; black legs.

XIV. Reptiles, Fish, etc.

Indefinite.	Definite.	English.
Nye.	nye.	fish.
Kali.	kali.	snake.
Ndili.	ndili.	python.
Tupu.	tupuī.	puff-adder; ? cerastes.
Ndovopŏle.	ndovopŏlē.	small fat snake, a foot long. Poisonous, but not deadly.
Kenji gọ̄rọ.	kenji gọ̄ri.	tree-snake; thin; 3 to 4 ft. Brown stripe along it.
Ndawundo kali	ndawundo kali.	green snake.
Nguru.	ngurui.	black snake.
Ndamba.	ndambe.	crocodile.
Pama.	pame.	iguana.
Kọ̄lọ.	kọ̄lī.	red-headed lizard.
Kpeni.	kpeni.	speckled lizard.
Kogo-nje.	kogo-njei.	slow-worm. Said to have a head at each end, owing to its tail being the same shape as its head.
Ndọ̄kulọ.	ndọ̄kule.	chameleon.
Ngaku.	ngakuī.	crab.
Ndọ̄vọ.	ndọ̄vọi.	toad.
Jībele.	jibele.	bull-frog.
Kpwegbi.	kpwegbi.	croaking frog.
Gbasonde.	gbasonde.	green tree frog.
Banasowe.	banasowe.	flesh-coloured climbing frog.
Kondo.	kondui.	small fish found in mangrove swamps. Jumps, and climbs trees. Swims with its head out of water.
Haku.	hakwe.	turtle.
Nwoniga.	nwonigei.	oyster, or rather oyster-shell.
Bonge.	bonge.	a fish; ? herring.
Pọ̄lī.	pọ̄lī.	same as *bonge*.

Indefinite.	Definite.	English.
Kenje	kenje	fresh water flying-fish.
Tumu.	tumui.	shark.

XV. Insects.

Indefinite.	Definite.	English.
Fuhani.	Fuhani.	insect generally.
Fo.	Foi.	big biting fly.
Pundi.	Pundi.	mosquito.
Fufu.	fufuī, *or* fufuihũ.	moth.
Komi.	komī.	bee.
Higbo.	higboï.	a wasp of sorts. Makes a white hanging comb.
Dọmbe.	dọmbe.	wasp that digs a hole in the ground.
Bewe.	bewe.	a bright-coloured beetle that digs a hole in the ground.
Silo.	siloï.	spider.
Kogonde.	kogonde.	butterfly.
Papapoli.	papapoli.	grasshopper.
Kimbọ̄.	kimbọ̄i.	a big cricket. Roasted and eaten.
Kondo.	kondui.	locust—destructive kind.
Petu.	petui.	grasshopper ; ? cricket.
Kongowetu.	kongowetui.	grey striped locust—not hurtful.
Kpekpe.	kpekpei.	cockroach.
Kpekpeli.	kpekpeli.	caterpillar.
Nya.	nyāi.	tick.
Jike.	jike.	jigger.
Kpindiyia.	kpindiyiei.	cicada.
Fuvulu.	fuvuluï.	wood-borer.
Ndondo.	ndondui.	millipede.
Kalondo.	kalondoi.	centipede.
Kekeme.	kekeme.	scorpion.
Kọlo.	kọlī.	snail.
Kọ̄wọ̄, kọ̄wọ̄nga.	kọ̄wīsia.	driving ants. *Ants* usually in plural.
Gili.	gili.	white ant.
Pupu	pupui, pupuisia.	small ant—a general term.
Falọ̄.	fale, falesia.	red ant ; makes its nest in leaves. Very painful sting.

Indefinite.	Definite.	English.
Kpaina.	kpaine.	stink ant.
Leleme.	leleme.	green mantis.
Divovo.	divovoi.	fly that bores a hole in trees and bites.
Jokọ̄ndi.	jokọ̄ndi.	tarantula.
Bulọ̄.	bulī.	any worm.
Dańińye.	dańińye.	a crawling insect that bores a horizontal hole below the surface and bites.
Gọ̄ndọ̄ fo̱fo.	gọ̄ndọ̄ fo̱foe.	horned beetle in the pambe palm.
Mbawe.	mbawe.	big white grub in oil palms.
Ndī (*usually pl.* ndīnga).	ndīngesia.	flies.
Bowī vofo.	bowī vofoi.	beetle that rolls a ball of dung.

XVI. Stars, etc.

Indefinite.	Definite.	English.
Fọ̄lọ̄.	fọ̄lī.	sun.
Ngalu.	ngalui.	moon.
Dumbeka.	dumbeke.	star.
—	Konungui.	Orion.
—	Ndelọ̄i.	Southern Cross.
—	Sokoleguli.	Pleiades.
—	Tonyahei	Venus. (lit. Jealous woman.)

XVII. Spiritual Terms.

Indefinite.	Definite.	English.
Ngewo.	ngewoi.	God.
Haniwa, *or* Hawa.	haniwāi, *or* hawai, *or* haiwai.	a devil, sprite.
Ngafa	ngafé (yafé).	spirit, whether abstract or materialized.
Ngelegohũ.	—	heaven.
Ngelemahũ	—	land of the living.
Ndọ̄.	—	lower world.
Ndọ̄mo (*pl.* ndọ̄bela).	ndọ̄moi (*pl.* ndọ̄beleisia).	inhabitants of the lower world.

XVIII. Natural Features.

Indefinite.	Definite.	English.
Batihũ	batihũ.	swamp.
Kpetihũ.	kpetihũ.	swamp with running water.
Bulihũ.	bulihũ.	ground raised above the water.
Bulomi.	bulomi.	flat ground.
Popa.	popé.	pond.
Popawa.	popawāi.	large lake.
Kpọ̄li.	kpọ̄li.	river.
Kpọ̄li la.	kpọ̄li lei.	river mouth, entrance in the mangroves.
Fọ̄fọ.	fọ̄fọi.	clearing.
Fọ̄fọwahũ.	fọ̄fọwahũ.	big clearing in the bush.
Ngiye.	ngiyé.	hill.
Ngiye gombu.	ngiye gombui.	valley.
Ko.	—	east.
Kpundohũ.	—	west.
	(No words for north and south.)	
Mahũ.	—	up-country = north.
—	mbui.	down-country = south.
Njego̱.	njego̱.	up-stream.
—	nje mbui.	down-stream.
Kpoye.	kpoyé.	sea.

Njei i venda.	it is high tide.
Njei lo vendama.	the tide is rising.
Njei i belī.	the tide is low.
Njei lo belīma.	the tide is ebbing.
Njei i belīa kpolīhũ.	the water has drained out of the lagoon.

XIX. Names.

Men's.

Abo.
Abu.
Agidi.
Ama.
Awukpe.
Babai.
Bagoe.
Baio.
Bandeba.
Bassi.
Bawumba.
Benda.

Bendu.
Benga.
Benya.
Beté.
Beya.
Bindi.
Bobo.
Boma.
Bongu.
Boni.
Bori.
Bovoa.
Bōwī.
Boya.
Bundo.

Daima.
Dapi.
Dīmo.
Dingi.
Dongboi.

Feundru.
Fidi.
Filika.
Fina.
Foli.
Fomodia.
Fongujia.

Gaimo.
Gando.
Gapu.
Gava.
Gbando.
Gegbwa.
Gevo.
Goba.
Gyalonga.

Hegwe.
Hindōlo.
Holima.
Hunyo.

Jaiya.
Jaka.
Jiba.
Jibao.
Jina.
Jobai.
Jongopi.
Joon.
Jusu.

Kabanga.
Kaifuma.
Kaikura.
Kaila.
Kaili.
Kailundu.
Kaitibbi.
Kaiyenge.
Kamanda.
Kamoe.
Kanboi.
Kangwai.
Kapindi.
Kapu.
Kapuje.
Kaveota.
Kawundi.
Kiowa.
Koji.
Koka.
Kole.
Komahũ.
Komawa.
Komo.
Konga.
Kowai.
Kpana.
Kwesia.

Lagga.
Lahai.
Lambọ̄i.
Lamina.
Lasana.
Lasani.
Lavari.
Lebi.
Lemu.

Masenja.
Makaia.
Mboma.
Moivumba.
Mosé.
Motwa.
Mundá.

Navọ̄.
Ndọ̄vi.
Ngeba.
Ngili.
Numai.
Nyagoa.
Nyakoi.
Nyangbawula.

Pessima.
Pilima.
Ponga.
Povandi.
Puja.

Samo.
Sandi.
Sangawuru.
Sanu.
Sao.
Sei.
Selu.

Si.
Siki.
Simo.
Sĭna.
Sita.
Songo.
Sukri.

Tiama.
Tong.

Vanboi.
Vandi.

Yakwai.
Yambasu.
Yendewa.
Yewa.
Yopoi.
Yunga.
Yungawo.

Names used by Mendes, but borrowed from Susu, Timmani, Vai, Sherbro, etc.

Amara, S.

Baggi, Sher.
Bai, T.
Bana, Sher.
Bangali, S.
Bili, V.
Biya, Sher.
Bongawutu, S. Leone.

Bundukar, V.

Fama, Sher.
Fani, V.
Foday, T.

Jo, Sher.

Kabona, S. Leone.
Kanda, Sher.
Kelfala, S.

Malaki, T.
Moiwa, V.
Morlai, S.

Santigi, T.
Siafa, V.
Sori, T.
Soriba, T.

Yamba, T.

Mori Names.

Ali.

Bakari.
Boima.

Fatoma.

Isa.

Jibira.

Mahmadu.
Moriba.
Momo.
Musa.

Osene (Wuseni).
Osumana (Mana).

Saidu.

English names are largely taken, such as—

Africa.

Blackie.

Fineboy.

Joe.
John Bull.
Johnny.

Tommy.

Women's names.

Baiye.
Bamania.
Bandī.
Bepui.
Bendu.
Betī.
Binda.
Boi.
Bondo.

Foma.

Gwanyia.

Jassa.
Jato.
Jeromo.
Jiabo.
Jinamba.
Joli.
Ju.

Kefui.
Kema.
Koinya.
Kona.
Kwala.
Kwandi.

Lebu.
Lombe.

Mafande.
Mahenda.
Mamagula.
Mamui.
Mandoro.
Mangaiye.
Mangundia.
Mangwe.
Manje.
Marabwinde.
Masiye.
Mavángiri.
Mawokuli.
Memeniya.

Nyava.
Njembe.
Nyange.

Sabama.
Sao.
Sita.
Sombo.
Sowulu.
Suku.

Talo.
Tiama.
Tuma.

Yenge.

Mori name.

Hawa.

XX. Mende-English.

Note.—Words marked * do not change their initial letter. In looking out a noun the beginner is warned to select the definite form unless there be any good reason to the contrary.

Vowels have in some words been specially marked in this vocabulary as an aid to pronunciation, though it has not been considered necessary to so mark them in other parts of the book.

Words not found under the hardened initial consonant may be found under the softened and *vice versâ*.

*A, *prep.*	with.
*A, *adv. interrog.*	where?
*A, *pron.*; ā	he; he not.
*A, *pron.*	you.
*Abië, *pron.*	you.
*Amuë, *pron.*	we.
*Ange, *pron.*	I.
*Angië, *pron.*	he.
*Atië, *pron.*	they.
*Awuë, *pron.*	you.
*Ba, *pron.*	you.
*Bā, *pron.*	you not.
*Bā, *n.*, Bāi.	price.
*Bāgbango.	dear.
Ba = mba, *n.*, mbei.	rice.
Bala = mbala, *n.*, mbalé.	sheep.
Bale, *or* Bwāle = kpāle, *tr.* & *intr. v.*	pain.
*Bālī, *tr.* & *intr. v.*	vomit.
Bande = kpande, *n.*, kpandé.	gun.
Bandi = kpandi, *adj.* & *v.*	hot.
Bāọ = bāwọ, *tr. v.*	cure.
Bate = gbate.	make.
*Bato, *adv.* (= Ba to, *you see.*)	perhaps.
*Bāya, *n.* & *tr. v.*, bayé.	deceit, deceive.
*Be, *adv.*	also, indeed.
*Bē, *v.*	you say, *or* saying.
*Bē, *pr.*	you not.

*Bē, _prep._	here.
Bē = mbē, _tr. & intr. v._	dry.
Beí = _def. form of_ mba.	rice.
*Bēka = bē yaka.	this side.
*Bē-ndo, _adv._	here.
Bēkē = mbēkē, _n._, bēkéi.	branch.
*Bela, _pl. of suffix_ mō.	people.
Bĕla = mbĕla, _tr. v._	split, tear.
*Belī, _tr. & intr. v._	drain, ebb.
*Belī, _adj._, belingo.	skilful.
Bembe, _tr. v._, _or_ bimbe, mbimbe.	surround, encircle
*Bēre, _n._, bēré.	trousers.
*Bi, _pron._	you (_sing._).
*Bī, _pron._	you not.
*Bia, _pron._	you.
Bīa = kpīa, _tr. & intr. v._	pull out, come out.
*Biē, _pron._	you.
*Biē = bi ye.	to you.
Bīje = mbīje = bīye, _n._, bījeí.	name.
*Bima, _pr._	to you.
*Binda, _pr._	yours.
*Bise, _n._	thanks.
*Bo̱, _n._, bo̱i.	thing.
Bo̱ = mbo̱, _tr. v._	dig.
Bọ̄ = mbọ̄.	pierce, shoot.
*Bọ̄a, _salutation._	how do you do?
Bọ̄la = mbọ̄la, _n._, mbọ̄lé.	neck.
Bọ̄le = gbọ̄le, _v._	drink.
Bọ̄ma = mbọ̄ma, _n._, mbọ̄mé.	hammock, net.
Bọ̄nda = mbọ̄nda, _n._, mbọ̄ndé.	kindred.
*Bo̱ra, _n._, bo̱ré.	hat, cap.
Bo̱wa = mbo̱wa, _n._, mbo̱wé.	knife.
Bo̱ya = mbo̱ya, _v. & n._, mbo̱yé.	present, gift.
Bū = mbū, _adv. & prep._	under.
Bū, _n._, būi.	lower part.
*Bua = bọ̄a.	how do you do?
*Bubu, _intr. v._	fly.
Bukpia = pugbia, _tr. v._	uproot.
*Būla, būlo, _n._, būlí, _usually_ bulíhū.	plain, open swamp.
*Bule, _intr. v._	burst.

Bumbu = mbumbu = wumbu, *tr. v.*	take, lift up, take away.
De = te = le, *intr. v.; tr. v.*	climb; lift.
Dē = dēwē = tewe, *tr. v.*	cut, pass.
Dē = dēwē = ndewe, *tr. v.*	beat.
Deli = ndeli, *adj.*, delingo.	wet.
Deli = teli, *adj.*, delingo.	black.
Demu = temu = lemu, *tr. v.*	beg pardon, acquit.
Do = to = lo, *tr. v.*	see.
Dọ = tọ = lọ, *tr. & intr. v.*	stand, build.
Dọ̄ = tọ̄, *tr. v.*	send.
Do̱gbē = to̱gbe, *adj.*	young.
Dogbo̱ = ndogbo̱, *n.*, dogbo̱i.	bush.
*Do̱mē, *n.*, do̱meí (dommay).	story.
*Do̱mē gbīa.	tell a story.
Do̱me = ndo̱me, *n.*, do̱mé (dormé).	ground.
Dọ̄me = ndọ̄me = lọ̄me, *n.*, dọ̄mé (doomé).	shirt.
Dumbēka = lumbeke, *n.*, dumbēké.	star.
Dumbele = lumbele, *n.*, dumbelé.	lime, lemon.
Duli = dọ̄li = lọ̄li, *n.*, dulí.	dance.
*E, *adv.*	yes.
*Ē, *pr.*	he not.

F changes into *V*.

Fa, *prep. & conj.*, *usually* va.	of, for, an account of.
Fākali, *n.*, fakalí.	pawpaw tree and fruit.
Fakalewe, *adj.*, Fakálēmōï.	lazy, slack; a lazy man.
Fāla = vāla, *intr. v.*	to be ready (to start).
*Fale, *conj.*	therefore.
Fale = vāle, *intr. v.*	grow (of plants).
Fandē, *n.*, fandé.	cotton.
Fawéhū, *n.*	flat ledge of rocks.
Fāya = vaya, *tr. & intr. v.*	scatter, spill, waste.
Fe = ve, *adv.*	completely.
Fē = vē, *n.*, feí.	pot.

Fe = ve, *tr. v.*	give. Object, precedes; person follows with preposition 'to.
Fē, *v., trans.*	fill.
intrans.	swell (of the body).
Fefe, *n.*, fefeí.	wind.
*Fele, *adj.*, Fere.	two.
Fefele.	two by two.
Fọ̄, *tr. v.*	reach, arrive at, pass through.
Fọ̄ = fọ̄lọ̄, *n.*	day.
Fọ̄, fọ̄ọ̄, *n.*, fọ̄i	year.
Fo̱, *n.*, fo̱i.	big biting fly.
Fọ̄fọ̄, *n.*, fọ̄fọ̄i.	open place.
Fọ̄fọ̄hũ.	publicly.
Fọ̄gba, *tr. v.*	whip.
Fọ̄lọ̄, *n.*, fọ̄lī́.	day, sun.
Fọ̄ma, *n.*, fọ̄mé.	whip.
Fọ̄mbọ̄, *tr. v.*	extend, unroll.
Fo̱ni, *n.*, fo̱ní.	grass.
Fo̱nya, *tr. v.*	squeeze.
Fūhani, *n.*, fūhani.	insect.
Fūka, *tr. v.*	grind, pound.
Fūkọ̄, *n.*, fūkọ̄i.	ring, circular pad for the head when carrying a load. Coast English, kātā.
Fūla, *tr. v.*	hasten.
Fūla, *n.*, fūlé.	village.
Fūlọ̄, *tr. v.*	loosen.
Fulu (= fu = vu), *adj.*, fulungo, vungo.	living.

Gb changes into *Kp*.

Gā, *tr. v.* = gara, kara.	teach, learn.
Gahũ = kahũ, *n.*	body.
Gāka = kāka, *tr. v.*	coil up, encircle.
Gama, *adv. prep.*	towards, to.
Gbā = kpā, *adj.*	different.
*Gbā, *adv.*	first.
*Gba, *tr. v.*	stop.
Gbahã, *intr. v.*	be tired.
Gbale, *v.*	pain.
*Gbāma, *adv.*	to no purpose.

Gbāọ̄ = kpāọ̄, *intr. v.*	cry out, scream.
Gbate = kpate, *tr. v.*	make, construct, repair.
Gbate, *intr. v.*	be, *or* become rich.
Gbāya, *adj.* & *n.*	strong, force.
*Gbe, *pron.*	what.
Gbe, *tr. v.*, gbele.	drive away, dismiss.
*Gbe, *intr. v.*	let, allow.
Gbē, *tr. v.*	cease.
Gbĕma !	stop that ! wait !
Gbē, *n.* & *v.*	business, be busy.
Gbē, *intr. v.*	look.
Gbegbe, *n.*, gbegbé.	parrot.
Gbela, gbeanga, *prep.*	near.
Gbele.	what is the matter ?
Gbēlē = gbe, *tr. v.*	leave, dismiss, look at, etc.
Gbenda, *tr. v.*	pluck fruit, snatch.
Gbenge, gbengeme, *adv.*	yesterday.
*Gbeva, *adv.*	why ?
*Gbī, *n.*, gbī.	rudder.
Gbīa, kpia, *tr.* & *intr. v.*	pull out, come out.
Gbīahū̆, *adj.*	tall.
Gbiaye, *n.*, gbiayeí.	likeness.
Gbo, *tr. v.*	help.
*Gbo, *pr.*	what ?
Gbō, *intr. v.*	relieve one's self, go w.c.
*Gboma, *adv.*	again.
Gbọ̄tọ̄, *adj.*, gbọ̄tọ̄ngo.	many, much.
Gbọ̄wu, *intr. v.*	be tired.
Gbọ̄wungo.	tired.
Gbọ̄wu, *intr. v.*	ripen.
Gbọ̄wu, *tr. v.*	bury.
Gbọ̄ye, *n.*, gbọ̄yé.	sea.
Gbo̱yō, *tr. v.*	finish.
Gbu *and* gbue, *adv.*	last night.
*Ge, *adv.*	some time ago, the other day.
Ge = ke, *tr. v.*	show.
Ge ange, angië.	show me, him.
Gele, *n.* & *tr. v.*	end.
*Getete, *adv.*	tightly.
Gilī = kilí, *intr. v.*	think, brood over, remember.
Gili a na.	think of that.

Go = ko, koi.	war.
Gō = kō, *n.*, gōi.	belly.
Go = ko, *tr. v.*	fight.
*Go, *tr. v.*	give.
Bi ngi go a mehe.	give him food.
*Gogoli, *adj.*	white.
*Go̲la, *v.*, *used with* nde, *as* ndégola.	tell a lie.
Go̲la = ko̲la, *tr. v.*	surprise.
Go̲le = ko̲le, *tr. v.*	divide.
*Go̲li, *tr. v.*, go̲'i.	pluck (fruit).
Gọ̄li, *tr. v.*	buy a wife.
Gọ̄me = kọ̄me, *tr. v.*	collect, assemble.
Gọ̄na = kọ̄na, *tr. v.*	introduce.
*Go̲ro, *n.*, go̲re.	wall round a town, etc.
Go̲rola, go̲roleí.	gateway in same.
Gọ̄wọ̄, *intr. v.*	fly.
Gu = ku, *intr. v.*	can, able, enough, reach.
Gu = ku, *n.*, kui.	smell.
Guhã = kuha, *adj.*, guhango.	far.
Gula = kula, *tr. & intr. v.*	drop, fall.
Gula = kula, *n.*, kuré.	cloth.
*Gulo, *adv.*	in front.
Gulo = kulo, *adj.*, kulongo.	small.
Guru = kuru, *tr. v.*	accept.
Gutu = kutu, *adj.*, kutungo.	short.
*Ha, *n.*, hei.	female.
*Ha, *adv.*	to-day.
*Ha, *n.*, hei.	death.
*Ha = hani, *n.*	thing.
*Hā, *v.*, hango.	die, dead.
*Haga, hawa, *adj.*, hawango.	lazy.
*Haga, hawa, *tr. v.*	clear, carve.
*Hāka, *n.*, hākeí.	load, utensil, thing
*Hāka, *adj.*, hakango.	empty.
*Hala, halage, *adj.*	first.
*Halē, *n.*, halé.	medicine.
*Hāma, *n.*, hāmeí.	wet season ; waist.
*Hango, *adj.*	dead.
*Hani, *n.*, haní.	thing.

*Hāpē, *n.*, hapé.	root.
*Hawa, *adj.*, hawango.	lazy.
*Hege, *n.*, Hegé = hewe.	soap.
*Hei, *tr.* & *intr. v.*	sit, set, plant.
*Heiwulu, *n.*, heiwulī.	stool.
*Hele, *tr. v.*	hang.
*Hemu, *n.*, hemui.	light, candle, etc.
*Henga, *n.*, hengé.	dream.
Hengá wile.	to dream.
*Hewu, *adj.*, hewungo.	equal.
*Hī, *tr. v.*	plant.
*Higbe, *intr. v.*, higbengo.	sick.
*Hija, *tr. v.*	beat, stamp.
*Hije, hiye, *intr. v.*	get up.
*Hina, *n.*, hiné.	male.
*Hinda, hingda, *n.*, hindeí.	thing, affair, place.
*Hindō, *n.*, hindōi.	man.
*Hindōlọ̄, *n.*, hindōlọ̄i.	son.
*Hini, *n.*, hiní.	husband.
*Hite, *tr. v.*	let down.
intr. v.	reach, consult.
*Hiye, *adv.*	indeed, yes.
*Hiye, *intr. v.* = hije.	arise.
*Ho̱, *tr. v.*	sew.
*Ho̱, *tr. v.*	knock, strike against.
*Ho̱, *adv.*	then, used at end of interrogative sentences.
*Họ̄ē, *interj.*	shall we?
*Họ̄kpa, *n.*, họ̄kpe.	nose.
*Ho̱na, *tr. v.*	practise witchcraft against.
*Hondo, *adj.*	hundred.
*Họ̄ta, *n.*, hōté.	guest, stranger.
*Hou, *tr. v.*	catch.
Houma!	catch hold!
*Hũ, *n.*, hui.	inside.
prep.	in.
*Hũ, *prefix.*	an intensitive prefix to verbs.
*Hũa, *n.*, hũeí.	animal, meat.
*Hũgbe, *tr. v.*	look into.
*Huge, *tr. v.*	explain, relate.
*Hugo̱, *tr. v.*	understand, attempt.

*Hũguhango (pronounced almost *ngwango*).	distant.
*Huma, *tr. v.*	steal.
*Huma, *tr. v.*	measure, compare.
*Hupu, *tr. v.*	mix.
*Huyela, *tr. v.*	sweep, wipe.
*I, *pr.*	he.
*I̱, *pr.*	he not.
*Ī, *adv.*	yes.
*Ina, *conj.*	if, suppose.
*Ita, *adj.*	one (used in counting).
*Jā, *tr. v.*	touch.
Jā a ngie.	touch it.
Jama = sama, *n.*, jameí.	distinguished person.
Jango = sawango, *adj.*	three (special use).
Wu jango.	you three.
Jēgá = jia kā.	walk quickly.
*Ji, *dem. pr.*	this.
*Ji, *conj.*	when, if.
Ji = je = nje, *n.*	mother.
*Jia, *intr. v.* (*also* ji).	walk, travel.
n., jiei.	journey.
Jia = njia, *n.*, njiei.	word, palaver.
*Jialō, *n.*, jialō̱i.	child that can just walk.
*Jiwi, *n.*, jiwi.	key.
Jo̱ = so̱, *also* jo̱lo, *tr. v.*	obtain, get, marry a wife.
Jo̱la = so̱la, *n.*, so̱le.	noise.
Jō̱ndu = sō̱ndu, *tr. v.* & *n.*	swear, curse.
Jo̱ngo = so̱ngo, *n.*	equivalent.
Ngi jo̱ngoi.	its equivalent, its cost.
Gbe jo̱ngo?	how much?
Jo̱so = so̱so, *tr. v.*	load a gun, pack a hole.

K changes into *G*.

Kā, *n.*, kāi.	dirt.
*Kā, *adv.*	very, very much.
Kā = kara, *tr. v.*	teach.
Ka, *n.*, kei.	husk, empty shell, etc.

Kafa, *tr. v.*	cheat.
Kahã, *n.*, kahei.	basket.
Kahũ, *n.*, kahui.	body.
Kaye, *n.*, kayé.	rust.
*Kaká, *adv.*	quickly.
*Kākā, *adv.*	very.
Kaka = gaka, yaka, *n.*, kakeí.	side.
Kake, *n.*, kakeí.	wall.
Kala, *n.*, kaleí.	circle.
Kale, *n.*, kalé.	seed, bone, cartridge.
Kali, *n.*, kalí.	hoe.
Kali, *n.*, kalí.	snake.
Kalō, *n.*, kalọi.	basin.
Kama hani, *n.*	wonderful thing.
Kamba, *n.*, kambé.	grave.
Kańa, *n.*, kańa.	box.
Kani, *n.*, kani.	—
Kani gboli.	gold.
Kani gogole.	silver.
*Karō, *n.*, Karōmo.	Vai, a neighbouring people to the Mendes.
Kasọ, *adj.*	cunning.
Kata, *n.*, kateí.	hedge.
Katéhũ.	garden, enclosure.
Kaye, *n.*, kayé.	fault.
Ke = ge, *v.*	show.
*Ke, *conj.*	and.
*Ke, *n.*, kei.	father, master.
*Kea = kia *and* kina, *conj.*, &c.	when.
Kea ji na.	like this.
Kele, *tr. v.*	end.
*Kelei, kere?	is it not so?
Kelema, *n.*, kelemeí.	end.
*Kene, *n.*, kene.	old man, a title of respect.
Kenye, *n.*, kenyeí.	country.
*Kia, *conj.*	whilst, when, etc.
*Kina, *conj.*	ditto
Kọ = gọ, *n.*, gọi.	belly.
Ko, *n.*, koi, *also v.*	war.
Ko̱, ko̱lo, *tr. v.*	know, try.
Kọhũ, *n.*, koihũ *or* kohui.	belly.

Kọ̄hune, *n.*, kọ̄huné.	joy.
Koko, *n.*, kokoi.	ant-hill.
Koko, *tr. v.*	find.
Kokoli, *tr. v.*	ditto
Ko̱lama, *tr. v.*	surprise.
Ko̱li, *n.*, ko̱lī.	scissors.
Kọ̄le, *tr. v.*	wash, clean.
Kọ̄le, *adj.*, kọ̄lengo.	clean.
Ko̱le, *tr. v.*	divide.
Ko̱le, *adj.*, ko̱lengo.	cold.
Ko̱li, *n.*, ko̱li.	leopard.
Ko̱li, *tr.*	pluck fruit.
Ko̱lo, *n.*, ko̱le.	paper, book, skin.
Kọ̄lọ̄, *n.*, kọ̄lī.	fire-place, barrel.
Ko̱lo̱, *tr. v.*	try, feel.
*Ko̱lu, *n.*, ko̱lī.	iron.
Ko̱ma, *n.*, ko̱mé.	assembly.
Kọ̄me, *tr. v. & noun.*	collect, meet.
Komi, *n.*, komí.	bee, honey.
Kọ̄nda, *n.*, kọ̄ndé.	mortar for pounding grain.
Kọ̄nu, *n.*, kọ̄nī.	axe.
Kọ̄tọ̄, *adj.*; kọ̄tọngo, *v.*	bent ; roll up.
Ko̱tu, *n.*, ko̱tī.	rock, stone.
Ko̱we, *n.*, ko̱wé.	log, fallen tree.
Ko̱wo, *adj.*	left (hand).
Kọ̄wọ̄, *intr. v.*	fly.
Ko̱wu, *n.*, ko̱wī.	wood.
*Ku, *n.*, kui.	day.
Ku, *n.*, kui.	smell.
Kuhama, *adj.*	far.
Kuimeni, *tr. v.*	smell.
Kui neingo.	it smells sweet.
Kui nyamungo.	it smells bad.
Kū = gu, *v.*	can, able.
Kula = gula, *tr. & intr. v.*	drop, fall.
Kula, *n.*, kulé, kuré.	cloth.
Kula gutu, *n.*, kula gutī.	lit. small cloth, rag or any piece.
Kulọ̄, *adj.*, kulongo, kulī, gulongoi, wulī, wulongoi.	small.
Kulu = kuru, *tr. & intr. v.*	agree, accept.

Kundéhũ, *n.*	corner, *or* recess for a bed.
Kungoi hũ, *n.*	annex to a house, room.
Kuru = kulu, *tr.* & *intr. v.*	agree, accept.
Kutu, *adj.*, kutungo.	short.

Kp changes into *Gb*.

Kpa, *n.*, kpaé.	debt.
Kpa, *adj.*	different.
Kpã = kpala = kpaé.	farm.
Kpa, *adv.*	fast.
Kpā, *tr. v.*	count.
Kpaki, *n.*, kpakí.	arm, shoulder, wing.
Kpakpa, *tr. v.*	fasten, nail.
Kpakpau, *adj.*, kpakpaungo.	difficult.
Kpala, *n.*, kpalé.	farm.
Kpale, *n.*, kpalé.	pain.
Kpambi, *n.*, kpambī.	line, mark.
Kpande, *tr.* & *intr. v.*	shout out.
Kpande, *n.*, kpandé.	gun.
Kpandi, *tr. v.*; *adj.*, kpandingo.	heat, hasten; hot.
Kpangba, *n.*, kpangbé.	broom.
Kpāō, *n.* & *v.*	cry, call.
Kpate, *tr. v.*	make, repair.
Kpate, *adj.*, kpatengo.	rich.
Kpawu, *n.*, kpawuī.	bridge.
Kpē, *n.*	business.
Kpengo, *adj.*	busy.
Kpē, *tr. v.*	stop.
Kpe, *adv.*	still, quiet.
Kpe, *tr. v.*	drive, dismiss.
Kpē = kpēlē, *tr. v.*	look at.
Kpēkpē, *v.* & *adj.* = yekpe, yekpengo.	good.
Kpele = kpere, *adj.*	all.
Kpele, *n.*, kpelé.	beard.
Kpēlē, *n.*, kpēlēi *and* kpēí.	time.
Kpēma = kpelema, *n.*, kpēmé.	time.
Kpīa = gbia, *v.*	pull out, come out.
Kpindi, *n.*, kpindi.	night.

Kpini, *tr. v.*	twist
Kpiti, *n.*, kpitī.	grass.
Kpohũ, *n.*	flour.
Kpoko, *n.*, kpokoi.	evening.
Kpọku, *intr. v.*	sprout.
Kpọ̄lē, *adj.* kpọ̄lengo.	unripe.
Kpọ̄li, *tr. v.*	drink.
Kpọ̄li, *n.*, kpọ̄lī́.	river.
Kpọ̄lọ̄, *n.* kpọ̄lī́.	salt.
Kpọ̄wa, *adj.*, kpọ̄wango.	foolish.
Kpoye, *n.*, kpoyé.	sea.
Kpọyō *tr. v.*	finish.
Kpūeila, *n.*, kpūeilé.	hut.
Kpūko, *n.*, kpūkoi.	bed.
Kpuli, *tr. v.*	shave the head.
Kpulo, *n.*, kpuli.	knot.
Lā = ndā, *n.*, lāi.	leaf.
La = nda, *n.*, lei.	mouth, opening as a gate, etc.
Lā = ndā, *tr. v.*	pull.
La = nda, *tr. & intr. v.*	lay, lie, place.
*Lā, *adv.*	not.
*Lā, *n.*, lei.	name.
Labu = ndabu, *adv.*	in front.
Lagbou = ndagbou, *tr. v.*	shut.
Lahī = ndahī, *tr. v.*	warn.
Lakpa = ndakpa, *v.*	grow up.
Lala = ndala, *n.*, laleí.	oar.
Lama = ndama, *n.*, lameí.	lying down place, bed.
Lapi = ndapi, *v. & n.*	fight (not war), wrestle, swim.
Latọ̄ = ndatọ̄, *tr. v.*	praise.
Lave = ndave, *tr. v.*	fill.
Lavengo.	full.
Lawọ̄ = ndawọ̄, *tr. v.*	open.
Layia = ndayia, *n.*, layiei.	word, order.
Lẹ̄ = ndē, *tr. v.*	bear, beget.
Le = de = te, *tr. v.; intr. v.*	lift up; climb.
*Le, *adv.*	still.
*Lē, *adv.*	a little.
Lē = ndē, *intr. v.*	speak, tell.
Le = de, *tr. v.*	condemn.

*Le, *v.*	to be.
Le = nde, *n.*, ndei.	a lie.
Le = lewe = tewe.	cut, pass.
Lekpe = ndekpe, *tr. v.*	arrange in order.
*Lele, *adv.*	slowly.
*Lele, *adj.*	wrong.
Lēli = ndēli, *tr. v.*	appease.
Lema = ndema, *tr. v.*	forget.
Lembi = ndembi, *tr.* & *intr. v.*	delay.
Lemu = temu, *tr. v.*	acquit.
Lenga = ndenga, *pl. n.*	children.
Lenga = tenga, *adv.*	together.
Lewe = tewe, *tr. v.*	cut, pass.
= ndewe, *tr. v.*	beat.
Lī = ndī, *n.*, lī.	heart.
*Li, *intr. v.*	go.
past tense, ya.	
Lia = ndia, *n.*, ndiei.	middle.
Lila = di la, *tr. v.*	take away.
Līma = ndima, *n.*, līmeí.	choice.
Līwi = tīwī, *tr. v.*	close (the eyes).
*Lo, *v.*	to be.
Lo = to, *tr. v.*	see.
Lọ̄ = ndọ̄, *n.*, lọ̄i.	child.
Lọ̄ = dọ̄ = tọ̄, *tr.* & *intr. v.*	stand, stop, build, follow.
Lo̱ = ndo̱, *n.*, lo̱i.	rum, wine.
*Lo̱, *n.*, lo̱i.	day.
Lọ̄ = dọ̄ = tọ̄, *tr. v.*	send.
*Lọ̄, *tr. v.*	like, want.
Lọ̄ = ndọ̄, *tr. v.*	leave.
Lọ̄hũ = ndọ̄hũ, *tr.* & *intr. v.*	lose, be lost.
Lọ̄kọ̄ = tọ̄kọ̄, *n.*, lo̱kọ̄i.	hand, arm.
Lo̱le = ndole, *n.*, lo̱lé.	hunger.
*Lọ̄le, *adv.*	how many.
Lọ̄li = dọ̄li, *n.* & *v.*	play, dance.
Lo̱lo = ndo̱lo, *n.*, lo̱lé.	ground, country.
*Lo̱lu, *adj.*	five.
*Lọ̄me-lọ̄me, *adv.*	noiselessly.
Lọ̄ndọ̄ = ndọ̄ndọ̄, *v.*	be silent, cease.
Lo̱wu = ndo̱wu, *tr. v.*	hide.
Lua = ndua, *n.* & *v.*	fear.
Lugo = tugo, *adv.*	in front.

Lula = ndula, *intr. v.*	rot, decay.
Luma = duma, *intr. v.*	consent.
Luva = nduva, *intr. v.*	spend the day.
*Ma, *prefix.*	intensitive prefix to verbs.
*Ma, *pr.*	we.
*Mā, *pr.*	we not.
*Ma, *prep.*	for, on, to.
*Mā, *tr. v.* & *n.*	desire.
*Mābāli, *tr. v.*	refuse, hinder.
*Made *tr. v.*	raise.
*Madewe, *tr. v.*	cut off, detain.
*Magbia, *tr. v.*	undress, pluck a bird.
*Māgọmbọ̄, *tr. v.*	strip leaves off a branch.
*Mahã, *n.* maheí.	king, chief.
*Mahëu, *tr. v.* & *adj.*	equal, make equal.
*Mahou, *tr. v.*	choose.
*Mahũ, *prep.*	on, above.
*Mahũgbēle (-gbe), *tr. v.*	watch over.
*Majia, *tr. v.*	sell.
*Make, *tr. v.*	feed.
*Malē, *tr. v.*	meet, overtake.
*Male, *tr. v.*	cover, roof.
*Malewe, madewe, *tr. v.*	cut off.
*Maluve, *tr.* & *intr. v.*	charge.
*Mama, *n.*, mamé.	elderly person, grandparent.
*Mamage, *n.*, mamagei.	foolishness.
*Mamamau, *n.*, mamamaui.	pity.
*Mamō, *n.*, mamōi.	owner.
*Mamạ, *adj.*	foolish.
*Mana, *n.*, mané.	plantain.
*Manda, *adv.*	tightly.
*Mane, *adj.* & *tr. v.*	sweet, sweeten.
*Mane, manehe, *tr. v.*	watch.
*Mani, *n.*, manī.	trap.
*Mani, *tr. v.*	want, be in need of.
*Manu, *tr. v.*	forgive.
*Matọ̄, *tr. v.*	add to, increase.
*Mavula, *tr. v.*	hasten.
*Mawali, *n.*, mawali.	bet.
Mawali hou.	make a bet.
*Mawele, *tr. v.*	cover.

*Mawulọ̄ (mau'ro), *tr. v.*	wait for.
*Mayafa, *tr. v.*	backbite.
*Maye, *tr. v.*	stoop, lower.
*Mayela, *tr. v.*	brush.
*Mayia, *n.*, mayiei.	accusation.
Mayia ge.	accuse.
*Mayili, *tr. v.*	dress.

Mb changes into *B.*

Mbā, *n.*, mbāi.	friend.
*Mbā, *prep.*	top.
Mba, *n.*, mbei.	rice.
Mbaka, *n.*, mbaké.	music.
Mbala, *n.*, mbalé.	sheep.
Mbali, *tr. v.*	vomit.
Mbalu, *n.*, mbalí.	cane loop to climb trees.
Mbawa, *n.*, mbawé.	soap.
*Mbe, *adv.*	to me here.
Mbela, *tr. v.*	split, tear.
Mbēle = mbewele.	this road.
Mbēmbē, *tr. v.*	swing round, encircle.
Mbo̱, *tr. & intr. v.*	dig.
Mbọ̄, *tr. & intr. v.*	pierce, penetrate.
Mbo̱gba, *n.*, mbo̱gbé.	cutlass.
Mbola, *n.*, mbolé.	cup.
Mbọ̄lē, *intr. v.*	be blind.
Mbọ̄lọ̄, *n.*, mbọ̄lī, mbọ̄lọ̄hū.	throat.
Mbọ̄ma, *n.*, mbọ̄mé.	hammock.
Mbọ̄nda, *n.*, mbọ̄ndé.	kindred.
Mbọ̄wa, *n.*, mbọ̄wéi.	knife.
Mbu, *adv. & prep.*	under.
Mbūmbu, *tr. v.*	take up.
Mbumbu, *n.*, mbumbui.	fish-trap.
*Mē.	we not (*condit.*).
*Mē.	we say.
*Me, *tr. v.*	eat.
*Mehe, *n.*, meheí.	food.
*Meni *and* me, *tr. v.*	hear, understand, perceive.
*Mi, mindo, *adv.*	where.
*Mia, miando, *adv.*	yonder.

*Mia, *v.*	is.
*Migbe, *adv.*	when?
*Miji, *n.* miji.	needle.
*Mini, *n.* & *adj.*	
Miningo.	heavy.
*Mīta, *n.* mīté.	spoon.
*Mo, *tr. v.*	burn.
*Mo̱li, *tr. v.*	ask.
*More, Moremo, Moremōi.	More man, *i. e.* Moor by derivation—any Mahommedan.
*Mu, *pr.*	we.
*Mū, *pr.*	we not.
*Mua, *pr.*	we.
*Mua, *intr. v.*	bathe.
*Mumu, *adj.*	small, applied to young birds, nails, etc.

*Na, *adv.*	there.
*Na, *dem. pr.*	that.
*Nā, *adv.*	now.
*Nama, *n.*, namé.	blood.
*Namu, *intr. v.*	slip.
*Nani, *adj.*	four.
*Navọ̄, *n.*, navọ̄i.	money.
Ndā, *n.*, ndāi = lāi.	leaf.
Nda, *n.*, ndei = lei.	mouth, door.
*Nda, *n.*, ndei.	portion.
Ngi nda, *poss. pr.*	his own.
Nda = la, *tr. v.*	lay, lie down.
Ndā, *tr. v.*	pull.
*Ndahani, *n.*, ndahani.	meat, fish, etc., used as food.
Ndakpa = lakpa, *intr. v.*	grow.
Ndakpa, *n.*, ndakpeí.	young man.
Ndakpalọ̄, *n.*, ndakpalọ̄i.	ditto.
Ndalọ̄ = lalọ̄, *tr. v.*	join.
Ndapi = lapi, *tr. v.*	fight, wrestle, swim.
Ndavē = lave, *tr. v.*	fill.
Ndawọ̄ = lawọ̄, *tr. v.*	open.
Ndē = le, *n.*, lei.	child.
*Nde = ndewe, *n.*, ndei.	brother.

Ndē = le, *tr. v.*	tell.
Nde = le, *n.*	a lie.
Ndē = lē, *tr. v.*	bear, beget.
*Ndego̱la, *intr. v.*	tell a lie.
Ndeli = deli, *v.* & *adj.*, ndelingo.	wet.
Ndende = lende, *n.*, ndendei.	boat.
Ndevu = levu, *n.*, levui.	life, rest.
Ndewe = lewe, *tr. v.*	beat.
*Ndewe, *n.*, ndewei.	brother.
Ndī = li, *n.*, lī.	heart.
Ndia = lia, *n.*, ndieí, *also prep.*	middle.
*Ndiamo, *n.*, ndiamōi.	friend.
Ndile *or* ndili = dile, *n.*, ndīlī.	boa-constrictor.
Ndọ̄ = lọ̄, *n.*, lọ̄i.	son, daughter.
Ndọ̄ = lọ̄, *tr. v.*	leave.
Ndo̱ = lo̱, *n.*, lo̱i.	rum, wine.
Ndogbo̱ = dogbo̱, *n.*, ndogbo̱i.	bush.
Ndọ̄ke = lọ̄ke, *tr. v.*	clear bush, etc.
Ndo̱le = do̱le, *n.*, ndo̱lé.	hunger.
*Ndọ̄lē, *tr. v.*	bear children.
Ndọ̄li = dọ̄li, *n.*, ndọ̄lī.	hook, fish-hook.
Ndo̱lo = lo̱lo, *n.*, ndo̱lé.	ground, world, country.
Ndọ̄ma = lọ̄ma, *n.*, ndọ̄mé (doomé).	shirt.
Ndo̱ma = doma, *n.*, ndo̱mé (dormé).	ground.
Ndondo = londo, *v.*	cease.
Ndopa = dopa, *n.*, ndopé.	antelope, deer.
Ndọ̄pọ̄ = lọ̄pọ̄, *n.*, ndọ̄pọ̄i.	boy, girl, inferior.
Ndo̱vo = lo̱vo, *intr. v.*	be unsuccessful.
Ndọ̄wa = lọ̄wa, *n.*, ndọ̄wé.	hole.
Ndọ̄wọ̄ = lọ̄wọ̄, *n.*, ndọ̄wọ̄i.	horn.
Ndo̱wu = lo̱wu, *tr.* & *intr. v.*	hide.
Ndufe = lufe, *tr. v.*	extinguish.
Ndūla = lula, *tr.* & *intr. v.*	rot.
Nduli = duli, *n.*, ndulí.	smoke.
Nduwe = luwe, *tr. v.*	clear the bush.
*Ne, *n.*, nei.	tongue.
*Ne, *n.*, neí, & *tr. v.*	pleasure, please.
Nengo.	sweet.

*Nemáhũ, *n.*	sense.
Nemáhũ lengo.	clever.
*Nene, *n.*, neneí.	shade.
*Neni & ne, *v.*	sweeten.
*Nete, *n.*, neté.	door (= the door itself).
Nga = ga, *pr.*	I.
Ngā = gā, *pr.*	I not.
Nga, *adv.* & *prep.*	on top.
Ngāfa = yafa, *n.*, ngafeí.	spirit.
Ngāfa = yafa, *tr. v.*	slander.
Ngahango = yahango, *adj.*	blunt.
Ngahuma = yahuma, *tr. v.*	steal from.
Ngāla = yala, *n.*, ngalé.	mat.
Ngāle = yale, *tr. v.*	break.
Ngalī = gali, *n.*, ngalī.	thorn.
Ngalu = ngau = yau, *n.*, ngalui.	egg, moon.
Ngama = yama, *n.*, ngameí.	eye, face.
Ngama = yama, *tr.* & *intr. v*	return.
Ngāngē = yange, *tr.* & *intr. v.*	scratch, itch.
Ngape, *tr. v.*	turn upside down.
Ngara = gara, *n.*, ngaré.	a coarse grass.
Ngate = yate, *tr.* & *intr. v.*	kindle.
*Ngē, *pr.*	I not.
*Ngē, *v.*	I say.
Ngela = yela, *tr. v.*	sweep, clean, wipe.
*Ngela-ngela.	one by one.
*Ngēlē, *n.*, ngēlēí.	heaven, sky, cloud.
*Ngēlēwọ̄, *adv.*	at daybreak.
*Ngeleya, *adv.*	aloft.
Ngelī = yelī, *tr. v.*	abuse.
*Ngenda, *n.*	morning.
Ngenge = yenge, *n.*, yengé.	work.
Ngengemō, *n.*, ngengemōi; *pl.* gengebra.	workman, labourer.
*Ngēvọ̄, *n.*, ngevọ̄i.	dry season.
*Ngēwo̱, *n.*, Ngewo̱i.	God.
Ngeya = yeya, *n.*, ngeyeí.	rope.
Ngeya = yeya, *tr. v.*	buy.
Ngi = gi, *pr.*	I.
Ngi, *pr.*	his, him.

Ngī = gī, *pr.*	I not.
*Ngië, *pr.*	him.
Ngila = gila, *n.*, ngilé.	dog.
Ngīlī = yīlī = yī, *tr. v.*	cook.
Ngīlī = yīlī; *tr. v.*	bind.
*Ngītīya, *adv.*	outside.
*Ngīyē, *n.*, ngīyḗ.	hill.
*Ngiye, *conj.*	until, except.
Ngo̱ = wo̱, *n.* & *v.*, ngo̱i.	cry.
Ngọ̄ = wọ̄, *n.*, ngọ̄i.	voice, word, message.
*Ngọ̄la, *n.*, ngọ̄lé.	bush.
Ngọ̄lē = gọ̄le, *v.*	shave the face.
Ngọ̄li bọ̄, *intr. v.*	piss.
Ngo̱lo = wo̱lo, *adj.*, ngo̱longo.	large.
Ngo̱lo = wo̱lo, *intr. v.*	weep.
Ngombu = yombu, *n.*, ngombui.	fire.
Ngongo = ngolongo, wongo, *adj.*	large.
Ngongolu = yongolu, *n.*, ngongolui.	tooth.
Ngọ̄va = wọ̄va, ngọ̄vango, *adj.*	old.
Ngu = wu, *n.*, ngui.	head.
Ngu = wu, *tr. v.*	wake up.
Ngua = wua, *n.* ngueí.	fruit.
Ngua = wua, *tr. v.*	wash (clothes), put on, thrust in.
Ngulē = wule, *n.* & *v.*, ngulḗ.	song.
Ngulī = gulī, *tr. v.*	paddle.
Ngulo = wulo, *n.*, ngulé.	oil.
Ngulu = wulu = nguru, *n.*, ngulī.	tree, stick.
Ngundu, *adj.*, wundungo.	green, raw.
*Ṅi, *adv.*	so, thus.
*Nika, *n.*, nikeí.	cow.
*Nina, *adj.*, ninango.	new.
*Nīni, *n.*, nīni.	female breast.
Nja = ya, *n.*, njei.	water, rain.
*Njala, *n.*, njaleí.	landing-place.
*Njalọ̄wa, *n.*, njalọ̄wé.	water-hole.

Njasa = yasa, *n.*, yasé.	thatch—generally, and from the oil-palm in particular.
Nje = yi, *n.*, nji.	mother.
*Njē, *n.*, njēi.	goat.
Nje = yē, *tr. v.*	lower.
Njepe = yepe, *n.* & *v.*, njepé.	talk.
Njī = yi, *n.* & *v.*, njī.	sleep.
Njīa = yīa, *n.*, njiei.	word, affair, palaver.
Njuo = yuo, *n.*, = njuọ̄i.	finger.
*Nu = numu, *n.*, numuí; *pl.* nunga.	person.
*Nwo̱na, *adj.*, nwo̱nango.	bitter.
*Nwo̱nī, *n.*, nwo̱ní.	bird.
*Nya, *pr.*	my, me.
*Nyaha, *n.*, nyaheí.	woman, wife.
*Nyamu, *adj.*, nyamungo.	bad.
*Nyande, *adj.*, nyandengo.	fine.
*Nyani, *tr. v.*	spoil.
*Nyapọ̄, *n.*, nyapọ̄i.	young woman.
*Nye, *n.*, nyé.	fish.
*Nyegi, *tr. v.*	mark, write.
*Nyī, *tr. v.*	bite.
*Nyo̱ko, *n.*, nyo̱koi.	manner, sort.
*Nyo̱nyo̱, *pr.*	each other.
Pa = wa, *tr. v.*	kill.
Panda = wanda, *adv.*	properly.
*Pawa, *tr. v.* & *n.*, pawé.	pay.
Pē = pēlē = wē = wēlē = pilē = wile = wiri, wi, *tr. v.*	do.
*Pei *or* peṅ, *adv.*	first.
Peka = weka, *n.*; *adj.*, pekeí.	other.
Pela = wela, *tr. v.*	finish.
Pela = wela, *intr. v.*	flee.
*Pē-lá, *n.*, pē leí.	doorway.
*Pēle, *n.*, pēlé *or* pĕ̄lí.	road.
Pēlē = wēlē, *n.*, pēleí.	house.
Pēbu.	indoors.
*Pēna, *n.*, pēné.	clay for pottery.
Pīlī = wīlī = p'lī, *tr. v.*	throw.
Pīme = wīme, *intr. v.*	run.

Pinde = winde, *intr. v.*	jump.
*Po, *tr. v.*	cut with an axe.
*Poloṅ, *adv.*	far.
Pọ̄ma = wọ̄ma, *n.*, pọ̄mé.	corpse.
Pọ̄ma = wọ̄ma, *prep.* & *adv.*; *n.*, pọ̄mei *or* wōma.	behind.
Po̱na = bo̱na, *tr. v.* & *adj.*, po̱nango.	straighten, straight.
*Pọ̄nje, *tr. v.*	strip leaves.
*Po̱pa, *n.*, pọ̄pé.	pond, lake.
Pọ̄pọ̄ = wọ̄po, *tr. v.*	carry on the back.
*Po̱ro, *n.*, po̱ré.	earth, soil.
Pọ̄te = wọ̄te, *tr. v.*	turn.
Pọ̄wa = bọ̄wa, *n.*, pọ̄wé.	flower.
*Pu, *adj.*	ten.
Pu = wu, *tr. v.*	put, pour.
*Pū.	European.
Pūmō, pūmōi.	European person.
Puyia, puyiei.	European language.
Pukpia = wukpia, *tr. v.*	uproot.

S changes into *J*.

Sago, sao, *adv.*	no.
Sama = jama, *n.*, samé.	person of distinction.
Samba, *n.*, sambé.	basket.
*Sande, *n.*	a female society = *Poro* for men.
*Sangbā, *n.*, sangbāi.	drum.
*Sange, *adv.*	just now, recently.
*Sani, *n.*, sanī́.	bottle.
*Sawa, *adj.*	three.
*Se, *n.*, sé.	thanks.
*Segbula, *n.*, segbulé.	rattle.
Seje, sese, *tr. v.*	slice.
Sejia, *tr. v.*	shake.
Seli, *n.*, seli.	judge, witness.
*Sema, *n.*, seme.	bamboo.
Sia, *tr. v.*	rub.
*Silọ̄, *n.*, silọ̄i.	spider.
*Sina, *adv.*	to-morrow.
So̱ = jo̱ = so̱lo = jo̱lo, *tr. v.*	marry, get, obtain.

So̱ku, *adj.*, so̱kungo.	bend.
Sokuihũ, *n.*	cape, corner of a wood, etc.
So̱le = jo̱re, *n.*, so̱lé.	noise, shouting.
So̱lo = so̱.	see *so̱*.
Sọ̄ndu = jundu, *tr. v.*	curse.
So̱ngo = jongo̱, *n.*, so̱ngoĩ,	price.
prep.	instead of.
Susu, *adj.*, susungo.	deep.
*Ta, *pr.*	he, she, it.
*Tā, *pr.*	he not, she not, it not.
*Ta, *conj.*	and, with.
*Ta, *n.*, tei.	town.
*Tamia, *conj.*	therefore ; so it is.
*Tanga, *n.*, tangé.	cassada.
Tātọ̄ = tọ̄tọ̄ = lọ̄tọ̄, *tr. v.*	begin.
*Tau, *adj.*	nine.
*Tāve, *n.*, tavé.	tobacco-pipe.
*Tāwa, *n.*, tawé.	tobacco.
*Tē.	they not.
*Te, *n.*, te.	fowl.
*Tē, *v.*	they say.
Te = le = de, *tr. v.*	raise.
*Tē, *adv.*	almost ; also indicates continuous action.
*Tekpe, *n.*, tekpe.	basket.
Teli = deli, *adj.*, telingo.	black.
Temu = lemu = demu, *tr. v.*	acquit, ask pardon.
Tenga = lenga, *adj.*	some.
* *adv.*	perhaps.
= lenga, *prep.*	towards, together with.
Tewe = lewe = dewe, *tr. v.*	cut, pass, cross, decide.
*Tewu, *n.*, tewui.	palm-nuts.
*Ti.	they, them.
*Tī.	they not.
*Tia.	they.
*Tiē.	them.
*Tifa, *n.*, tifé.	twig.
Tikpo = likpo, *n.*, tikpoi.	walking-stick.
Tiwi = liwi, *tr. v.*	close (the eye).
To = lo = do, *tr. v.*	see.

Tọ̄ = lọ̄ = dọ̄, *tr. v.*	send, point at, stand, build, follow.
*Tohe, *n. & intr. v.*	cough.
Tọ̄kọ̄ = lọ̄kọ̄, *n.*, tọ̄kọ̄i.	hand, arm.
*To̱kpo, *n.*, to̱kpoi.	oil-palm.
*To̱kpolo̱, *n.*, to̱kpolo̱i.	palm wine.
Tọ̄li = lọ̄li = dọ̄li = ruri, *tr. v.*	call.
Tọ̄lọ̄ = lọ̄lō, *n.*, tọ̄lọ̄i.	jealousy.
*To̱ne, *tr. v.*	tickle.
*To̱nya, *n.*	truth.
Tọto = tāto = lọtọ.	begin.
To̱wo = lo̱wo, *n.*, to̱wé.	fame, report.
*Tọ̄wu, *n.*, tọ̄wui	palm-nut.
Tukpe = lukpe, *tr. v.*	push.
Tuwo = tugo = lugo = luwo, *adv. & prep.*	before.

V changes into *F*.

Va, *prep.*	of, on account of, for.
Va, *tr. v.*	salute, say good-bye.
Vala, *tr. v.*	get ready.
Vale, *intr. v.*	grow—of plants.
Vaya, *tr. v.*	scatter.
Ve = fe, *tr. v.*	give.
Ve, *adv.*	completely.
Veli, *tr. v.*	say good-bye.
Veli, *tr. v.*	ask for.
Vu, *intr. v. & adj.*	live.
Nu vu.	a living person.

*Wa, *pr.*	you.
*Wā, *pr.*	you not.
*Wa, *intr. v.*	come.
Wa a.	come with = bring.
Wala, *intr. v.*	bring.
*Wā, *adj.*, wāi.	great.
Wā = pā, *tr. v.*	kill.
We = ye, *prep.*	to, for.
Wē = wēlē, *n.*	house.
Wē = pē, *tr. v.*	do.
*Wē, *pr.*	we not.

Wēhinda = pēhinda, *n.*, wē-hindeí.	conduct.
Weka = peka, *adj.*	other.
Wela = pela, *tr. v.*	finish.
Wela = pela, *intr. v.*	run away.
Wēlē = pele = pe = we.	do.
Wīlī = pīlī, *tr. v.*	throw, shoot.
Wīme = pime, *intr. v.*	run.
*Wọ̄, *pr.*	own.
Wọ̄ = ngọ̄, *n.*, wọ̄i.	voice.
Wō = ngō, *tr. v.*	break.
*Wo̱, *adv.*	formerly.
*Wofela, *adj.*	seven.
*Woita, *adj.*	six.
Wo̱la = ngo̱la, *v. n.*	weeping.
*Wọ̄lọ̄ = wọ̄, *intr. v.*	listen.
Wo̱longo = ngo̱longo, *adj.*	great.
Wōma = pōma, *n.*, wōmei.	back.
prep.	behind.
*Wọ̄nga, *n. pl.*, wọ̄ngeisia.	relations.
Wo̱ngo = ngo̱ngo, *adj.*	big.
Wọ̄pọ̄ = pọ̄pọ̄, *tr. v.*	carry on the back.
Wọ̄te = pọ̄te, *tr. v.*	turn, answer.
Wōva = ngōva, *adj.*, wōvango.	old.
*Wu, *pr.*	you.
*Wū, *pr.*	you not.
Wu = ngu, *tr. v.*	awake.
Wu = ngu, *n.*, wui.	head.
*Wua, *pr.*	you.
Wua = ngua, *intr. v.*	bear fruit.
Wua = ngua, *tr. v.*, or wa.	wash.
*Wuë, *pr.*	you.
Wulọ̄ = kulọ̄, *adj.*, wulongo.	small.
Wulo = ngulo, *n.*, ngulé	fat, oil.
Wulo, *adj.*, gulongo	fat.
Wulu = ngulu, *n.*, wulī.	tree.
Wumbu = mbumbu, *tr. v.*	take up, carry.
Yā, *n.*	edge, surface.
Yā, *adv. & prep.*	on top.
*Ya, *intr. v.*	go.

*Yā, *v.*	to be not.
Yā, *adv.*	not.
Yaka = kaka, *n.*, yakeí.	side, direction.
*Yakpē, *adj.*	same.
Yale = ngale, *tr. v.*	break.
Yama = ngama, *n.*, yamé.	eye, face.
*Yama, *intr. v.*	return.
Yate = ngate, *tr. v.*	kindle.
*Ye, *v.*	be.
*Yē, *v.*	he says.
Ye = we, *prep.*	to.
*Ye, *pr.*	who? how?
Ye = nje, *intr. v.*	descend.
*Ye, *n.*, yei.	country.
Yeja = ngeja, *adj.*	right (not left).
Yeka = ngeka, *adv.*	almost.
Yekpe = kpekpe, *adj.*, yekpengo.	good.
Yela = yira = ngera, *adj.*	one.
Yela = ngela, *tr. v.*	wipe.
*Yele, *v.*	be.
Yele = ngele, *intr. v.*	laugh.
Yele = ngele, *intr. v.*	scream.
Yenge = ngenge, *intr. v.*	work.
Yepe = ngepe, *intr. v.*; *n.*, yepei.	talk.
*Yese, *adj.*	first.
*Yetahũ, *n.*	own town, home.
Yeya = ngeya, *n.*	hand.
Talo ngi yeya.	it is (in) his hand = he has it.
Yeya = ngeya, *tr. v.*	buy.
Yeya = ngeya, *n.*, yeyeí.	rope.
Yī = nji, *intr. v.*	sleep.
n., yī.	sleep.
Yī = nji, *n.*	mother
*Yia, *intr. v.*	speak.
n., yiei.	talk, language.
Yīli = ngīli, *tr. v.*	cook.
Yīli = ngīli, *tr. v.*	tie.
Yira = yīla, *adj.*	one.
*Yo, *pr.*	who.

XXI. English-Mende.

(The definite form is put in brackets.)

Able, he is = he can.	i gũ.
About.	see under Prepositions.
Above.	ma, mahũ.
Accept, agree.	kuru.
Accuse.	mayia ge.
Acquit.	temu.
Across.	wọ̄ma.
Action.	pēhiṅda (pēhiṅdei).
Add.	mātọ.
Affair.	hiṅda, njia (hiṅdei, njiei).
Afraid, he is.	i lũa.
After.	wọ̄ma.
Afternoon.	kpokovọ̄li.
Afterwards.	na wọ̄ma.
Again.	gboma.
Against.	ma.
Ago.	wo̱.
Agree, accept.	kuru.
Aim at, aim at it.	tọ̄ ; tọ̄ ngi ma.
Alive.	vulungo.
All.	gbi, kpele.
Alone.	yakpe.
And.	ke, ta.
Animal.	hũa (hũei).
Another.	peka.
Answer, *v.*	duma.
Ant.	see under Insects.
Any.	gbi.
Appease.	lĩ leli.
Arm.	tọkọ̄ (lọkọ̄i).
Arrange.	magbate.
Ask.	mo̱li, veli.
Assemble.	kọ̄me.
At.	gama.
At once.	keyakpe.
Awake.	wu.
Axe.	konu (konī).

Baby.	ndọ̄la (ndọ̄le).
Back,	pọ̄ma (pọ̄mei), wọ̄ma or wōma.
to carry on the	pọ̄pọ̄, wọ̄po.
Backbite.	mayafa.
Backbiter.	ngafamo (ngafamoi).
Bad.	nyamu.
Bag.	baggi, sondubolo (sondubolé).
Bag (haversack).	gbafa (gbafé).
Bamboo, ordinary.	keni, semi.
palm from which piassava is made.	nduvu (nduvui).
Banana.	seli, sele.
Bank (of a river, etc.).	ngiye (ngiyei).
Barrel.	kọ̄lọ̄ (kọ̄lọ̄i).
Basket.	tekpe.
Bathe.	mūa.
Be, *v.*	lo, le, mia, ya, ye, yele.
Bear (children).	le, ndo le.
Beard.	gbele.
Beat.	ndewe.
Become.	wēlē, wē.
Bed.	gbuko (gbukwé), ndama (lamei).
Bee.	komi.
Before.	place—gulo, tugo, labu. time—peṅ, ngova, ge, gba.
Begin.	tāto, toto.
Beginning.	tātọ̄ma (tātọ̄mei).
Behaviour.	wehiṅda (wehiṅdei).
Behind.	wōma.
Believe.	hou a tonya.
Belly.	kọ̄hū (koihū or kohui).
Belonging to me.	nya wọ̄ le = it is my own.
Below.	mbū.
Bend.	kọ̄tọ̄.
Besides.	gboma, ji wōma.
Bet, *v.*	mawali hou.
Better, it is.	fisa.
Between.	lia.
Beyond.	wōma.
Big.	wā, ngọngo.

Bird.	nwoni.
Birth.	lē.
Bite.	nyī.
Bitter.	ṅo̱na.
Black.	teli, telingo.
Blame.	kāyē (kāyeí).
Blind.	mbọ̄le, mbọ̄lengo (mbọ̄lengoi).
Blood.	ṅāma (ṅamei).
Blunt.	ngāhango.
Board.	gbembele (gbembere).
Boat.	ndende.
Book.	ko̱lo (go̱lé).
Both.	venjo.
Bottle.	sani.
Bottom, the.	imbui.
Bow (for shooting).	ndikpa (ndikpé).
Box.	kaṅa (kaṅa).
Boy.	ndọ̄pọ̄ (ndọ̄pọ̄i).
Branch.	mbēkē (mbēkē).
Break, a house.	wo̱.
a stick.	yale.
a needle.	yale.
Bridge.	kpawu (kpawī).
Bring, *i.e.* come with.	wa a . ., wala.
Broom.	kpangba (kpangbe).
Brother.	ndewe, nde.
Brush, *v.*	mayela.
Bud.	kpo̱ku.
Build.	dọ̄.
Burn.	mo.
Burst.	būli.
Bury.	kpo̱wu.
Bush (the forest).	dogbo (dogboi).
Busy, I am.	gbe lo nya ma.
But (rather and).	ke.
Buy.	ngeya, yeya.
By.	a.
Calf (animal).	nika lọ̄ (nika lọ̄i).
Call.	tọ̄li, luli, ruri.
Can, *v.*	gū.

Carefully.	panda.
Carrier, *i.e.* labourer.	ngengemoi.
Carry (take up or away)	bumbu.
on the back.	wọ̄pọ̄, pọ̄pọ̄.
Cartridge.	kale.
Cask.	kọ̄lọ̄ (kọ̄lī).
Catch.	hou.
Cease.	ndondo, londo, gele (end).
Change.	pote (turn).
	maluwe (transform).
Cheap, *i.e.* not dear.	bā ī gbani.
	nyandengo (fine).
Chief.	maha (mahei).
Child,	ndọ̄, lọ̄, (lọ̄i).
able to walk.	jia lọ̄i.
Children.	lengesia.
Choose.	mahou, bumbu (take).
Circle.	kala (kalei), ka (kāi).
Clay.	po̱ro (po̱re), pena (pene).
Clean, *v.* & *adj.*	ko̱le, ko̱lengo.
Clear the ground.	nduwe.
Clever, he is.	ngi nemáhũ lengo.
Climb.	de.
Cloth.	kula (kule).
Cloud.	ngele (ngele).
Cold.	ko̱lengo.
Collect.	kome, yando.
Comb, *n.*	kpegbe
Comb your hair, *v.*	bi wui hũgbia.
Come.	wa.
Companion.	mbā (mbāi).
Complain.	mayia ge.
Condemn.	le.
Cook.	yīlī.
Cork (of a bottle).	sani lagbolui.
Corner,	kundo (kunde).
recess for a bed.	kundehũ.
Cough.	tohe.
Count.	kpā.
Country.	ye (yei).
	yetahũ (home town).

Cover.	mawele.
Crooked.	so̱kungo.
Cross, *v.*	tewe.
Cross-roads.	pele la bame, ganania.
Cry.	ngo̱, wo̱.
Cunning.	kāsǭ.
Cup.	mbola (mbole).
Cure.	bawǭ.
Cut.	tewe.
Cut your hair.	bi wui malete (or) bi wui wǭli.
Cutlass.	mbogbwa (mbogbwe), kpatǭ (kpatui).
Daily.	fǭlī gbi, kugbima.
Damp.	ndelingo.
Dance.	dǭli.
Dancer.	dǭlemo (dǭlemoi).
Dark.	kpindi.
"Dash," *i. e.* a present.	mboya (mboyé).
Dawn, at.	ngelewǭ.
Day.	lo̱ (lo̱i), ku, fǭlǭ (fǭlī).
Dead.	hango.
Death.	ha (hēi).
Debt.	kpa (kpei).
Decide.	tewe.
Deep.	susu, susungo.
Deer, *i. e.* antelope.	ndopa (ndopé).
Delay.	lembi.
Descend.	hite, ye.
Dew.	lugbu (lugbui).
Die.	ha.
Different.	gba.
Difficult.	kpakpaungo.
Dig.	mbo̱.
Dislike.	dǭlo.
Dismiss.	gbē.
Divide.	ko̱le.
Do.	pēlē, pīlī, pē ; wēlē, wīrī, wē.
Doorway.	pele la (pele lei).
Door itself.	nete.

Down, *i. e.* on the ground.	do̲mé (*pr.* dormé).
Drag, draw.	nda.
Dream.	hengá.
Dress.	magbate.
Drink.	gbọ̄le.
Drop.	gulā́.
Drum.	sangba (sangbai).
Drunk (wine holds him).	ndo̲ i ngi houa.
Dry, *v.*	bēli.
adj.	bēli, belingo.
Dry season.	ngọ̄vọ̄ (ngọ̄vọ̄i).
Dung.	kpọ̄ (kpọ̄i).
Dwarf.	tumbu (tumbui).
Each.	gbi.
Each other.	nyo̲ nyo̲ (nyo̲ nyo̲i).
Ear.	wọ̄li.
Early, morning.	ngenda tete.
Earth, *i. e.* all countries.	ndo̲lo (ndo̲le *or* ndo̲ei).
soil.	po̲ro (po̲re).
East.	ko̲.
Eat, *tr.*	me.
intr.	mehe me.
Ebb, of the sea.	belī.
Edge of a knife.	ya.
Egg.	ngalu (yalui), tē-yalui, te-yaui.
Empty.	haka, hakango.
End, *v.*	gele.
n.	ikelemeí.
Enough, it is.	i gua.
it is not.	ī guni.
Equal.	mahewu.
Evening (afternoon).	kpokovọ̄i.
Every.	gbi.
Examine (look into).	hũgbe.
Explain.	hũge.
Expose.	gbia fọ̄fọ̄ihũ.
Eye.	yama (yamei).
Face.	yama (yamei).
Fall	gulā́.

Fame.	to̱wo (to̱wé).
Family.	mbọ̄nda (mbondé).
Far.	kuhango, hũguhango (*pr.* ngwango), mahũguhango (*pr.* ma'ngwango), kuhama.
Farewell, to bid.	See under Salutations.
Farm.	kpãle, kpã (kpãei).
Fasten.	kpakpa.
Fat, *adj.*	gulongo.
Father.	ke (kei).
Fault.	kaye (kayé).
Fear.	lua.
Feast.	gọ̄ma (gọ̄me).
Feather.	njọ̄mbọ̄ (njọ̄mbọ̄i).
Fence.	kāta (kāté).
Few.	wūlo.
Field.	kpãle (kpãle), kpã (kpãe).
Fight (wrestle).	lapi.
(war).	kọ̄ (kọ̄ī).
Fill.	fe, fenda, ndave, lave, lavenda.
Find, something new.	koko, kokoli.
something looked for.	to (lit. see).
Finish.	gbo̱yō.
Fire,	gombu (gombui).
a gun.	pili (lit. throw).
First, the.	i halagei.
adv.	yese, peṅ, gba.
Fish.	nye (nyé).
Fisherman.	nyegbemoi.
Fishing-net.	nye boma (bomé).
Fish-hook.	ndoli.
Flower.	pọ̄wa (pọ̄wé).
Fly (insect).	See under Insects.
v.	go̱wo, buwu.
Follow.	tọ̄ *with* wọ̄ma.
Food.	mehe (mehei).
Foolish.	mamungo.
Foot.	go̱wo (go̱we).
For.	va.
Forget.	lēma.
Forgive.	manu.

From.	no word—see under Prepositions.
Fruit.	wua (wuei).
Full.	lavengo.
Gamble—with cowries.	kpoyo-go (goi).
with cards.	ko̱lo-go (goi).
Garden.	kpãle (lit. farm).
	katéhũ (lit. compound).
Gate.	ngoréla (ngorelei).
Gather.	ngando, yando.
Get, obtain.	jo̱, so̱.
Girl.	nyapọ̄ (nyapọ̄i).
Give.	fe, go (for uses see Part I).
Go.	li, ya.
Gold.	kani gbōle.
Good.	yekpengo, nyandengo.
Grind.	fuka.
Ground, *n.*	ndo̱mē (ndo̱mei).
Grow,	lakpa.
of plants only.	vale.
Hammock.	mbōma (mbōmé).
Hand.	lọ̄kọ̄ (lọ̄kọ̄i).
Hang.	hele.
Happen.	wēlē, malē.
Hard.	kpakpaũngo.
Hasten, *tr. v.*	mavula.
intr.	pe kaká.
Hat.	bo̱le.
Have, rendered by to be in the hand.	I have it, Ta lo nya yeya. I have nothing, Hani gbī nya yeya.
He.	ta, a, i.
Head.	ngu, wu (wui).
Heal.	bawọ̄.
Hear.	meni, me.
Heart.	lī.
Heat, *v.*	gbandī.
Heavy.	miningo.
Help.	gbo ; gbo nya ma, help me.

Here.	be.
Hide.	lo̲wu.
High.	kuhango.
Hill.	ngiyē (ngiyēi).
Hit against.	ho̲.
Hold.	hou.
Hole.	ndowa (ndowe).
Home.	yē (yei).
Honey.	komi (bee), komi yei (bees' water).
Hook.	ndọ̄li.
Hoop for climbing trees.	mbalu (mbalī).
Horn.	ndọ̄wọ̄ (lọ̄wọ̄i).
Hot.	gbandi, gbandingo.
House.	pe, pele, wele.
How.	ye (comes second in sentence). See under Adverbs.
Hunger.	ndo̲le (ndolé).
Hunt.	kpe.
Hurry, *tr*.	mavula.
intr.	pe kaka.
Husband.	hini.
Hut.	kpueila (kpueilé).
If.	ina.
Immediately	keyakpe.
In.	hũ.
Insect.	fūhani, *usually plural* fuhanisia.
Inside.	hũ, gohũ.
Instead.	jongo.
Intended, I.	ngi yeto.
Into.	hũ.
Iron.	ko̲lu (ko̲li).
Jealous.	tọ̄lọ̄.
Join.	ndālo.
Journey.	jia (jiei).
Joy.	ko̲hũne.
Judge, *n*.	seli.
v.	tewe.

Jump.	wīnde, pīnde.
Keep.	hou.
Kernel.	kale (kalé).
Key.	jiwi.
Kill.	pa, wa.
Kindred.	wo̲nga (wongé).
Knife.	mbowa (mbowé).
Knock against.	ho̲.
Knot.	kpūlo (kpuli).
Know.	ko̲, go̲.
Labourer.	ngengemo (ngengemoi).
Lame.	kpo̲rongo.
Language.	yīa (yiei).
Large.	wa, ngo̲longo, ngo̲ngo.
Last, the.	ikelemage.
Late, come.	lembi.
Lately.	sange, ge.
Laugh.	yele.
Lay.	nda, la.
Lazy.	hawango.
Leaf.	ndā (ndāi).
Leak, *v.*	mbo.
Lean, *v.*	digbī.
Learn.	gā.
Leave,	kpēlē, kpē.
behind.	lọ̄.
Left hand, the.	kowo lọ̄kọ̄i.
Leg.	go̲wo (go̲wé).
Let down, *tr. v.*	hité.
Lie, tell a.	ndé gora.
down.	la.
Lift.	de.
Light, *n.*	hemu (hemui).
not heavy.	ī minini.
Like—	kea . . . na.
like this.	kea ji na.
tr. v.	longo, followed by "a" and the object.
Likeness.	kpiaye (kpiayei).

Line marked out.	kpambi.
Listen to.	meni.
Little.	kulo, wulongo, mumu.
Living.	vulungo.
Living person.	nū vu.
Load, *n*.	haka (hakei).
a gun.	joso.
Lock.	kpolu (kpoli).
Log.	kowe (kowé).
Long.	kuha, kuhango.
Look.	kpele, gbe.
for, *i. e.* search.	ko̱koli.
Looking-glass.	meme.
Loose, *v*.	fūlọ̄.
Lose.	ndo̱hũ.
Lower, *tr. v*.	hité, maye.
part.	imbui.
Mad.	gbuwa.
Make a thing.	gbate.
i. e. do.	we.
Man.	hiṅdọ̄ (hiṅdọ̄i).
Many.	gboto, gbotongo.
Mark, *v*.	nyegi.
Marry.	nyaha jo (*or* jolo).
Master.	ke (kei).
Mat.	yala (yale).
Measure, *v*.	hūma.
Meat,	hũa (hũei).
including fish.	ndahani (ndahani).
Meet.	male.
Mend.	gbate.
Mende.	Mende.
Mendeman.	Mendemo (Mendemoi).
language.	Mende yia (yiei).
Message.	ngọ̄ (ngọ̄i).
Middle.	lia (liei).
Mix.	hupu.
Money.	navọ̄ (navọ̄i).
Month.	ngalu, ngau (ngalui, yalui).
Moon.	ngalu, ngau (ngalui, yalui).

Morning.	ngenda.
Mortar for pounding.	kọ̄nda (kọ̄nde).
Mother.	njẹ̄ (yi).
Mouth.	la (lei).
Much.	gboto, gbotongo.
Mud.	pawa (pawé).
Music.	mbaka (mbaké).
Must.	= shall (future tense).
Nail, *n.*	lo̱ndema (lo̱ndeme).
v.	kpākpa.
of the finger or toe.	yengalu (yengalui).
Name.	bije (bijei), la (lei).
Near.	gbela.
Nearly.	yeka.
Necessary, to be.	māni.
Needle.	miji.
Nest.	nwoni-ta (nwoni-tei).
Net.	mboma (mbome).
New.	nīna, nīnango.
Nice.	nyande, nyandengo.
Night.	kpindi.
No.	erer, saō (emphatic).
Noise.	sore (soré).
None.	gbī.
Not.	See chapter on Negative.
Nothing.	hani gbī.
Now.	sange.
Oar.	lala (lalei).
Obey.	wọ̄ meni.
Obtain.	jo̱.
Of.	va.
Often.	pepe.
Oil.	ngulo (nguli).
Old.	ngova, wovango.
On.	ma, mahũ.
On account of.	va.
Only.	yakpe, leke, yeke.
Open.	ndawo, lawo.
Order, a direction.	layia (layiei).
Other.	peka (pekei), weka (wekei).

Out.	No word. See Prepositions.
Out-house (room).	kongu (kongui).
Outside, *i. e.* in the open.	ngitiya.
Over, *i. e.* upon.	ma.
i. e. beyond.	wọ̄ma.
Overtake.	male.
Own.	wo, nda.
my own.	nya wo, nya nda.
Pad for the head when carrying a load.	fūkọ̄ (fukọ̄i).
Paddle, *n.*	guli.
v.	nje guli.
Pain, *n.* & *v.*	gbale.
Palm.	See under Plants.
Palm oil.	ngulo gbou (ngulo gboui).
Palm wine.	tọkpo lọ (tọkpo lọi).
Paper.	kọlo (kole).
Pardon, ask.	demu.
Part.	kaka.
Pass.	tewe.
Path.	pele (peli).
Pay, *n.* & *v.*	pawa.
People.	nunga.
Perhaps.	tenga.
Person.	numu (numui).
Pick-up.	bumbu.
Pinch.	fọnī.
Pity.	manu.
Place.	hiṅda (hiṅdé).
Plant, *v.*	hī.
Play, *n.* & *v.*	lọ̄li.
Please, to.	kọne.
Pluck, a bird.	magbia.
a flower, fruit.	gole, go'e, gbenda.
Point to.	tọ̄.
Point to it.	tọ̄ ngi ma.
Poison.	pā-hale (pā-halé).
Pond, pool.	pọ̄pa (pọ̄pé).
Possess, *v.*	yeya, *n.*
he possesses it, *i. e.* it is in his hand.	ta lo ngi yeya.

Pot.	fe (feí).
Pound, *v.*	kpakpa.
Pour.	pu, wu.
Powder.	dehe.
Powerful.	gbayango.
Pray.	he.
Praise.	lato.
Prepare.	hũgbate.
Present, *n.*	mboya (mboyé).
adv. i. e. here.	be.
Price.	jongo (jongoi).
Properly.	panda. Very common word.
Public, in.	fọ̄fọ̄ hũ.
Pull,	ndā, lā.
out.	kpia.
Purpose on.	a kege.
Pursue.	kpē.
Push.	tukpe.
Put.	pu, wu.
Quick.	káká.
Quietly.	lome-lome.
Rag.	kula gutu (kula gutī).
Rain.	nja, njei.
Rainy season.	hama (hamé).
Raise.	te.
Raw.	ngundu, wundungo.
Reach.	hité.
Ready.	vala.
Remain, *i. e.* sit down.	hei.
Remainder.	mo̱nu (mo̱ní).
Remember.	gili.
Repair.	gbate.
Reply.	pọ̄te, wọ̄te.
Rest, *v.*	ndevu, levu.
Return, *v.*	yāma.
Rice.	mba (mbeí).
Rich.	gbatengo.
Right hand.	yeja lọ̄kọ̄i
Right, *adj.*	lemungo.

Ripe.	bengo.
Rise.	hije, hiye.
River.	kpọ̄lī.
Road.	pele (pelí).
Rob.	yahuma.
Rock, *n.*	ko̱tu (ko̱tí).
Roll, *v.* (of a ship).	lekpe.
Roll up.	kọ̄tọ.
Room, *n.*	pēlē, wēlē, kongo, kongōihũ.
inner recess (corner).	kundehũ.
Root.	hapē (hapḗ).
Rope.	ngeya (ngeyeí).
Rot, *v.*	ndulu.
Round, *adj.*	kikili, kekele, kere.
v. to put round, encircle, pass round.	mbimbi, gala.
Round about.	ikakamage.
Row, a boat.	guli.
Rub.	sia.
Rudder.	gbī.
Rum.	ndo̱ (ndo̱i), lo̱ (lo̱i).
Run.	pime, wime.
Runner of a plant.	ngeyako̱ (ngeyako̱i).
Rust.	kaiye.
Sacrifice, *n.*	sā hani.
v.	sā gbia.
Sake of.	va.
Salt.	kpọ̄lọ̄ (kpọ̄lọ̄i).
Same.	yakpe, se.
Sand.	ṅgaṅga (ṅgaṅgé), ṅgaṅya (ṅgaṅyé).
Saw, *n.*	so̱wi.
Say.	nde, le.
Scatter.	faya.
Scent (perfume).	ku yei.
Scrape.	gbenye.
Sea.	kpoye (kpoyḗ).
Search.	kokoli.
Seat.	he wuru (he wurí).
See.	to, do, lo.

Seed.	kale (kalɛ́).
Seek.	ko̱koli.
Sell.	majia.
Send.	dewe, lọ̄.
Sense.	nemáhũ̄.
Separate.	go̱le.
Servant.	bo̱ilọ̄pọ̄ (bo̱ilọ̄pọ̄i).
Set, *v.*	hei.
Settle a dispute.	tewe.
Sew.	ho̱.
Shake.	jesia, jeji.
Shallow.	tetele.
Sharp.	yāndingo.
Shell, of an oyster, husk, empty snake skin, etc.	gā (geí).
Shirt.	ndọ̄ma (lọ̄mɛ́).
Shoot.	pili.
and hit, *i.e.* pierce.	mbọ̄.
Short.	kutu, kutungo.
Shout, *n.*	sole, sore.
v.	sore we.
Show.	ke.
Show him.	ke a ngie.
Shut, *v.*	lagbou.
adj.	lagboungo.
Sick, to be.	higbe.
adj.	higbengo.
Side.	kāka (kākei), yāka, gāka.
Sing.	ngulē, wulɛ̄.
Sit.	hei.
Skin.	ko̱lo (ko̱lɛ́).
Sky.	ngɛ́lɛ̄ (ngɛ̄lé).
Sleep.	yī.
Slowly.	lɛ̄lɛ̄.
Small.	kulo, kulongo.
Smell.	ku (kūi).
sweet.	ku ne.
bad.	ku nyamu.
v.	kui meni.
Smoke.	ndūli, lūli.
Sneeze.	diso.

So, thus.	ṅi, hi.
Soap.	mbawa (mbawé), hega (hegé).
Some.	lenga.
Song.	ngulē, wulē.
Soon, *i. e.* quickly.	káká.
Sow.	hī.
Speak.	nde, yia le.
Spend, money.	majia.
the day.	luva.
Spill.	pu, faya.
Spirit.	ngafa (ngafé), yafa.
Split, *v.*	mbela.
adj.	mbelango.
Spread.	fọ̄mbọ̄.
Sprout, *v.*	kpo̱ku.
Squeeze.	fo̱nya.
Stand.	tọ̄.
Star.	dumbeka (dumbeké).
Start.	hije.
Steal.	huma.
from.	yahuma.
Steer.	gbī hou.
Stick, *n.*	nguru (ngurī).
walking-.	tikpo (tikpoi).
Still, *adv.*	kpe.
Sting.	mbọ̄.
Stone.	ko̱tu (ko̱tī).
Stop.	kpele, kpe.
end.	gele.
Story.	do̱me (do̱mé).
Straight.	po̱na, po̱nango.
Straighten.	po̱na.
Stranger.	ho̱ta (ho̱té).
Strength.	kpaya (kpayé).
Stretch.	fọ̄mbọ̄.
String.	ngeya (yeyeí).
Strip, undress.	magbia.
leaves.	mapọ̄nje, magọ̄mbo.
Strong.	gbayango.
Stupid.	mamu, mamungo.
Sugar.	sugar.

Summit.	ngumba.
Sun.	fǭlǭ, (fǭlī).
Surface.	ngā, yā.
Surpass.	tewe.
Surround.	bimbi.
Swallow, *v.*	gbolē.
Sweep.	ngela, mayela.
Sweet.	ne, neingo.
Swell, *v.*	fe.
Swim.	lapi.
Swing round.	bimbi.
Take.	bumbu.
Talk.	njepe, yepe, yia le.
Tall.	gbiahungo.
Taste.	ko̱, go̱.
Teach.	kā, gā.
Tear, *v.*	mbela.
Tell.	nde.
Thank, *v.*	segbia.
Thank you.	bise.
That.	na.
There.	na, mia, miando.
Thick.	kpo̱tu, kpo̱tungo.
Thin.	teve, tevengo.
Thing.	hani, bo̱ (bo̱i).
Think.	gili, to̱ye.
Thirsty, my throat is dry.	nya bo̱lohũi bengo.
This.	ji.
Thorn.	ngari.
Throw.	pīlī, wīlī.
Thrust in.	ngua, wua, joso.
Thus.	ṅi.
Tickle.	to̱ne, dote.
Tightly.	panda (properly), getete.
Time.	kpēlē (kpēlē), kpē.
Tire.	gbowu.
Tired.	gbahã, gahũ hango.
Are you tired?	bi gbahã?
To.	See Prepositions.
To-day.	ha.

To-morrow.	sina.
Too.	tunu.
Top, the.	imahui, ngumba.
Touch.	jā.
Toward.	gama, tenga.
Town.	tā (tei).
Trap.	mani.
Travel.	jia.
Tree.	ngulu (ngulí), nguru (ngurí).
Trousers.	bere (beré).
Truth.	tonya.
Try.	ko̱, ko̱lo.
Turn.	pọ̄te, wọ̄te.
Twins.	felanga.
Twist.	kpini.
Umbrella.	Tebele, nja-gbuwa (nja-gbuwé).
Under.	mbu.
Understand.	meni, hũgo.
Undress.	magbia.
Unexpectedly, to meet.	kolama.
Unfold.	fọ̄mbọ̄.
Unlike.	gbā.
Unlucky, to be.	ndo̱vo.
Unripe.	kpọ̄le, kpọ̄lengo.
Untie.	fulọ̄.
Up.	ma.
Upon.	ma, mahũ.
Uproot.	pugbia.
Useless.	gbamafu.
Valley.	ngiye gombu (ngiye gombui).
Valuable.	bā gbango.
Very.	kā.
Village.	fula (fulé).
Visit, *v.*	va.
Voice.	ngọ̄ (ngọ̄i), wọ̄ (wọ̄i).
Vomit.	bali.
Wait.	mawulu.

Wake.	wu.
Walk.	jia.
Wall.	kaka or kake (kakeí).
Want, *v.*	longo a.
War.	ko (koi).
Warm, *v.*	kpandi.
adj.	kpandingo.
Warn.	lahĩ.
Wash, clothes, plates.	wua, wa.
i. e. bathe.	mua.
Watch, *v.*	mānē, mahũgbe.
Water.	nja (njeí).
Way.	pele (pelí).
Wear clothes.	yili.
Weed, *v.*, *i. e.* pull up weeds.	kpiti gbia.
Weep.	wo̱lo.
Welcome, *v.*	va.
Well, water-hole.	nja lowa (nja lowé).
Well, *adv.*	panda.
West.	kpundohũ.
Wet.	deli, delingo.
What?	gbe?
When?	See Adverbs.
Where?	mi? mindo?
Which?	igbé?
Whip.	fọma (fọmé).
White.	kọlē, kolengo, gogole.
White man.	pumo (pumoi).
man's language.	pu yia (pu yiei).
Who?	ye? yo?
Whole, all.	gbi, kpere.
Why?	gbeva?
Wicked.	nyamu.
Wife.	nyaha (nyahei).
Win, in a game, *i. e.* kill.	pā.
take the money.	hou.
Wind.	fefe (fefé).
Window.	ndaome.
Wine.	ndo̱, lo̱ (lo̱i).
Wing.	kpaki.
Wipe (plates).	hũyela.

Wise, he is.	ngi nemáhũ lengo.
Witch.	ho̱na (ho̱né).
With.	a.
Within.	hũ, gohũ, bu.
Without.	See Prepositions.
Woman, wife.	nyaha (nyahei).
unmarried girl.	nyapọ̄ (nyapọ̄i).
Wood.	ko̱wu (ko̱wī).
Word, speech.	njia (njiei), yia (yiei).
direction, order.	layia (layiei).
voice.	ngọ̄ (ngọ̄i).
Work, *n.*	ngenge (ngengé), yenge.
v.	ngenge *and* ngenge wili.
Workman.	ngengemo (ngengemoi).
pl. (*indef.*).	gengebra.
World.	ngelebu, ndo̱le gbi.
Worm.	buli.
Wrap up.	bimbi.
Wrestle.	lapi.
Write.	nyegi.
Wrong, to be.	lele.
Yard, enclosure.	katéhũ.
Year.	fọ̄ (fọ̄i).
Yes.	ī, ē.
Yesterday.	gbenge, bengeme, gbĭ.
Yonder.	miando, mia.
Young man.	ndakpalọ̄ (ndakpalọ̄i).
Young of an animal.	. . . lọ̄i.

PART IV

STORIES

Reading Materials

I.

The Spider and his Hungry Children.

Kasiloi i ndenga le.	The spider bore children.
Ndole gbo.	They were very hungry.
I hiye lime go'ime dogboi hũ.	He arose to go and gather food in the bush.
I li, i male.	He goes, he meets it.
Sele gboungo.	It was a ripe banana.
Fomamoi i hei lo sele gama.	A man with a whip sat at the banana.
Kasiloi i jã sele.	The spider touched the banana.
Fome i gbia.	The whip came out.
I ngi vogba.	It beat him.
Kena i ngi vogba	When it beat him
Kasiloi gbwenda.	The spider snatched (the fruit).
I yala a pime ngi lenga we.	He ran off with it to his children. (lit. He took it with running).
Ti me a kpindi na.	They ate that night.
Ngewonga i ngi nyahei gbe.	At daylight he drove away his wife.
Ngi nyahei i ya nye gbeme njei hũ.	His wife went to catch fish in the water.
Ye, kea bi nya gbe gɛ̃ bi go.	She said, If you drive me away I will not give you (some).
Ye, nga nye me lo.	He said, I will eat fish.
Ye, nya be gɛ̃ bi go.	She said, I certainly will not give you (any).
Ke i ya.	And she went.
I ngi mayia ge a ngi kei.	She complained to her father.
Ye, nga nyahei gbia lo bi yeya.	He said, I will take away your wife.

Incomplete.

II.

The Fate of the Man who abandoned his Wife and Child.

Tamoi i ya wọ.	A person went once upon a time.
I nyahei jo.	He took a wife.
I koi bumbu.	She conceived.
I ngi nyahei gbe.	He drove away his wife.
I li dogboi hũ.	She went to the bush.
I nyahei lọ.	He left his wife.
I ndọi de dogboi hũ.	She bore a child in the bush.
Ti fere gbi	Both of them.
Ta ngi loi i jia.	She and her son they walk about.
Mehei gbī na ta me.	No food there for them to eat.
Ngi njei a li,	His mother goes,
A mboli gbia dogboi hũ.	She pulls up a yam in the bush.
I lọi na bawoni.	She preserved her child.
Ngi loi a lakpa.	Her child grows up.
Ngewo i wa.	God comes.
I gbatenga dogboi hũ.	He was rich in the bush.
I ti male dogboi hũ.	He met them in the bush.
Ngewo ye,	God said,
Wa yo wu mbe?	Who are you that are here?
Ye, ma nya njei.	(He answered) I and my mother.
Ngewo i ho navoi ma.	God took money.
I fe tiye.	He gave it them.
Ngewo i li dogboi hũ.	And God went away into the bush.
Nyahei ngi lọi i gbate dogboi hũ.	The woman's son grew rich in the bush.
I gbia dogboi hũ;	He came out of the bush;
A hite pē wai ma.	He reaches the high road.
Ke ta ngi kei ti gome.	And he and his father they met.
Ye, kia wọ bi nya njei gbeni,	He said, Since you formerly drove away my mother,

Nga bi wā lo.	I will kill you.
Ye, kia na ma bie mu longa,	He said, Since now you and I see each other,
Nya be, gi bi houma,	I also, I will catch you,
Gi bi wā.	I will kill you.
Ta wa ye,	Himself he said,
Bā nya hō.	Do not seize me.
I ya i ngili;	He went to tie him;
I ngi ho;	He caught him;
I ngili;	He bound him;
I mbowei bumbu;	He took a knife;
I nda 'gi bo̱le la;	He drew it across his throat;
I tē;	He cut;
I ha—ngi kei.	He died—his father (did).
Kele mia.	It is the end.

III.

The Fate of the Man who cleared the Bush when told not to do so.

Tamo yira i ya dogboi hũ nduweme.	A certain person went into the bush to clear (a piece of ground).
Hāwai ye, bã nduwe.	The devil said, Do not clear.
(Hāwai *or* Haniwai is a materialised spirit inhabiting the forest.	
Ye, nga duwe lo.	He said, I shall clear.
Bi nduwenga lo	(The devil said) If you clear
Bē mbei me.	You will not eat the food (lit. rice).
Ke ngelewo	And at daylight
Ke i mbogbwei bumbua.	He took a cutlass.
Hawai ye ngima,	The devil said to him,
Bã nduwe.	Do not clear.
Ye, nga nduwe lo.	He said, I shall clear.
Ye, bi nduwinga lo	(The devil) said, If you clear
Ye mbe gbī na bi me.	There will be no rice there for you to eat.
Ke i ya dogboi hũ ndu'iva.	And he went into the bush to clear.
Ke i nduwía.	And he cleared.
Ke i gombui ; Ke i mbumbua ;	And he took fire ;
Ke i ye kpalehũ ;	And he went to the farm ;
Ke i gombui dọa kpalema.	And he put fire to the farm.
Ke i kpalei moa.	And he burnt the farm.
Ke i kali bumbua.	And he took a hoe.
Ke i ya,	And he went,
Ke i mbei wuli,	And he took rice (lit. draw as water),

Ke i mbei bumbua,	And he carried the rice,
Ke i ya kpalehũ.	And he went to the farm
Ke i ndea ngi nyahei ma,	And he said to his wife,
Ke ngi lọi,	And (to) her son,
Ye, wa be,	He said, Come here,
Mu mbei bo.	Let us plant the rice.
Ke ti punga ndoli ma,	And they put it in the ground,
Ke ti ya pe bu.	And they went home.
Ke ti yinga.	And they slept.
Ngēwa ti ya gbueila.	At dawn they went to their farm-hut.
Ye ti mbei bonga.	He said they were to plant the rice.
Ye, kea ti mbei boa.	He said, When they had planted the rice they could go away.
Ke mbei gbia.	And the ears of rice appeared.
Ke ti ya kpaleima	And they went to the farm
Ti mbei lē.	To cut the rice.
Ti nganga,	They threshed it,
Ke ti punga hambui ma,	And they put it on the drying-frame,
Ke i benga.	And it dried.
Ke ti bumbúa,	And they took it,
Ti pu kọnde hũ.	They put it in the mortar.
Ye, kea ti pui kọnde hũ ti hija.	He said, When they put it in the mortar, they were to beat it.
Ke ti gbia kọnde hũ,	And they took it out of the mortar,
Ke ti punga fe hũ.	And they put it in the pot.
Ke ti ngīnga,	And they cooked it,
Ke ti gbia hũ,	And they took it out,
Ke ti menga.	And they ate it.
Ke ti jango,	And they three,
Ke ti mbei menga,	They ate the rice,
Ke ti ha.	And they died.
Ke nu wāi i ndea,	And the big man said,
Ye, ji wọ gi ndea.	Saying, I told you before.
Nge, ba dogboi luwi ba ha lo.	I said, do not clear the bush (or) you will die.
Ye, ta ji bi hanga.	He said, Therefore you have died.

Ye, nū ji mbe indea bima,	He said, This person here told you,
Ye bā ji we;	Saying, Do not do this;
Bi penga lo,	If you do it,
Ba ha lo fe.	You will surely die.
Nū wai i ye bā ji pe, bā pe.	If a big person says do not do this, do not do it.
Igboyoai.	It is finished.
Mu kelema mia lo.	Ditto.

IV.

The Devil who took a Human Wife.

Haiwāi i ya komé tei hũ.	The bush-devil went to a meeting in the town.
Ke nyahei, i longa a ngie.	And the woman, he liked her.
Ye nga bia jolo.	He said, I will marry you.
Ke i nyahei wumbu,	And he took the woman,
Ke ti ya peli hũ,	And they went into the road,
Ke ngi lọi.	And her child (also).
Ke ti ya dogboi hũ.	And they went into the bush.
Ke ti ya tei hũ.	And they went into the town.
Haiwai a numu me.	The devil eats man.
Nyahei na ke ngi lọi ti ya dogboi hũ.	That woman and her child went into the bush.
Haiwai ye, ngē bi me.	The devil said, I will not eat you.
Ye, nga bi jolo lo.	He said, I will marry you.
A ngi bumbu i li pele bu.	He takes her, he goes into the house.
Ngelewo Haiwai i li pelíma.	At daylight the devil goes into the road.
I nunga lo,	He sees (some) people,
I to ho,	He catches them,
I ya a tie pele bu,	He took them home,
Ngi nyahei ē numui me.	His wife would not eat man.
I li dogboi hũ.	He went into the bush.
I li, i hũei hou.	He goes, he catches an animal.
I wala ngi nyahei we.	He brings it to his wife.
Ngi nde wulī i hiya.	Her little brother got up.
I nde ngi ndei ma,	He said to his sister,
Mu li.	Let us go.
Ke ti hijenga,	And they got up,
Ke ti ya.	And they went.

Haiwai i ngi nde wulī honga.	The devil caught her little brother.
Ye, bi li bi wala bi ndewe.	He said, Go and fetch your sister.
I hiya, i li.	He got up, he went.
I ngi ndewe male.	He met his sister.
I nde ngi ma, ye,	He said to him, saying,
Hiye mu li.	Get up, let us go.
Ke Haiwai i nde ngi mbilema, ye,	And the devil said to his brother-in-law, saying,
Bē li a nya nyahei gbindi.	You must not go with my wife to-night.
Ke ngelewa, ke ngi ndei ke i mbumbúa,	And at daybreak her brother took her,
Ke ti hitia peli hũ.	And they reached the road.
Ke ti ya,	And they went,
Ke ti njei malenga,	And they came to a river (water),
Njei ngọlongo,	A large (piece of) water,
Ke ti gele njei ma.	And they stopped at the water.
Ke Haiwai i hiya.	And the devil got up.
I tọnga ti ma péli hũ,	He followed them in the road,
Ke i ti malenga,	And he overtook them,
Ke i ya peli hũ,	And he came into the road,
Ke i ndea tima, ye,	And he said to them, saying,
Wē li.	You must not go.
Wa, a mu yama.	Come, let us return.
Ta wa ye, bi nyaha joro wọ,	Moreover he said, If you have married a wife,
Ye, ē gua ti wele.	He said she cannot return home.
Ye na ngi nyaha gọ̄lini wọ.	He said, Now I have married a wife.
Ye, ē gua ti wele	He said, She must not return unto her country
Yeka njei i beli.	Until the water dries up.
Ye ke njei i gule mu gulo,	But (the other) said, May the water dry up in front of us,
Mu li ma nya ndewe,	So that I and my sister may go on,
Ye mu gbi mu hite mu yei ma.	He said, and that we may all reach our country.

Ye gbe gombui i gula mu lua hũ.	He said, Let fire fall between us.
Ke gombui i gula ti lua hũ.	And fire fell between them.
Ke Haiwai i wotia i yama ngi weletahũ.	And the devil turned and returned to his own (lit. home) town.
Ke i yama,	And he returned,
Ke i ndea ngi lọ̄i ma, ye,	And he said to his son, saying,
Nunga wo ngi ti houni,	The people I caught the other day,
Ye ti ya ti wetahũ, ke nya ndopoi.	He said, they have gone back to their country with my boy.
Ke i ndea ngi kei ma,	And he said to his father,
Ye, nga lilo.	He said I will go.
Ye, ngi wa be nyaheina, ke bi lenga lo.	He said, I bring the woman here, and your children.
Ke i ya i hite tei hũ.	And he went, he arrived at the town.
Ke i ndea nyapui ma,	And he said to the girl,
Ye, nga wa ngi nde bima,	He said, I come to tell you,
Ye, mu yama.	He said (that) we (must) return.
Ke i ndea ngima, ye,	And she said to him, saying,
Ngē wama.	I shall not come.
Ye, gbele ?	He said, What is the matter ?
Ke Haiwai i wa,	And the devil came,
Ti ngi hounga,	(and) they caught him,
Ke ti bumbu.	And they took him.
Ti ya peli hũ,	They went into the road,
Ke ti yombui ngatea,	And they lit a fire,
Ke ti Haiwai hounga,	And they seized the devil,
Ke ti ngi ngilinga,	And they bound him,
Ke ti bumbu,	And they took him,
Ke ti pilia ngombui ya,	And they threw him on the fire,
Ke i hanga.	And he died.

End.

V.

The Twins and their Brother.

Tamoi mia wo̱,	Once upon a time there was a man,
I hiye i nyahei so̱lo.	He arose, he married a woman.
I ndọ̄i le fere.	She bore two children.
Felanga atie.	They were twins.
Ti lakpa.	They grew up.
Ke ti nde wulọ̄i fela angie.	And their little brother was their senior.
I li ko̱lo.	He went up country.
Ti yei a mbe yili ;	Their mother cooks rice ;
I kpia hũ ;	She takes it out ;
I pu peleti hũ.	She puts it into a plate.
Ti wa mbei mema ;	They come to eat rice ;
Ti mbei me ;	They eat rice ;
Ti peleti ngulo.	They break the plate.
I nde ti ma, ye,	She said to them, saying,
Gbele?	What is the matter?
Ye, nga mbei yili we,	That I cook the rice,
Ke wa peleti wulo.	And you break the plate.
Ye, wu ndewe i ya wo̱ kolo.	She said, Your brother has gone up country.
Ye, we li na,	She said, Suppose you go there,
Ye, wa wa ngi.	And you bring him.
Ta va ye mu lima na.	Accordingly he said, Let us go there.
Ye'mu wa angie.	He said, Let us bring him.
Tolī i lọ̄i ngitiya.	A kola tree stood outside.
I veli ngi ma ;	He said good-bye to her ;
Ye, mu lima lo.	[1] He said, We are going.
Ye, tōli gi nda be.	He said, The kola I planted here.

[1] Apparently one of the twins speaks for the two.

Ye, i gbenda i gula ndo̱me,	He said, When it ripens and falls to the ground,
Ye ke mua wama.	He said, we will come back.
Ke ti ya ti ndewe woma	And they went after their brother
Ke ti wala ti nje we.	To bring him to their mother.

Incomplete.

NOTE.—Twins do not count. Their younger brother is reckoned their senior. The child born after twins is called "fela."

VI.

The Boy who fell into a Hole.

Tamoi mia wo̱.	There was once a man.
I hiye i nyahei so̱lo.	He got up, he married a wife.
I ndoi le gbotō.	She bore many children.
Ngi lenga ti lakpa.	Her children grew up.
Moremo a ti lenga.	Some of them were Mori[1] men.
Ti li dogboi hũ.	They went into the bush.
Ti ndowe male foni hũ.	They met a hole in the grass country.
Ti ndewe ti wili dowei hũ.	They threw their brother into the hole.
Ti wama tei hũ,	When they came into the town,
Ti kei i ti moli, ye,	Their father asked them, saying,
Wu ndewe ta mindo?	Where is your brother?
Te, i wa.	They said, He is coming.
Te, mū ngi loni.	They said, We have not seen him.
Ke ti kei i velia tima, ye,	And their father sent them off, saying,
A li, nya ndiamoi gama kolo.	Go to my friend up country.
Ti hiya, ti ya.	They got up and went.
Ngi ndiamoi i hiya kolo.	His friend started from up country.
Ta wama ngi ndiamoi gama.	He was coming to his friend.
I gbia foni hũ,	He came out of the grass country,
Ye, nja gboli māi lo nyama.	He said, I want water to drink.
I ndea ngi lengá ma, ye,	He said to his children, saying,
A li, wu nje wulī wala mbe.	Go and bring a little water to me.

[1] Mori, corruption of Moor, means magician, or Arabic charm writer, etc.

Ke ngi lenga ke ti ya nja lowei me (= ma),	And his children went to a water hole,
Ke ti nje ndowe hũ,	And they descended into the water hole,
Ke ti nde wulī malia na dowei hũ.	And they found their small brother there in the hole.
Ke ti geyéi ke ti ngilia fe ngi bolui ma,	And they tied a rope to the neck of a pot,
Ke ti ndewe i fei honga,	And their brother caught the pot,
Ke i vembia la.	And he caught hold of it.
I hoa,	He held it,
Ke ti tenga ngiyema.	And they raised him to the edge.
Ke ti yama,	And they returned,
Ke ti denga ti kei ma, te,	And they told their father, saying,
Mu ndewe ji wo̱ i wili dowé hũ.	This is our brother who threw himself into the hole.
Te, mu gbia ndowé hũ.	They said, We have pulled him out of the hole.
Ke ti kei ngi yamai abwale.	And their father's eyes hurt.
Ē nū lo.	He saw no body.
Ke ti hale ti gbia angie.	And they found medicine for him.
Ti sia ngi yama,	They rubbed it on his eyes,
Ke i bawonga.	And he was cured.
Ke ngi kei nyahei jo̱longa.	And his father took his wife again.
Ke ngi kei i ngi hounga.	And his father caught him.
E li.	He goes.
Ngombui i ngate.	He lit a fire.
I nde nunga ma, ye,	He said to the people, saying,
A wa mu nya loi hou,	Come let us catch my child,
Mu lila.	Let us take him.
Mu pili ngombui hũ.	Let us throw him in the fire.
Ke ngi yei i ndenga ngi kei ma, ye,	And his mother said to his father, saying,
Bi nya lọ̄i hoa,	You have caught my child,
Ye bi panga,	She said, if you kill him,
Ye nya be, ye, ngi hama.	She said, I too shall die.
Ke i ya a pime.	And she ran off.

I njei malenga.	She came to the water.
I wili njei hũ.	She threw herself into the water.
I ha.	She died.
Ke ngi kei ke ta be i hiyenga.	And his father he too arose.
Ye nya be gi lima.	He said, I too am going.
Ye, ngi li gi lō njei hũ.	He said, I am going to put an end to myself in the water.
I gboyoa.	It is finished.

VII.

The Boy stolen by a Devil.

Nyapui i hiye.	A woman got up.
I hini jo̱ro.	She married a husband.
Ti ndọ̄i de.	They bore children.
Hindọ̄i hijia ngelewo,	The man rose early,
Ti li kpãleí ma.	They went to the farm.
I ndọ̄i la,	She laid down her child,
I hiye i li ngurī gbua (gbia) me.	She got up, she went to pull up sticks.
Haiwai i wa,	A devil came,
I ndopui mbumbu,	He took the child,
I lila ngi wetahũ.	He took it home.
Ngi yei i wa gbwela ;	Its mother came to the hut ;
I ndọ̄i loni ;	She did not see the child ;
I wolo.	She cries.
I hiye, i li tei hũ.	She got up, she went into the town.
I nde ngi hini ma, ye,	She said to her husband, saying,
Ngī ndọ̄i loni.	I do not see the child.
Ngi hini i hiye,	Her husband got up,
I wa gbwe la.	He came to the hut.
Ĭ kok'oi ;	He looked for it ;
Ī tōni.	He did not see it.
Ti yama tei hũ.	They returned into the town.
Hawai a li dogboi hũ ;	The devil goes into the bush ;
A mehei bumbu,	He takes food,
A wala ndọ̄i we a me.	He brings it to the child to eat.
I lakpa.	It grew up.
Hawāi i li.	The devil goes.
(Hawāi gbatengo.)	(The devil was rich.)
I hiye.	He gets up.
Ndọ̄pọ̄i i hiye i li.	The boy gets up, he goes.

Hawai i li pebu.	The devil goes indoors.
Ndopoi i kulé bumbu.	The boy takes a cloth.
I njī bumbu.	He takes a goat.
I hiye, i li ngi kei gama.	He gets up, he goes to his father.
Ta ngi kei ti lo.	He and his father saw each other.
I nde ngi ma, ye,	He said to him, saying,
Hewa lo wo̱ i ya ange dogboi hũ.	It was a devil who took me into the bush long ago.
I nde ngi kei ma, ye,	He said to his father, saying,
Mu li Hewai ngi wetei hũ,	Let us go to the devil's own town,
Mu navọ̄i bumbu.	And take away his money.
Ke ti ya sawa Hewai we ta wāi hũ.	And they three went to the devil's house in the town.
Ti li ti jango,	They went, they three,
Ti navoi bumbu.	They took the money.
Ke Hawai i lọ̄ tima.	And the devil followed them.
I li.	He goes.
Ti gbua pelagbame,	They came out to the cross road,
Ti hei na.	They sat down there.
Ke ndọ̄pọ̄i i ndea ngi kei ma, ye,	And the boy said to his father, saying,
Hewai ta wama.	The devil is coming.
Ke Hewai i wa;	And the devil came;
Ke i ndea ndopoi ma, ye,	And he said to the boy, saying,
Gbwele, gbe nya navoi bi bumbu?	Why have you taken my money?
Ye, Bē lila.	He said, You must not take it away.
Ke ndopoi i hiya.	And the boy got up.
I nde ngi kei ma, ye,	He said to his father,
A li.	Go.
Ye, ma Hewai mu lō,	He said, I and the devil remain,
Ke ngi kei i ya ngi weta hũ,	And his father went to his own town,
Ke ndopoi ta hewai ti ya-ma Hewai wetahũ.	And the boy and the devil returned to the devil's town.
Ke Hewai i ndopoi hōnga,	And the devil caught the boy,
I ngua pebu.	He put him in the house.
I pele gbo ngi ma.	He shut him into the house.
Ke kpindi i wa.	And night came.

Ke ndọ̄pọ̄i i maluvinga a Hawai.	And the boy turned into a devil.
I gbua i li ngi kei gama.	He came out, he went to his father.
I li ta ngi kei ti hiye ti li dogboi hũ.	He went, (and) he and his father they got up (and) they went into the bush.
Hale ji wọ ngi kei vea;	His father had given him this medicine of old;
I mbumbu;	He took it;
I fengie.	He gave it to him.
Ti li pe wai ma;	They went to the road;
Ti hi.	They sat down.
Ke nunga ke ti wa,	And people came,
Ke Hawai ke i hindoi hou.	And the devil caught a man.
I pa, i mbumbu,	He killed him, he carried him,
I fe ngi lọ̄i we.	He gave him to his son.
Ke ti hiya,	And they arose,
Ke ti wa ti wetahũ.	And they came to their town.
Ke i ngilia, i mbumbu,	And he cooked him, (and) he took him,
I fe ngi ye.	He gave to him.
Ye, ngē me.	He said, I will not eat it.
Ke kpindi i welenga.	And night came.
Ke i gbua ngitiya.	And he went out.
Ke hale gbwele i mbumbua.	And he took all the medicine.
Ke i mbogbwe bumbua.	And he took a cutlass.
I ya ngi kei gama;	He went to his father (the devil);
Ke i wa pele bu;	And he came indoors;
Ke ngi kei nji hũ;	And his father (devil) was asleep;
Ke i ngi kei hoa;	And he seized his father;
Ke i ngi kei wanga.	And he killed his father.
Ke i hiya i hitia peli hũ.	And he went (and) he reached the road.
Ke i ndenga ngi ke lenga ma,	And he said to his father's children,
A mu li.	Let us go.
Ke ti ya,	And they went,
Ke ti fonga.	And they arrived.
Ke i ngi kei malea,	And he met his father (*i. e.* own father),

Ke i ndea ngi kei ma,	And he said to his father,
Ye, Hawai wo̱ ngi ngi pã.	Saying, I have killed the devil.
Ye, ngi lengá lo.	And his children.
Ke i ndea ngi kei ma, ye,	And he said to his father, saying,
Ngi wai lo a hale.	I have brought the medicine.
Ke kpindi wela.	And night came.
Ke ti wa pelebu,	And they came into the house,
Ta ngi kei ti fere.	He and his father, they two.
Ke i hale gbua.	And he took out the medicine.
Ke i henga.	And he sat down.
Ke ngi kei i ndea ngima, ye,	And his father said to him, saying,
Hale ji bi wai la,	This medicine that you have brought,
Ye, mu ko̱le.	He said, Let us divide (it).
Ye, nya ndei ve.	He said, Give me my share.
Ke ngi kei ngi ndei vea.	And his father gave him his.
Ke ti ya ngi kei we pebu.	And they went to his father's house.

VIII.

The Woman who did not wish her Daughter to be Married.

Nyapọ̄i mia wo,	There was once a woman,
I ndoi leni.	She bore a child.
Ye, numu gbī e soro.	She said nobody shall marry her.
Ndakpalọ̄i ye ga soro.	The young man said, I will marry her.
Ye, numu gbī nya lọ̄i jo̱lo ke a pe lọ̄ koti ma.	She said, Nobody shall marry my daughter except he can build a house on a rock.[1]
Ye, yiei ngi kulua.	He said, I accept the condition (lit. saying).
Ye ke nyahei fembe.	He said also, Give me the woman.
Mame be ye, ngi kulua ;	The old woman also said, I agree ;
Ki i nyahei fe ngie.	And she gave the woman to him.
Ngelewo ke i mbowé bumbúa.	At daybreak he took a cutlass.
I li dogboi hũ.	He goes into the bush.
I ngurī lewe,	He cuts sticks,
I wa ngurī,	He brings the sticks,
I pu.	He lays them down.
Ī pele lọ̄ni.	He did not build the house.
I male ngi yemoi i mbei yilia.	He found his mother-in-law cooking rice.
Ye, bi lokoi wu fei hũ bi mañye gbia,	He said, Put your hand into the pot (and) bring out the delicacies (from the bottom),
Bi fembe ngi me.	Give them to me to eat.
Nyapōi ye sao.	The woman said, No.
Ndakp'oi ye, ba na wi lo.	The young man said, You must do that.
Ye, ngē pili.	She said, I cannot.
Ye, bi na wi lo ga bi mayia ge lo.	He said, Do that, or I will make a complaint against you.

[1] This is the equivalent to an impossibility, as holes cannot be dug in a rock to put the posts in.

Ye nya lọi va ngi nya loko wu mba gbwandi hũ,	She said, For the sake of my child to put my hand in the hot rice,
Ye, ngā pili.	She said, I will not do so.
Ndakpo'i ye ba pilo.	The young man said, You shall do so.
Ke i ya i ngi mayia ge.	And he went to make his accusation.
Ti tewe.	They decide.
Ti ndakpaloi lemu.	They give the case in favour of the young man.
Nyapoi i jelisia molia, ye, gbe va ngi nde jo̱ni?	The woman asked the judges, saying, Wherein was I wrong? (lit. Why did I get the lie?)
Mahanga kpele ti li ti wu tema.	All the chiefs they go, they debate.
Tē, hani fa mu na weni, tē mū ya gama loi wo̱,	They said, We did that, because, they said, we have never seen such a case before,
Ngiye bi yakpei bi ji wilia.	Until you did this.
Tē numu gbī bi ndọ̄ le numu hani gbī fa be,	They said, Nobody who has ever borne a child has made such a condition that no man shall get her,
Ke ta pe lọ̄ ko̱tu ma.	Except he build a house on a rock.
Tē ji na dakpaloi kabande i gula bi ya.	They said, See how the young man has put you into the wrong.
Ke bi lọi fe ngi ye i lila.	So give him your daughter and let him take her away.
Ke i ndọi fenga.	And she gave her daughter.
Ta yakpei i longa heini.	She remained sitting there alone.
Ndakpaloi be ī pe lōi kotui ma.	And the young man did not build the house on the rock.
Nyapoi be ī ngi loko wuai mbei bu,	The woman also did not put her hand in under the rice,
A kpia a fe ngi mbele we.	To take something out and give it to her son-in-law.
I li i hei na gbwama fu ikelemei.	She goes, she sits down there, having gained nothing.
	The end.

IX.

The Spider and the Maggot.

Kasiloi ke bawe.	The spider and the maggot.
Kasiloi i kpale la,	The spider laid out a farm,
Ke bawe be i gbale la.	And the maggot too laid out a farm.
Kasiloi i nunga lōnga,	The spider sent men,
Ye, ti li ti ngi yenge wili.	Saying, they were to go and do his work.
Ke bawe i gbia,	And the maggot went out,
Ke i nunga lōnga,	And he sent people,
Ye, a mu li mu nya yenge wili.	Saying, Let us go and do my work.
Bawe ye siloi lengá ma, ye,	The maggot said to the spider's labourers (lit. children),
Wā yenge siloi we.	Do not work for the spider.
Kasiloi na ye gbolĭ lo kohũ.	That spider has only dirt in his belly.
Ye, bia bi lini silo i yengeme,	He said, If you go and work for the spider,
Ye, bē mehe nene me.	He said, you will not eat nice food.
Ye, a mu li mu yenge we.	He said, Let us go and work.
Ga wu go lo a mehe neni.	I will give you nice food.
Ke ngelewonga,	And when daylight came,
Ke ti ya bawe yengeme.	(And) they went to work for the maggot.
Ke bawe ngi nyānga	And the maggot's wives
Ke ti mbei yilia gengebra we.	Cooked rice for the labourers.
Ndahani gbī ta pu bei ma.	There was no meat to put on the rice.

Ke bawe nyahangesia ti ngi lọ̄linga,	And the maggot's wives called him,
Tē, mu mbei yilinga ngengebela we,	Saying, We have cooked rice for the labourers,
Ke hani gbī ma.	And there is nothing on it.
Ye a fe hei ngombui ya.	He said, Put the pot on the fire.
Ke fe i gbwande kākā igbowu.[1]	And the pot got very hot (until) it boiled over.
Bawe ye ngi nyānga ma a nya wī fei hũ.	The maggot said to his wives, Throw me into the pot.
Ke ti ngi wilia fe gbande hũ.	And they threw him into the hot pot.
Ta ngi wote,	They turn him,
Ngi wului i gbia gboto.	(So that) his fat came out plenty.
I fe wai na lave kpa ke ládi na.	He filled that big pot completely with his fat (*ládi* = lard—an adopted word).
Ti ngengebela lọ̄li, ti wa.	They call the labourers, they come.
Ke bawe vulunga ti pu mbei ma.	And the maggot was alive, and they put him back on the rice.
Ngengebla ti me.	The labourers ate.
Bawe ī hani.	The maggot did not die.
Ngengebra ke ti ngi lato.	And the labourers praised him.
Ke siloi be ke i ndea gengeb'ra ma, ye,	And the spider also said to the labourers, saying,
A mu li nya kpãe,	Let us go to my farm,
Ma yenge pi lo; kea kpwawe i peni,	We will work; as the maggot did,
Ye, ga pe lo.	He said, so will I do.
Ke ngengebra ti ya ngiye kpãma.	And the labourers went to him to the farm.
Kasiloi ngi nyānga	The spider's wives
Ke ti mbei yilia;	Cooked rice;
Ndahani gbī ma.	There was no meat on it.
Ke ti siloi lọlea,	And they called the spider,
Te, wa mbei gama.	Saying, Come to the rice.
Ke ngengebra ti me.	And the labourers ate.
Ke hani gbī ma.	And there was nothing on it.
Ye, a fe he nga.	He said, Put the pot on.

[1] Same as ripening of fruit.

Ke ti fei henga.	And they put the pot on.
Ke fei gbwandinga.	And the pot got hot.
Ye ngi nyānga ma,	He said to his wives,
Nya fei gbwandi hũ.	My pot is hot.
Ke ngi nyānga ti ngi wilia fe gbwandi hũ.	And his wives threw him into the hot pot.
Ke ngi yongolui gewia (gewo).	And his teeth burnt.
Ke i gbua fei hũ.	And he made dirt in the pot.
Ke i yili gulanga.	And he screamed out (dropped lit.) a yell.
Ke i ngengebra lọlinga.	And he called the labourers.
Hani gbī mbei ma ta me.	There was nothing on the rice for them to eat.
Ke ti ngi yelea, tē,	And they laughed at him, saying,
Bē ge, hindé bawe a pi ba pi lo.	You said the other day that what the maggot did you would do.
Tē, bi bele nyania.	They said, Your reputation is spoiled.
Ke bawe ta ngi wili fe gbwandi hũ,	But the maggot whom they threw into the hot pot,
Ngi wuli i gbia lo,	His fat came out,
I fei ve kpã.	(And) he filled the pot completely.
Ke ngengebra ti me ;	And the labourers ate ;
Ti goi ve,	They filled their bellies,
Ke ti ya tei hũ.	And they went home (lit. into the town).
Ke kasiloi gbele nyania.	But the spider's reputation was spoilt.

X.

The Spider and the Bush Goat.

Kasiloï mia wo ;	There was once a spider ;
I ndenga leni.	He bore children.
Twa wuli i ndenga le gboto.	The bush goat bore many children.
Kasiloi ke i kpãe la.	The spider laid out a farm.
Twa wulī i kpãe la.	The bush goat laid out a farm.
Mehe gbī na a pu kpãlei hũ.	There was no rice to plant in the farm.
Kasiloi be i kpãe la.	The spider also laid out a farm.
Mehe gbī na a pu kpãe hũ.	There was no rice to plant in the farm.
Twa wuli lenga ti jijiama dogboi hũ,	The bush goat's children walked about in the bush,
Ke ti ya ti gũwe male.	And they went and came across a silk cotton tree.
Mehe yīngoi (= yilingoi) ngǫwi ya gbĭ.	There was cooked food at the very top of the cotton tree.
Ke ti yama, dole tima, ti yetahũ.	And they returned, hungry, to their home.
Ke ti ndenga ti kei ma,	And they said to their father,
Tē, mu ya dogboi hũ,	Saying, We went into the bush,
Mu ya ;	We went ;
Mu mba yīngoi lo nga ngǫ-we hũ.	We saw cooked rice in the cotton tree.
Ke ti kei i ndea tima, ye,	And their father said to them, saying,
Ngelewo sina mu li na.	At daybreak to-morrow we go there.
Ti yī gbuĕ.	They slept that night.
Ngelewo ke ti ya na bei gama nguwe hũ.	At daybreak they went there to the rice in the cotton tree.

Ke ti ya.	And they went.
Ke ti hitia bei ma ;	And they reached the rice ;
Dole tima.	They were hungry.
Tē, ma ye pe mu mbei ji me ?	(And) they said, How can we arrange to eat this rice ?
Ke ṅgafe i yia nguri hũ, ye,	And the spirit spoke in the tree, saying,
Wu yia, wu pe, wu mbei ji me.	You talk about what you must do to eat this rice.
Ye foma i ye na,	He said, A whip is there,
I la mbei na mahũ.	It lies on the top of that rice.
Ndewe yira mia,	It is one cut,
Ke mbei na ta ngi menga.	And that rice can be eaten.
Ke twa wuli na i ndea mbei ma,	And the (lit. that) bush goat said to the rice,
Ye, mbei na mia !	Saying, You rice there !
Bi hei gurī hũ !	That are sitting in the tree !
Wa bi nya lē yira,	Come and beat me once,
Gi bi me.	So that I may eat you.
Ke mbei na i yenga ;	And the rice came down ;
I ngi vogba ;	It thrashed him ;
I gula ndo̱me.	He fell to the ground.
Lo̱ woita i bumbu do̱me,	Six days (later) he picked himself up from the ground,
Ke i ngi mbei venga,	And he gave him his rice,
Ke i yala ngi yetahũ.	And he took it away home (lit. home, town, inside).
Kasiloï ke i mbei ji longa.	And the spider saw this rice.
Ke i twa wuli molia, ye,	And he asked the bush goat, saying,
Bi mbei ji jo̱i mi lo ?	Where did you get this rice ?
Ye, ngi mbei ji loni dogboi hũ nguwe wai hũ.	He said, I saw this rice in the bush in the big cotton tree.
Ye, na ge ange nya be gi mba me.	He said, Now show me (so that) I too may eat rice.
Twa wuli ye ngi ma,	The bush goat said to him,
A mu li ngelewo.	Let us go at daylight.
Ke ti yinga.	And they slept.
Ngelewa, ke ti ya dogboi hũ mbei gama.	At daybreak they went into the bush to the rice.
Kasiloi ke i mbei longa.	And the spider saw the rice.

I twa wuli moli ye,	He asked the bush goat, saying,
Ba ye pe ge ba mbei ji me?	How did you manage the other day to eat this rice?
Ye, mbei na mia gi li na yira gọ̄wé na hũ.	He said, (As to) that rice over there, I went there once to that cotton tree.
Ngafei lo, ngi wọ̄ mia a mbei na.	It is a devil, (and) that rice belongs to him.
Ye, bia bi mbei na me,	He said, You who eat the rice,
Ye, bi fomesia loma?	He said, do you see the whips?
Ye, ī.	He said, Yes.
Ye, ndē yira i ye lo na.	He said, One cut is there.
Ye, ndē pu i ye lo na.	He said, Ten cuts are there.
Ye, ndē nu fere gboyongó i ye lo na.	He said, Forty cuts are there.
Ye, ndē nu sawa gboyongó i ye lo na.	He said, Sixty cuts are there.
Ye, ndē nu lo̱lu gboyongó i ye lo na.	He said, One hundred cuts are there.
Kasilọ̄i ye, hindolọ̄i ange nya yakpei va.	The spider said, I am a man myself.
Ye, nya longo a ndē nu lo̱lu gboyongo mba galui va.	He said, I am willing (to take) a hundred cuts for a bowl of rice.
Kasilọ̄ï ye, mbei na mia!	The spider said, You rice there!
Bi heini ngọ̄we na hũ,	Who are sitting in that cotton tree,
Wa bi nya lewe numu lo̱lu gboyongo,	Come and give me a hundred cuts,
Gi bi me.	And I will eat you.
Mu nya lenga gbwele mu gō i ve.	It will fill mine and all my children's bellies.
Ke mbei i yenga i ngi lewe yira.	And the rice came down and gave him one cut.
Ke i gula ndo̱me.	And he fell to the ground.
Nika nani ba galúi ta mia i ngi leweni.	It beat him terribly (lit. as big as a dish to hold rice and four cows).
I ngi lewe i gula ndo̱me.	It beat him; he fell to the ground.

I lọ̄ i ngi lema.
I gu a fọ̄ yira
Ī mbei meni.
Ke ndo̱le i ngi wā.

Kelemei.

It left off beating him.
For a whole year (lit. it reached one year)
He ate no food (lit. rice).
And hunger killed him.

The End.

XI.

The Okro Tree.

Nyapọ̄i mia wō,	There was once a woman,
I ndọ̄i le.	She bore a child.
Ngi lọ̄i nyandengo wa.	Her child was very beautiful.
Ngi lọ̄i i nyālọ̄i.	Her child was a girl.
Ye numu gbī e soro.	She said, Nobody shall marry her.
Ke i bonde henga.	And she planted the okro tree.
Bondo wulī ke i wŏlŏa.	And the okro tree grew big.
Ke bonde ke i wa.	And the okro fruit came also.
Numu gbī ē bonde me.	Nobody could eat the okro.
Bonde nyapọ̄i wele wōma.	The okro was behind the woman's house.
Kọ̄lī i bondo wuli hū̃.	There was a snail in the okro tree.
Nyapọ̄i ye nya lọ̄i ngi ndeni.	The woman said, I have borne the child.
Numu gbī ā bi solo,	Nobody shall marry you,
Ke i nya bondo wuli ji wo.	Except he cut down this my okro tree.
Ke numu yira i wa;	And one man came;
Hota lakpalọ̄i angie.	He was a stranger.
Ye, bi bi lọ̄i vembe.	He said, Give me your child.
Ye, nga bi bondo wuli ji wo lo.	He said, I will cut down this okro tree of yours.
Ke i kọ̄nī vea ngiye.	And she gave him an axe.
Ta nyahei ti yi lailo.	He and the girl lay down to sleep.
Ngelewo i mbogbwe wumbu,	At daybreak he took the cutlass,
I kọ̄nī wumbu,	He took the axe,

I ya bondo wuli wome.	He went to cut down the okro tree.
I po ka ka.	He cut hard.
I nguli gohũ gbia.	He took out the tree's inside.
I ye kine gulama,	It was nearly falling,
Ke kọ̄li ji i jia guli wōme,	But this snail it walked down the back of the tree,
Ke nguli i yama,	And the tree was restored,
I lọ̄;	It stood;
Ē gulani.	It did not fall.
Ndakpalọ̄i na i nguli wo fọ̄ pu;	That young man cut at the tree for ten years;
Nguli ē gula.	The tree did not fall.
Ke i lowua,	And he hid himself,
Ke i ya ti yei;	And went to his (lit. their) country;
I gbahã guli ma.	He was tired of the tree.
Ke numu yira ke i wa.	And another person came.
Ye, nga nguri ji wo lo gi kulá.	He said, I will cut this tree and fell it.
Numu gboto ta nguli ji wo ta gbaha ma.	Plenty of people cut at this tree (until) they were tired.
Ke ndakpalọ̄i yira tei ji hũ yafango.	But there was one young man in this town who was a tale-bearer.
Ke i ndea ndakpalọ̄ïma ye,	And he said to the young man, saying,
Nyaha yira ī gele nyahei ji ma.	This is not the only woman.
Ye, gbe nyahei ji hinda ma.	He said, Leave this woman's affairs alone.
Ye, ga bi go lo a nyaha.	He said, I will give you a wife.
Ndakpalọ̄ï be ye sao.	But the young man said, No.
Ye, nyahei ji ta bondo wuli ji wo̱ ngi wōma,	He said, This woman and this okro tree it is that I am after,
Ye, nga ye nyahei ji lo soro?	He said, How can I manage to marry this woman?
Ke i ya nyapọ̄i gama	And he went to the woman
Ngi wọ̄ a ndoi.	Whose was the child.

Ye, ngi wa ngi bi lọi jo̱lo.	He said, I come to marry your daughter.
Ye, kulongo le.	She said, All right.
Ye ke, nyalọ̄i ji nu gbi a bi soro.	She said also, This my daughter, anybody can marry you.
Ye bē nya go a navo fa,	She said, You must not give me money for her,
Bi nya bondo wuli wo.	But you must cut down my okro tree.
Ye ngi kurua.	He said, I accept (the condition).
Ngelewo ti kọ̄nī ve ngi ye.	At daybreak they gave him the axe.
Ti kpe mbogbwe ma.	They add the cutlass.
I li nguli wo̱me.	He goes to cut down the tree.
I luva poma kpeng.	He spent all day cutting.
I ye kine gulάma.	It was nearly falling.
Ke kọ̄lī ji i jia gulī ma,	But this snail walked over the tree,
Ke ngulī i yama,	And the tree returned,
I lọ̄.	It stood.
Ndakpoi be ī yiani.	But the young man did not speak.
Mbogwe ke koni ke i ndowa bondo wuli bu.	He hid the cutlass and the axe under the okro tree.
Ke i ya,	And he went,
I nde ngi yemoi ma,	He said to his mother-in-law,
Ye, ngi nguli wonga,	Saying, I cut the tree,
Ke kọ̄lī ji i jia nguli ma,	But this snail walked over the tree,
Nguli ē gulani.	(And) the tree did not fall.
Ke ti ya kpokoi,	And they went at evening,
Ke ti la ta ngi nyahei.	And they lay down, he and his (intended) wife.
Ke i ngi nyahei molia,	And he asked his (intended) wife,
Ye, bi longo ange?	Saying, Do you like me?
Nyahei ye, I.	The woman said, Yes.
Ye, nya longo abie.	She said, I like you.
Ye ke pīlī ngi bondo wuli gulá.	He said, Then make me able to throw down the okro tree.
Ye ngi kurua.	She said, I agree.

Ye nga pe bi nguli gula.	She said, I will make you able to throw down this tree.
Ye hani fa gi ji wīlīma bi ye	She said, The reason I do this for you
Ngi nya longo abie fa mia.	Is that I like you.
Ye, yi bondo wuli wu toma.	She said, It is my mother's okro tree you are looking at.
Ye, nu bia ba po,	She said, If you are going to cut it down,
Ye, bã po a kọ̄nu.	She said, you will not cut it with an axe.
Ye, miji bumbu bi pola.	She said, Take a needle to cut it.
Bi hō yeya ñi.	You hold it in your hand so.
Ye bi kpakpa ma yira.	She said, You hammer on it once.
Ye, bi ndi(= nde), be, kulo! bondo! abie!	She said, You say, saying, Snail and okro! you!
Ye, bi wa bi la.	She said, (Then) come and lie down.
Ye, ba lo lai ji hũ lo ke nguli i gula.	She said, You will go and lie down to sleep, and the tree falls.
Ke ngelewa.	And day dawned.
Ndakpalọ̄i i miji bumbu,	The young man took the needle,
I hō yeya,	He held it in his hand,
I li.	He went.
I nde guli ma,	He said to the tree,
Ye, Bondo! kọ̄lo! abie!	Saying, Okro! snail! you!
I miji kpakpa nguli ma.	He stuck the needle into the tree.
I hiye na,	He arose thence,
I li,	He went,
I la,	He lay down,
I yi.	He slept.
I lọ̄,	He left it,
I lai lo ji hũ.	He lay down to sleep.
Ke nguli i gula.	And the tree fell.
Ke na i gboyoa a ngi ndeí na.	And now he finished his own part.
Ngelewo ndakpalọ̄i ye nyapọ̄i ma,	At daybreak the young man said to the woman,

Ye nya nyahei ve.
Ngelewo nyapọ̄i i ngi nyahei ve.
Ke nyapọ̄i ke i yīnga a njei.
Ndakpalọ̄i na i nyahei na bumbua,
I lila ti ye.

I gbate,
Ngi lowé i gu ndohũ gbi.

Domei gboyoa.

Give me my wife.
At daybreak the woman gave him his wife.
And the woman went down to the river (*i.e.* to drown herself).
The (lit. that) young man took the woman,
He took her away to his (lit. their) country.
He grew rich,
His fame reached every country.

The story is finished.

XII.

The Race between the Deer and the Snail.

Dope mia wo̱.	There was once a deer.
Ta kọ̄lī ti mawăli hōni.	He and the snail made a bet.
Kọ̄lī ye,	The snail said,
Nga wime gi lē ndopéma.	I can run faster than the deer.
Dope ye,	The deer said,
Nga wime gi lē kọ̄līma.	I can run faster than the snail.
Ke ti mawăli honga.	And they made a bet.
Dope nginda bondesia ke ti navoi yandoa.	The deer's own people collected the money.
Ke kọ̄li be,	And the snail too,
Ke nginda wongesia	His own relations
Ke ti navoi yandoa.	Collected the money.
Ti navoi yando kuhama polon.	They collected the money in a far place.
Ji pele hũ woita na mia.	It was six days' journey.
Ti li ti navoi gandó na.	They go, they bring the money there.
Mahanga kpele ti li,	All the chiefs go,
Ti hei na.	They sit there.
Ke kọ̄li i jia ngi wonga kpele mahũ.	And the snail travels to all his relations one after the other.
Ye, ma ndopa mu mawale honga.	He said, I and a deer have made a bet.
Ye, nā mawuë mu gbi lo nde ma,	He said, Now I and you we are all brothers,
Ke a nya bo̱,	And you must help me,
Mu li mu navoi ji me.	So that we go and win this money.
Ke kọ̄li wonga kpele ke ti lumá.	And all the snail's relations agreed.
Te, ke ji na bi wa mu gama,	They said, You come to us now,

Ma yepe,	And what are we to do,
Ke ji dope ta a wime	For when the deer runs
I lē muma.	He passes us.
Wa ta wu mawali hounga.	You and he have made the bet.
Ye, na wu toma—	He said, You see now—
Ye, ma ndopa mu mawali honga;	He said, I and the deer have made the bet;
Ye, kia muë gu a wimela a mu yala hũ-gbate.	He said, As we cannot run we must devise a trick.
Tamia ma gu ndopé ma,	So we shall overreach the deer,
Tamia mu mawali a gula dopé ma.	And the deer will lose the bet.
Te ke,	And they said,
Ma ye pe na mawali ji i gula?	How now can we manage to win the bet?
Ye, na wu toma—	He said, you see now—
Ye, ma ta mu mu mawali hōni.	He said, I and he made the bet.
Ye, nya gi kongo	He said, *I* know
Kia nga yalé ji gula gi gu ndopé ma.	How to do this trick on the deer.
Te ke mu kulua.	And they said we agree.
Ye, ngewa sina,	He said, At daybreak to-morrow,
Ye, wu gbi a wa nya gama.	He said, you all come to me.
Ke ngelewa kolisia gbi ti ndohũ	And at daybreak all the snails in the country
Ke ti wa ti mbai gama.	Came to their companion.
I ngi mbaisia lo̱wu pelehũ.	He hid his friends in the road.
I li, a ti lekpe pelehũ	He goes, he puts them one by one in the road
Ji woita welé nahũ:	For six days in that road:
I li, a ti lekpe na	He goes, he arranges them there
I fọ̄ fa navọ̄i gama.	Until he reaches the money.
I yela lo̱wu kawoli hũ te gbelanga.	He hides one in the rubbish hole close to the town.
Ke ngelewonga.	And daylight came.
Dope ta kpọ̄wango;	The deer was a fool;
Nemáhũ gbīna.	He had no sense.
Ke i wa kọ̄lī gama,	And he came to the snail,
Ye, mabia ma mawali honga.	He said, I and you have made a bet.

Migbe nā mu li na	When do we go now
Mu navoi gama ?	For our money ?
Kọ̄lī ye ndopé, ye,	The snail said to the deer, saying,
Bā me nyama.	You will not beat me.
Dopa wa ye kọ̄lī, ye,	The deer himself said to the snail, saying,
Bī guma a jiala,	You cannot walk,
Be, mua bia mu mawali hou.	You said, however, You would make a bet with me.
Ye, nya mawali a gula lo bima.	He said, You will lose the bet.
Ye, migbe na mu li ?	He said, When now do we go ?
Ye, lo̱ woita,	(The snail) He said, In six days,
Ye ke mu li navọ̄i gama.	He said also, we shall go for the money.
Ye kọ̄li, ye,	(The deer) said to the snail, saying,
Bia yese bi hitia navoi gama,	If you reach the money first,
Ye ke bi wongá gbele ti batea.	He said, All your relations are made rich.
Bi navọ̄i bumbu bi la,	Take the money you put down,
Kebi mawali i gula nyama.	And you will win the bet.
Ke kọ̄li be ke i ndea ndopé ma,	And the snail too said to the deer,
Ye, bia yese bi hũgba li navoi gama,	Saying, You go first to the money,
Ke bi mawali i gula nyama ;	And you will win the bet ;
Bi navoi bumbu,	Take your money,
Wā bi wonga kpele,	Bring all your relations,
Ke wu gbatea.	And you will (all) be rich.
Bi navoi wumbu bi me.	Take up the money and spend it.
Ke ngelewa.	And day dawned.
Ke ndopé i wa kọ̄li gama,	And the deer came to the snail,
Ye kọ̄li, ye,	He said to the snail, saying,
Mu li na-oh.	Let us go.
Kọ̄lī ye dopema, ye,	The snail said to the deer, saying,
Bia yese lọ̄ kulo bia li.	Stand in front of me and go first.
Dopé ye kọ̄li ma,	The deer said to the snail,
Ye, sao.	Saying, No.
Ye, bā me nyama,	He said, Do not follow me,

Bē gu a jiala.	You cannot walk.
Kọ̄li ye, gi kulua.	The snail said, I agree.
Ke ti jiei lọ̄toa.	And they started their journey.
Ke ndopé i longa kulo.	And the deer stood in front.
I wime kā.	He ran hard.
I gbia ke Kumasi nyo̱ko.	He came out as it were as far as Kumasi.
Ke i kọ̄li malea ngi gulo.	And he met the snail ahead of him.
Ke i kọ̄li mo̱lia, ye,	And he asked the snail, saying,
Bia ha	Just now
Gi bi longa nya wōma,	It was you I saw behind me,
Tamia bi bia mbe nya gulo.	Nevertheless here you are in front of me.
Ye, ngē ya be hũgba li.	He said, I am not hurrying.
Ke kọ̄lī be ke i jia,	And the snail too he walked off,
I ya,	He went,
Ke i lo̱wua.	And he hid.
Dopé na ke i wa,	And the deer came,
Ke i lia kọ̄lī ye na ma.	And he went on to the other snail.
I li a pime polon gbōma.	He ran on far again.
Kia wo i lini a wime kaka.	As before he ran hard.
Kọ̄lī ye na ngi mbai	The other snail, whom his
I ngi lo̱wui kawalehũ,	Friend hid in the rubbish hole,
Ke i gbia,	Came out,
Ke i ya navọ̄i gama.	And went to the money.
Dopé i lọ pọma,	The deer was (lit. stood) behind,
Ke kọ̄lī yese i fọ̄a navọ̄i ma,	And the snail reached the money first,
Ke mawali i gula dopé ma.	And the deer lost the bet.
Ke kọ̄lī i navọ̄ wāi na kpele bumbúa.	And the snail took all that large sum of money.
Ke ndopé fulenga,	And the deer reached there,
Te ndopé, te,	They said to the deer, saying,
Kọ̄lī mawali i gula bima.	The snail has won the bet.
Te, bi navọ̄i ji jo̱lo.	They said, You should have got this money.
Te, bia ba wime,	They said, You can run,
Kọ̄li ta ī gu a jiala.	(But) the snail himself cannot run.

Wa ta wu jia mawali hounga ;	You and he bet on your walking ;
Mawali i gula bima ;	You lost ;
Te, bē ya navoi ji jo̱.	They said, You did not get this money.
Ti ndewe,	They beat him,
Te, bi hawa wilenga.	They said, You were lazy (lit. made lazy).

Dọ̆mi vuli i gbo̱yoa.	The story is quite finished.
Numu a ye na ke a ngenda bia.	The person who is here says good-night to you.

XIII.

The Hornbill and the Dog.

Njeli.	Story.
Piangbe mia wo̱ ta ngila.	There was once a hornbill and a dog.
Kōi i gula.	War fell.
Ke ti welanga.	And they ran away.
Ke ti ya dogboi hũ.	And they went into the bush.
Ke ti tei lōnga na.	And they built a house there.
Ngelewo piangbe ye ngilé ma, ye,	At dawn the hornbill said to the dog, saying,
Mu mu mehe goé.	Let us go and find food.
Ke ti ya mehe goeme.	And they went to find food.
Ke ti tu gbole maléa (tu *short for* tọwe).	And they came across ripe palm-nuts.
Piangbe ye ngiléma,	The hornbill said to the dog,
Ye, mu tọwui le.	Saying, Let us cut the nuts.
Ke ti tọwui lenga.	And they cut off the palm-nuts.
Ke numu ē ngi mba layia gbia hũ.	Now nobody must disobey his senior's order.
Piangbe ye ngiláma, ye,	The hornbill said to the dog, saying,
Tu mu tenga,	We have cut down the bunch of palm-nuts,
Ye, numu ē sese.	He said, Nobody shall slice off the nuts.
Ye, lọngoihũ lọ mu me.	He said, Leave the remains for us to eat.
Ngila ye piangbe ma, ye,	The dog said to the hornbill, saying,
Kejina, nya laguli guhango ī le.	Now, my mouth is not long.
Bē, muë tọwui jese.	You say, We must not cut off the nuts.

Ye ke, kulungo le.	And he said, All right.
Ye, mu tọ̄wui me.	He said, Let us eat the nuts.
Piangbe ngi laguli guha wai na.	The hornbill's beak was very long.
A kpakpale tọ̄wui na ma.	He hammers on the nuts.
Piangbe i tọ̄wui na me fo.	The hornbill eats all that bunch of nuts.
Ī ngila goe.	He did not give any to the dog.
Kpē gbĭ a na wile ke a ngila.	Every time he does so with the dog.
Ngila be ye, kulungo le.	But the dog said, All right.
Ye, ke ji na, kōi gula ma bie.	He said, Now, there is war with you.
Ye, nya lei ī guhani.	He said, My mouth is not long.
Mu tọ̄wui lenga be,	We have cut the palm-nuts off,
Ilọngoihũ mu me.	And it is the remains that we (*i. e.* I) must eat.
Ye, kulungo le.	He said, All right.
Ke ngila be ke i ya	And so the dog went
Jijiamé dogboi hũ.	To walk about in the bush.
Ke i kōmi longa.	And he saw honey.
Kominga ti wulongo wa.	The bees were very fat.
Te le, ke ngila wa,	So it was, and the dog came,
Ke i ndea piangbia ma,	And he said to the hornbill,
Ye, ngi ya ha dogboi hũ,	I went to-day into the bush,
Ye, ngi kominga longa na.	He said, I saw bees there.
Piangba ye,	The hornbill said,
Ngelewo sina mu li na,	Let us go there to-morrow at daylight,
Mu komisia gbia.	And get the bees out.
Ke ngelewa	And at daylight
Ke ti ya na.	They went there.
Ti komi gbia kahã waya-kpa.	They took out eight baskets of honey.
Ngila ye piangba ma,	The dog said to the hornbill,
Ye, komi ji,	He said, This honey,
Ye, ma fọnya fawé ma.	He said, we will squeeze it on a ledge of rocks.
Piangbe ye sao.	The hornbill said, No.
Ye, mu kọle kā fefele (ka = kahã).	He said, Let us divide the baskets between us.

Ngila be ye sao.	But the dog said, No.
Ye, nga lo be wo̱ mu ya dogboi hũ,	He said, I was here first in the bush,
Mua ngi mba layia gbia hũ.	We must observe precedence.
Piangbe ye, ī;	The hornbill said, Yes;
Ye, mu komi fo̱nya.	He said, Let us squeeze the honey.
Ke ti komi vo̱nya fawe hũ.	And they squeezed the honey on the rock.
Fawe hũ a li polon.	The rock went far.
Ke ti tọ̄tọ̄a na a komi mela.	And they began there to eat the honey.
Ngila i li a komi.	The dog licks up the honey.
Piangbe ngi lei ī hite komi ma.	The hornbill's mouth did not reach the honey.
Ngi laguli na a jia le fawé-ma gbama.	His beak walks over the rock in vain.
Ke i gbalenga piangbe ma.	And it hurt the hornbill.
Ye, ngila,	He said, Dog,
Hindei ye na bi peni ange?	What have you done to me?
Ye, mabia muë ya he hinda yira.	He said, You and I will not sit down in one place.
Ngila be ye kulungo le.	And the dog said, All right.
Ngila i komi na me fu.	The dog ate all that honey.
Ye, ji ge mu gbonga tọ̄wui ma,	He said, When a short time ago we joined together for palm-nuts,
Bē, muë sese.	You said, Let us not slice them.
Bē ge, bi yakpei lo bi nemáhũ lengo.	You said, a few days ago, that you alone had any sense.
Ye nā ba li lo, kere.	He said, Now you can go if you like.
Ke piangbe ta ngila	And the hornbill and the dog
Ke ti ya kolonga mchei hindé ma.	They went away on account of the food in the place.
Ke ngila i piangbia lọ̄i menga.	And the dog ate the hornbill's child.
Piangbe i wa	The hornbill comes
I ngila jogba.	To choke the dog.
Ke ngilé i ngi nyia.	And the dog bit him.
Ke i gọ̄wọ̄a,	And he flew,

I lia ngē ma.	He went up to the sky.
Ta mia wo̱ na a kpaui na wili a ngila, ngila, ngila, ngila.	So it was that he made that cry of dog, dog, dog. (Ngila being an imitation of the bird's cry.)
Igboyoa.	It is finished.

XIV.

The Egg-plant and the Woman who talked.

Nyapọ̄i mia wọ.	There was once a young woman.
I gbema.	She was barren.
Ī ndọ̄ leni.	She bore no child.
Ta ngi banga ti gboni hini yira ma.	She and her companions shared a husband.
Kpele gbi a lewe dogboi hũ,	She was always wandering in the bush,
A wolo,	Weeping, (she weeps)
Ye, A! Ngewo wa!	Saying, Oh! Great God!
Ye, ngi gbọ wileni abië,	Saying, What have I done to you,
Nya ngē ndọ̄ leni?	That I have borne no child?
Kpele gbi a lewe	She was always wandering about
A ngole na wile.	And making that weeping.
Tamo i kpãe la tei gbela.	A man laid out a farm near the town.
Ti kọ̄jī hi.	They planted an egg-plant.
Kọ̄jī ke i wa.	And the egg-plant came up.
Te le, nyapọ̄i! mbawubela	So it was, that the rice planters
Ke ti wa ngi hini ye	Came to the woman's husband
Kpăhũ bawume.	To plant rice in his farm.
Te ngi ma,	They say to her,
Te, bī ndọ̄ leni.	Saying, You have borne no child.
Fale, bia ba li,	Therefore, go you,
Bi kọ̄ji ji goe,	(And) pluck this egg-plant,
Bi wa,	Bring it,
Bi ngili ngengebra we.	(And) cook it for the labourers.
Nyapọ̄i ke i sambe bumbúa,	And the young woman took a basket,
Ke i yá.	And she went.
I li,	She goes,
Ī fọ̄ kọ̄jema.	She reaches the egg-plant.

I ye kọ̄ji goema,	She was picking the eggs,
A ngole wile,	And weeping,
Ye, ma nya banga gbele	Saying, I and all my companions
Mu gboa hini ma,	We share a husband,
Ti gbi ti ndọ̄ lenga,	They have all borne children,
Nya ngī ndọ̄ leni.	(But) I have borne no child.
Kunayefo ndọ̄pọ̄ yenge gbi ta nya lọ̄ma.	They are always sending me to do all the inferior work.
Ye ke, ngewo le.	And said, It is God('s doing).
Te le, ke kọ̄ji ĭyila.	So it was, that it was the very egg-plant.
Ke i yiá.	And it spoke.
Ye nyapọ̄i, ye,	It said to the young woman, saying,
Ke ye wu layia ī gboto	If you talk less
Ke ngi bi bawọ̄a.	I may help you.
Nyapọ̄i i wọ̄te, ye,	The young woman turned, saying,
Yo jiei leni?	Who spoke?
Kọ̄ji ye,	The egg-plant said,
Ngē nya ge abiĕ.	I cannot show myself to you.
Ye, ba yepe.	It said, Do not talk.
Ye, ngē yepe.	She said, I will not talk.
Ye ke, jondu le.	It said also, Swear first.
Ke i jondua.	And she took an oath.
Kọ̄ji ye nyapọ̄i ma, ye,	The egg-plant said to the young woman, saying,
Nga pe lo bi ndọ̄ le.	I will make you bear a child.
Ye kulungo le.	She said, All right.
Ye ke, ba ye pe nā nga ndọ̄le?	And she said, How now will you make me bear a child?
Ye, bi yama lī́ (=lī́wī́).	It said, Shut your eyes.
Ke nyapọ̄i i ngi yama linga.	And the young woman shut her eyes.
Ke kọ̄ji na ke i maluvea a nyaha.[1]	And the egg-plant turned into a lady.
Nyaha lo nyande.	She was a beautiful lady.
Ye, nyapọ̄i ma,	She said to the woman,

[1] *Nyaha*, meaning woman or wife, is above *nyapọ̄*, girl or woman. See Vocabulary of Relationships, etc. In the Mende text the distinction is clear, but in the English it is necessary to use another word, *e. g.* lady, to distinguish the speakers.

Ye, bi yama volo.	Saying, Open your eyes.
Ke i ngi yama vongo.	And she opened her eyes.
A ye wọ̄te,	She turned round,
Ke i nyahalọ̄i loa lọ̄ni.	And she saw a young girl standing there.
Ngi nyini ji ngi yaka vengo.	Her breasts were full.
Ye nyapọ̄i, ye,	She said to the woman, saying,
Bē yepe.	You must not talk.
Ye, éh.	She said, Yes.
Ye, mu ya tei hũ.	She said, Let us go into the town.
Ye, ndē be, ye ndọ̄i ji?	She said, Say, (if any one says) whose child is this?
Nya ndewe lōi lo,	It is my sister's child,
I ndọ̄i ji yoyoi mbe.	She sent this child to me.
Ye, bā hũge.	She said do not explain.
Bā nde ba yema (= yiama),	Do not talk, saying,
Kọ̄ji lo maluveni a numui ji.	The egg-plant was changed into a person.
Ye, bi na léa,	She said, If you talk so,
Ye, nga yama lo gbon,	She said, I will surely go back again,
Ngi maluvi a kọ̄ji gboma.	I will turn into the egg-plant again.
Nyapọ̄i ye,	The woman said,
Bi hāi gbe ngeleya	You look for something in the air
Bi to dọma.	And you find (lit. see) it on the ground.
Ye, Ngewo yana ñi a bi go.	She said, It is God who gives you this.
Ye, ngē na wile.	She said, I will not do it.
Ye ke, mu li tei hũ.	And she said, Let us go into the town.
Ke ti yá tei hũ.	And they went into the town.
Numui gbĭ ke ti nyapọ̄i mọlia,	And everybody asked the woman, saying,
Te, ji bi ndọ̄ leni.	Seeing that you have not borne a child,
Bi ndọ̄i ji jọi mi lo?	Where did you get this child?
Ye, nya ndewe mia,	She said, It is my sister,
I ndọ̄i ji yoyui mbe.	Who (lit. she) sent this child to me.

Ti ndọ̄pọ̄i na lagoi.	They gave the young girl food.
Ti ngi kave.	They made a feast for her.
Ti pā ti me.	They kill, they eat.
Kene na ngi wọ̄ a nyapọ̄i na	The man whose own that woman was
Ī lọ̄i wo̱ angie.	Had not cared for her before.
Kpele gbi a nyapọ̄i hũmo̱li,	Every moment he asks the woman,
Ye, bi ndọ̄i ji jo̱i mi lo?	Saying, Where did you get this child?
Ye, nya ndewe lo	She said, It is my sister
I ndọ̄i ji yoyui mbe.	Who sent me this child.
Kpele gbi a ngi mo̱li.	Every moment he asks her.
Nyānga va ti nemahui ī guha.	As for women their sense is not great.
Ke i hũgenga a ngi hini.	And she told everything to her husband.
Ye, kpele na ge	She said, That time a little while ago
Ti ndeni, tē,	That they said, saying,
Ngi li kọ̄ji goeme,	That I was to go and pick the egg-plant,
Ngi li ge,	I went then,
Ngi wo̱lo kọ̄ji wulīma.	I wept at the egg-plant tree.
Ta ge i maluveni a numui ji.	It then turned into this person.
Ke nya hini mia abie ge,	And you have always been my husband,
Nya gohũ lowa bi ma.	I am entirely yours.
Ke ngi hũgenga abie.	And I have explained it to you.
Bā ya hũge a numu gbī.	Do not talk about it to anybody.
Bī hũgenga a numu,	(If) you talk about it to anybody,
Kọ̄jī hũmenia,	(And) the egg-plant hears,
A yama gboma	She will return
I wọ̄te a kọ̄ji.	And become an egg-plant again.
Fale bā hũge.	Therefore do not talk about it.
Te le, kene ye, ī.	So the man said, Yes.
Ye, ngē ya hũge.	He said, I will not talk about it.
Te le, ngi lima-nyahei	Now his favourite wife
Ke i ngi mo̱lia na,	She also asked him,

Ye, mbāi ji i ndọ̄i ji joi milo?	Saying, This other wife where did she get this child?
Kpele gbi i kene mo̱lia na.	She was constantly asking the man that.
Nyapọ̄i be tọ-nyaha mia.	This woman was a jealous woman.
Ngi longo i ngi mbai ji lọ̄i ji hinda hũgo.	She wanted to know all about her companion's child.
Ke kene i hũgenga a ngi lima-nyahei.	And the man told his favourite wife all about it.
Ye, ndọ̄i ji ge nyapọ̄i i wela.	He said, This child the woman produced a few days ago.
Ye, ba ngi gohũ lọ̄ yana.	He said, It is not the child of her belly.
Ye, i ye pileni i ndọ̄i ma joi.	He said, What she did to get the child (is this).
Ye, ji ge gengebla ti wai nya gama,	She said, when the labourers came to me,
Gbe na gi li kọ̄jọ̄ go'emi,	At the time that I went to pick the egg-plant,
Hũ mia ge kọ̄ji na	It was then that the egg-plant
I maluveni a numui na.	Changed into that person.
Kia gi hũgenga abie,	Seeing that I have told you,
Bā hũge a numu gbi.	Do not tell anybody else.
Bi hũgenga,	If you tell,
Bi mbai lọ̄i i yá,	Your companion's child is gone,
Ga pe bi ma a njia lo	(And) I will make trouble with you
Gau fere na i gboyo.	(Until) two months are ended.
Nyapọ̄i, ngi wọ̄ a ndọ̄i,	The woman, whose the child was,
Ke i ya nye gbeme.	Went to catch fish.
A hiye njei na hũ.	She comes up out of the water.
Ke nyapọ̄i na ke i ndọ̄pọ̄i lulinga a kọ̄jọ̄.	And the woman called the girl Egg-plant.
Ke i ya.	And she went.
Ye, gbe i hi,	She said, Let her sit down,
I ngi njei mawulo.	And await her mother.
Ye, ji wo̱ ngi ndea ngi ma,	(The egg-plant) said, I told her before,
Ngē, ā nya la ge,	Saying, she was not to show my name,

Tamia ā nya hinda hũge a ngi wongeisia,	Further, she was not to talk my affairs with her relations,
Ye, gbe i wa.	She said, Wait till she comes.
Ye sao, ī na.	She said, No, she is not there.
Nyā wama wilema.	The woman is coming in the road.
Ke nyapọ̄i i hiya nye gbeme.	And the woman came up from catching fish.
Kia wo̱ i wani,	When she came,
Ke i ngi mo̱lia, ye,	(The egg-plant) asked her, saying,
Ji wo̱ bi heni,	When you were sitting here before,
Ye, bemango, ndọ̄ ī bēya.	It said, You were barren, you had no child.
Ye, nya kọ̄jọ̄,	It said, I was the egg-plant,
Ba ndọ̄ wole wili dogboihũ,	You cried in the bush for a child,
Ye, nya kọ̄jọ̄,	It said, I was the egg-plant,
Ngi manu bi ma.	I pitied you.
Ngi wọ̄tea wo̱ a numu,	I turned into a person,
Ngi yenge bie,	I worked for you,
Tamia i wile bi limahũ ē gili a hinda gbī.	And also it came about that your mind was not to remember anything.
Tamia ba nde, bē,	Therefore you were not to say that (lit. saying)
Kọ̄jọ̄ lo ange.	I was the egg-plant.
Ye, ngi yama mbe-oh.	It said, I go back as I was before.
Ke i yama,	And it returned,
I li hindei	It went to the place
Wo̱ nyapọ̄i na i li na kọ̄jọ̄ goeme.	Where the woman had gone before to pluck the egg-plant.
Ke ngi lọ̄i i yama na,	And her child returned there,
Ĭ wọ̄te a kọ̄ji.	It turned into the egg-plant.
Nyapọ̄i na i hei wo̱ ndọ̄ gbī ya ngeya.	The woman used to sit there before without any child.
Ngi layia mia wo̱	It had been her complaint before
I ngi bani a ndọ̄i.	That she was without a child.
I kọ̄ji na hinda hũge wo̱,	She talked about the egg-plant's affairs,
I gbate wo̱ na	She had been well off when
Kọ̄ji na hinda hũ ;	The egg-plant was in the affair ;
Ke i ngi wọ̄ ngọ̄i lema.	But she broke her word.

XV.

The Magic Shirt.

Kene mia wo̱,	There was once a man,
I gbate,	He was rich,
I lewe dŏle gbele ma.	He surpassed all the country.
Numui kpele ti lọlọ angie	Everybody hated him
Nu gbate va.	Because he was rich.
Ke ti kōi hūbatéa ngi va.	And they prepared war for him.
Te, numu yakpei ji i lewe muma dŏle ji hū.	They said, This one man surpasses us in this country.
Te, mā kulu ngi ye.	They said, We do not agree to have him.
Te, a mu kōi we ngi ma,	They said, Let us make war on him,
Mu ngi vaya.	(And) let us spoil him.
Ke ti kōi wea ngi ma,	And they made war on him,
Ke ti ngi batehū vaya.	And they spoiled his wealth.
Ke i lo̱wunga.	And he hid.
Ke i ya dogboi hū.	And he went into the bush.
Kōi ī ngi loni.	The war did not see him.
Ke kōi i ngi nunga vuluisia kpele hou.	But the war caught all his people themselves.
Fọ yira i ndogboi hū.	One year he was in the bush.
I gbia.	He came out.
Ke kọi i gbo̱yoa.	And the war was finished.
I yama.	He returned.
I ngi lei lọ (lei *for* tei).	He (re)built his town.
Ke nunga ti wa ngi lei hū.	And people came into his town.
Ti bo ngima.	They helped him.
Ti ngi lei lọ.	They built his town.
Dakpāọ yira i bumbui gbate,	A certain young man made a fish trap,
Ke i yala njei hū.	And he took it to the water.

Ke i kale gọnũa.	And he made a weir.
Ke i bumbui welenga nga.	And he set the trap on it.
Ngelewo i wa kaleya.	At daybreak he came to the weir.
I male ti kale yahũma.	He found some one (lit. they) had stolen from the weir.
I lọ̄ na,	He stood there,
I mo̱li, ye,	He asked, saying,
Yo nya galé yahumamai?	Who has stolen from my weir?
Ye, nga mane lo.	He said, I will watch.
Mema! dogbọyusui mia	See! it was the wild man
I kale yahumama.	Who stole from the weir.
Ye, kalé ji nga mane lo.	He said, I will watch this weir.
Ye, numui ji i nya galé ji yahumama.	He said, This person is stealing from my weir.
Ye, nga hou lo.	He said, I will catch him.
Ke i ya tei hũ.	And he went into the town.
Ngi mbai ji ta ta ti longoma.	He and his friend were much attached to each other.
Ke i ya,	And he went,
I nde ngi ma, ye,	He said to him, saying,
Ngi kale konua,	I have made a weir,
Ke ti ya ngahumama.	And some one has gone and stolen from it.
Ye, mu li mu nga ne.	He said, Let us go and watch.
Mu ya,	Let us go,
Bi le nduvui hũ,	You climb into a (lit. the) bamboo palm,
Ye, nya ngi lo̱wu bele ku hũ.	He said, I myself will hide in the buttresses of a big tree.
Ke i ya,	And he went,
Ke i lo̱wú na bele kui hũ.	And he hid between the buttresses of the big tree.
Ke ngi mbai be,	And his friend too,
Ke i lo̱wua nduvui hũ ngeleya.	He hid aloft in the bamboo palm.
Ngenda tete	In the early morning
Ke dogboyusui [1] i wa	The wild man came
Kale yahumama.	To steal from the weir.
Ke i wa,	And he came,

[1] Dogboyusui is the chimpanzee, which, like the gorilla, is held to be half human, and to be a devil with magic powers.

Ke i ndọ̄mei gbia ngima,	And he took off his shirt,
Ke i gbo̱lé gbia wumba,	And he took off his hat,
Ke i belé gbia ngima,	And he took off his trousers,
Ke i vowé gbia ngi loko hũ,	And he took off his charms from his arm,
Ke i bumbua,	And he took them,
Ke i ndo̱wua gbele kuī hũ,	And he hid them between the buttresses of the big tree,
Ke i ya njei hũ kale ya.	And he went into the water on the weir.
Ke i mbombui gbia kale ya,	And he took the fish trap off the weir,
Ke i da vulonga,	And he loosed its mouth,
Ke nyenga ti wua do̱me.	And the fish poured out on the ground.
Ke i tọ̄a nyema,	And he pointed to a fish,
Ke na ha.	And it died.
Ke i gbaọ̄a, ye,	And he (the man) called out, saying,
Ko !	Ko !
Ye, bia ge ba nya gale yahumama.	He said, It is you who have been stealing from my weir.
Ye, Ko !	He said, Ko !
Ye, ndakpé-oh.	He said, My friend.
Ye, dogboyusui gbe,	He said, Look at the wild man,
I kale yahumama.	He is stealing from the weir.
Ye, a ye pe a kale yahuma ?	He said, How is he going about stealing from the weir ?
Ye, i nye wua ndo̱me,	He said, He poured the fish out on the ground,
Ke i lọ̄kọ̄ lọ̄a ngi lọ̄mé ma,	And he pointed his hand to his shirt,
Ke i tọ̄a nye ma,	And he pointed to a fish,
Ke na ha.	And it died.
Ke i ngi lọ̄kọ̄i lọ̄a ngi mbai ma,	And he pointed his hand to his friend,
Ke ngi mbai i ha ngeleya.	And his friend died aloft (in the tree).
Dogboyusui ke i lua,	And the wild man feared,
Ke i lia a pime,	And he went running,

Ke i ngi lọ̄mesia gbele lọ̄a na.	And he left all his clothes (lit. shirts) there.
Ke i ya.	And he went.
Ke dakpaọ̄i na ke i ngi mbai lọ̄linga,	And that young man called his friend,
Ke ye, ndakpe !	And he said, Young man !
Ye, wa a mu li-oh !	He said, Come, let us go !
Ke i ya.	And he went.
A ye na i wọ̄te na ;	It was then that he turned ;
Ngi mbai hango.	His friend was dead.
Ke ndogboyusui lọ̄mei na	And the wild man's shirt
Ke i mbumbúa,	He took,
Ke i ya a pime.	And he ran away.
Ke i ya a ndọ̄me,	And he took the shirt,
I fe mahei we.	He gave it to the king.
Ye, keke,	He said, My father,
Ye, bunde gula ngeya.	He said, trouble falls on me.
Ye, gbe bunde le ?	He said, What trouble ?
Ye, ngi ya gi kale gunuma,	He said, I went to construct a fishing weir,
Dogboyusui mia i ngahumama nyeya.	(And) the wild man stole from me.
Ngi hũgọ.	I did not understand.
Ngi ndea nya mbai ma,	I said to my friend,
Ngē, mu li nya gale mane we.	I said, Let us go and watch my weir.
Mu ya na.	We went there.
Dogboyusui i wa kale yahumama.	The wild man came to steal at the weir.
I ngi lọ̄me gbia ngima.	He took off his shirt.
I ngi pua ngulu kui hũ.	He put it between a tree's buttresses.
Nya mba i lọwua nduvuihũ.	My friend hid in a palm.
Nya be ngi lọwua ngulu kui hũ.	Myself, I hid between the buttresses of the tree.
Dogboyusui i wa kale yahumama.	The wild man came to steal at the weir.
I nye gbia njei hũ,	He took the fish out of the water,
I pua ngiye ma,	He put them on the bank,
I lọ̄kọ̄i lọ̄nga ngi lọ̄mema,	He pointed (his) hand to his shirt,

I tọa nyema,	He pointed to a fish,
Ke nyenga ti ha.	And the fish died.
Ngi bandéa dogboyusui ma,	I holla'd to the wild man,
Ngē, Ko !	I said, Hi !
Bia ge ba nya galéji yahumama.	It is you who have been stealing at my weir.
Ngē, ndakpe-oh !	I said, Friend !
Dogboyusui gbe,	See the wild man,
I kama hinda wilema.	He is doing something wonderful.
A ye pe, bi toa,	What he does is, you see,
A nye wu ngiyé ma,	He puts the fish on the bank,
I lọkọ lọ ngi lọme ma,	He points the hand to his shirt,
I lọ nye ma,	He points to a fish,
Ke nyé i ha.	And the fish dies.
Ye, na gi peni.	He said, I did that.
Ngi nya loko lo domé ma,	I pointed my hand to the shirt,
Gi to nya mba lenga,	I looked towards my friend,
Ke i ha do̱wume nduvui hũ.	And he died in his hiding-place in the palm.
Gī ko̱.	I do not know.
Ke dogboyusui i ya a pime.	And the wild man ran away.
Ta mia ta mahei ye,	Then the king said,
Na bi wileni.	You did that.
Ye, nga pe lo,	He said, I will arrange,
Ye, ngi njiei na bā wumba.	He said, to stop that affair on your head, *i. e.* that is hanging over you.
Ye, ke,	He said also,
Ye, a li wu wa dakpaoi na	Saying, Go and fetch that young man
I wileni beya (= bi yeya) dogboi hũ,	That died by your hand in the bush (*wile* = do, a euphemism for *die*).
Wu wala gi to.	Bring him for me to see.
Ke ti ya ti wala.	And they went and brought him.
Ye, dakpoi ji i hei ji wileni beya dogboi hũ,	He said, (If) this young man he died this death at your hand in the bush,
Ye, nga na go̱ pe.	He said, I shall know that soon.
Jialọi i lēma ngitiya.	A small child was passing in front.

Ke ta mahei ke i ngi lokoi lọ̄a dogboyusui lomema,	And the king pointed his hand to the wild man's shirt,
Ke i tọ̄a jia lọ̄i ma,	And he pointed to the child,
Ke i gula,	And it fell down,
Ke i ha.	And it died.
Ke i ndea dakpalọ̄i ma, ye,	And he said to the young man, saying,
Bi mbāi ji i hei wile beya dogboi hũ,	This your friend died by your hand in the bush,
Ye, njia gbī ya bi ma.	He said, There is no blame (lit. palaver) on you.
Ye ke, dogboyusui lọme ji i nya na va.	He said too, This wild man's shirt is now mine.
Ye, bamani mahei a nya na,	He said, Because I am the king,
Nya mia, ngi njia bāma bumba.	It is I who will stop the palaver on your head, *i. e.* will acquit you.
Dakpoi na ye,	That young man said,
Ngi kurua.	I accept.
I segbia mahei ma.	He thanked the king.
Ti jia lọ̄i gbọ̄wu.	They buried the child.
Ti ndakpoi be bõ.	They buried the young man also.
Mahei na i navo gboto majia	That king spent much money
Kọlongo dakpoi na va a hindei na hũ ;	On account of that young man and the whole affair ;
Kọlongo dogboyusui ma gulé na ma.	On account of the wild man and that shirt.
Ke njiei i gboyoa.	And the matter ended.
Ke mahei na fọ̄ i lewe nani	And that king for over four years
I gbate gboṅ,	Increased in wealth,
I lewe ngoveí ma.	More than before.
Ke i yunga longa a nasia gbele wọ	And he boasted over all those who before
Ti kõi goni angie.	Had made war on him.
Ye, nasia kpele ti kọ̄i goni ange,	He said, All those who made war on me,
Ye, ti wa,	He said, let them come,
Ye, mu go a fọ̄i ji.	He said, we will fight this year.

Ke i ti gonga a loe wayakpa.	And he gave them eight days.
Ke ti gbi, tia be, te,	And they all said,
Mu kulua,	We agree,
Te, kōi wo̱ ba mā wile,	They said, You have desired war,
Te, mu goa nā bi ma	They said, (If) we fight now with you
Mua bi wa lo.	We shall kill you.
Ye, ngi kurua.	He said, I accept.
Ke kōi wa.	And the war came.
Ye, numu gbi mawueni mu tei ji hũ.	He said, Everybody, I and you, we are in this town.
Ye, numu gbī ā kpande wili kọi ji ma.	He said, Nobody shall fire a gun in this war.
Ye, mu gbi, ye, a hei.	He said, All of us, he said, you must sit down.
Ye, nya kọi lo,	He said, It is my war,
Nga kōi ji go.	I will fight this war.
Ngi nunga gbi ke ti kurua.	And all his people agreed.
Ke ti lia ti hei.	And they went, they sat down.
Ke ta ngi mahei ke i wa pebu,	And the king of the town came into the house,
Ke i dogboyusui bele yinga (=yilinga),	And he pulled on the wild man's trousers,
Ke i dogboyusui lọme wunga,	And he put on the wild man's shirt,
Ke i dogboyusui gbo̱le welenga,	And he put on the wild man's hat,
Ke i dogboyusui vowi wua ngi baki hũ,	And he put the wild man's charms on his upper arm,
Ke i gbia ngitiya.	And he went outside.
Ke kọi i wa tei hũ.	And the fighting came into the town.
Ti nunga gbi hou tei hũ.	They (the enemy) caught all the people in the town.
Ke tī numu wani.	But they killed nobody.
Ti ngili lo ti kpelema.	They tied them all up.
Ti wa,	They come,
Ti mahei mo̱li, te,	They ask the king, saying,
Bi yema (yiama) ge	You were saying the other day
Mu wa	That we might come

Mu kōi go.	(And) make war.
Mahei be ye,	The king too said,
Nya ge ngi ndeni,	I myself said the other day,
Ngē, wu wa,	I said, Come,
Mu kōi go.	Let us fight.
Ye, kia bē (= gbele, time) na.	He said, It is now the time.
Ye, nya numu gbī kōi ji golama.	He said, I will take nobody by surprise in this war.
Ye, wu kia yira.	He said, You are all as one.
Ye, wū yama wu yei.	He said, You will not return to your country.
Nya kōi a houla.	My war will catch you.
Ke mahei ke i ngi lọkọ lọa	And the king pointed his hand
Dogboyusui lọme ji ma	To the wild man's shirt
I ngi ma,	That he was wearing,
Ke i tọ̄a kōi ma,	And he pointed to the enemy,
Ke ti gbi ti ha.	And they all died.
I ngi lọkọi tọ dogboyusui lọ̄mema ngi ma,	He pointed his hand to the wild man's shirt on himself,
Ke i lō kōisia ma,	And he pointed at the enemy,
Ke koisia gbi ti ha.	And the enemy all died.
Tī pande wili gōi ma.	They did not fire a gun in the war.
Kōsia ti gbọyoa hala.	The enemy all died (lit. finished dying).
Ta mahei i kōi gbi vaya a dogboyusui lọme na a ngi ma.	The king of the town destroyed all the enemy with that wild man's shirt that he wore.
I ndọ̄me gbia ngi ma.	He took off the shirt.
I pu kaña,	He put it in a box,
I ndagbou.	He shut it.
Kō gbī ī ya gui ngi lei ma.	No war could reach his town.
Nunga gbi ti nde, tē,	Everybody said, saying,
Kunafo wā gō a mahei ji.	You must never make war with this king.
Kamahinda i muma lia.	We have magic in our midst.
Mu wa kō ma,	We came to war,
Gbande ī wilini,	No gun was fired,
Tī numu wāni,	They did not kill a single person,

Numu ji kpele i ha.	(But) this people all died.
Tī ya we gboma.	They did not do it again.
Ke nunga ti ya,	And people went away,
Mahei na i lọ̄a.	That king was left (alone).
I gbate na hũ.	He grew rich there.
Igboyoa.	It is finished.

XVI.

The Woman whose Child returned to Life, and her Enemy.

Nyapọ̄i mia wọ.	There was once a woman.
Ta ngi bānga ti gbo hini ma.	She and her companions shared a husband.
Ti hini kpatengo.	Their husband was rich.
I gbēma,	She was barren,
Ī ndọ̄ leni.	She bore no child.
Ngi mbanga ti ndenga lē gboto.	Her companions bore many children.
I wa Mori ma.	She came to a Mori man.
Ye, pe ngi ndọ̄ le.	She said, Make me bear a child.
Ke Mori pea.	And the Mori man did so.
Ke i ndọ̄ léa;	And she bore a child;
Nyaha lo.	It was a girl.
Ngi lọ̄i nyandengo;	Her child was a fine one;
I lē ngi mbanga ti nda lenge nasia ma.	It was finer (lit. it passed) than her companions' children.
Ke ngi mba-nyahei i lọlọ a ngiĕ.	And her fellow-wife hated her.
Ke ngi lọ̄i na ke i gbelá.	And her child reached puberty.
Ke ti wa Sandi hũ.	And they came into the "Sandi" bush.
Dọpọ̄i la Mang-woni.	The girl's name was Mang-woni.
Ke ti ti gbia Sandi hũ.	And they came out of the Sandi bush.
Mańwoni nyandengo wa,	Mańwoni was very beautiful,
I lewe ngi mba Sandi yọ̄i nasia ma.	She passed her companions in the Sandi bush.
Ke nyapọ̄i ngi mba nyahei	And the woman's fellow-wife
Ke i họna lenga	Made witchcraft

Ngi mbai nyahei lọi ma,	Against her companion's daughter,
Ke i ho̱na lenga Mañwoni ma.	She made witchcraft against Mañwoni.
Ke i ha.	And she died.
Nyapọi i wolo ;	The woman wept ;
I wōnga ngau nani ;	She wept for four months ;
Ngi lọi yakpei i wōnga ngau nani.	She wept for her only child four months.
Ke ndọbela ke ti ngi mamamau golonga.	And the dwellers in the lower world felt sorry for her.
Ndọpọi hani.	The girl died.
I li ndọ.	She went to the lower world.
Ke pumō gowọli ke i lọ angie.	And a white man loved her.
Ke ta ta ti so wea.	And he and she married.
Dọpọi ke pumōi i ngi go a navō gboto.	And the white man gave the girl much money.
Nyapọi i wolo ngi lọi va ngau nani na.	The woman wept for her child those four months.
Ke pumōi na ta be ngi yafé na.	And that white man he too was a spirit there.
Ke i nyapọi mamamau loa.	And he saw the woman's sorrow.
Ye, nyapọi ji ge ngi ngi mamamau loma.	He said, I have seen this woman's sorrow for a long time.
Ngi ngi lọi yama ngelemahũ.	I will return her child to the land of the living.
Kpindi na ke nyapọi i la.	That night the woman lay down.
Ke i hengá a pumoi na,	And she dreamt of that white man,
Ta ngi lọi ti heni ko̱tu wele hũ,	(That) he and her child lived in a stone house,
Navọ gboto.	(With) plenty of money.
Dọpọi ye pumōi ma,	The girl said to the white man,
Ye, ngi nji lo.	Saying (that) it is her mother.
Ke pumōi ndea nyapọi ma,	And the white man said to the woman,
Ye, ngi bi mamamau go̱lo̱,	He said, I feel sorry for you,
Ye, ngo̱le ji gbi ba pile ngelemahũ.	He said, Making all this weeping in the land of the living.

Ye, nya mema ndō	He said, I am hearing down below
Kolongo bi lọ̄i ji hindahũ.	All about your child's affair.
Ye, ngelewa sina,	He said, At daybreak to-morrow,
Ye, bi li bi lọ̄i gambe ma.	He said, go to your child's grave.
Ye, bi segbule bumbu,	He said, Take your rattle,
Bi gbe ngale ma,	Add the mat to it,
Ke kọ̄nde bumbu ;	And take the mortar (for pounding grain) ;
Li bi lọ̄ kambé ma.	Go and put them on the grave.
Ye, bi lọ̄i, ye, nga velioma sina ;	He said, Your child, he said, I will present her (to you) to-morrow ;
I wa bi gama.	She will come to you.
Ye, kulongo le.	She said, All right.
Ngelewo i kọ̄ndé bumbu,	At daybreak she took the mortar,
Ke segbule,	And the rattle,
Ke ngale ;	And the mat ;
I li.	She went.
I ngale fọ̄mbọ̄ kambé ma,	She spread the mat on the grave,
I kọ̄ndé lọ̄ kambé ma,	She stood the mortar on the grave,
I segbulé ho mba.	She held up her rattle.
Ke pumōi nde ngi ma a kpindi,	And the white man told her in the night,
Ye, bi lọ̄i i gbia sina kambé hũ.	He said, Your child will come out to-morrow from the grave.
Ye, bā humbu a gbundé ma.	He said, Do not be in a hurry to embrace her.
Ye, gbema !	He said, Stop !
A tei gala sawa.	She will go round the town three times.
I wa bi gama ;	She will come to you ;
Bi hō.	Catch her.
Ke ngelewa nyapọ̄i i hi kambé ma.	And at daybreak the woman sat at the grave.
I ngule yīa.	She sang.
Ye Mańwoni !	She said, Mańwoni !
Ya ha Bondo.	Go to-day to the Bondo bush (same as Sandi bush).

Maṅwoni wa !	Maṅwoni, come !
Nyapọi i ngulé na yīa.	The woman sang that song.
Hawa pu gbē ma	In ten hours' time
Ke ndọ̄pọi ke i gbia kambe hũ.	The girl came out of the grave.
Ngi wui na kanī gbọ̄li na pun hondro nugboyongo.	Her head was of gold, twenty hundred pounds' worth.
Ngi lọkọi ji gbi kanī pumōi feni.	Her arm was all gold that the white man gave her.
I gbia,	She came out,
I li a pime,	She went running,
I tei gala sawa,	She went round the town three times,
I wa ngi njei gama.	She came to her mother.
Ke ngi njei bundea ma.	And her mother embraced her.
Ke navṓi na kpi,	And all that money,
Ke kambé na,	And the grave,
Ke i wotéa kotu wele ;	It turned into a stone house ;
Tawai i le na.	It was finer than any in the town.
Nyapọi na i ndọ̄i leni,	That woman she bore the child,
Ke i gbate a ngelemahũ.	And she was rich in the world.
Ke ngi mba nyahei ke i na lọa,	And her fellow-wife saw that,
Ke i gbalea ngima.	And it hurt her.
Ke ngi nda lọi na ke i yiama,	And she used to scold her own child,
Ye, gbe ?	Saying, Why is it ?
Gba ti nda lenga ta ha,	Other people's own children die,
Ta ti gbate ;	They grow rich ;
Bia bē ha.	(But) you will not die.
Ye, ha-oh !	She said, Die !
Gi gbate.	(So that) I get rich.
Ke i hona lea be ngi lọi ma.	And she made witchcraft also against her child.
Ke ngi lọi ha.	And her child died.
Ke ti kpowua	And they buried it
Ngi mba nyahei nda lọi gambé belanga.	Near the grave of her fellow-wife's own child.
Ke nyahei na ke ta be i yia pumōi gama ;	And that woman she too howled at the white man ;
I wolo lo fere.	She wept two days.

Pumōi be, ndọ̄pọ̄i nji i yia nya gama lo̱ fere ;	The white man too (said), This girl's mother has been howling at me for two days ;
Ye, ngi nje go̱lo ji wi lēma.	He said, her mother is making this weeping.
Ye, nga ngama lo sina.	He said, I will send her back to-morrow.
Ke nyapọ̄i be i hengá a pumōi,	And the woman dreamt of the white man,
Ye, wa sina bi ngule yia bi lọ̄i gambé ma.	(That) he said, Come to-morrow and sing at your child's grave.
Ye, ngi gbema i wa bi gama.	He said, I will let her come to you.
Ke nyapọ̄i i hengá.	And the woman dreamt.
Ngelewo ī yie (yiai) numu wọ̄ma.	At daybreak she spoke to nobody.
Ke i ya,	And she went,
Ke ta be ke i ngale wumbúa,	And she too took a mat,
Ke i segbula wumbúa,	And she took a rattle,
Ke i kọ̄ndé bumbúa,	And she took the mortar,
Ke i ya kambé ma.	And she went to the grave.
I kọ̄ndé lọ̄a kambé ma,	She stood the mortar on the grave,
Ke i ngale vọ̄mbọ̄a kambé ma,	And she spread the mat on the grave,
Ke i segbulé hōa mba,	And she held up the rattle,
Ke i ngule yia.	And she sang.
Ye, Mańwoni !	She said, Mańwoni !
Ye, ya ha Bondo ! Mańwoni wa !	She said, Go to-day to the Bondo bush ! Mańwoni, come !
Ke ngi lọ̄i i gbia kambe hū̃,	And her child came out of the grave,
I fọ̄ be ngi bwambu.	as far as its arm-pits.
Ī lī lọ̄ni.	She did not restrain her heart.
Ngi lọ̄i a gbia kambe hū̃.	Her child comes out of the grave.
Ā bo̱yo,	It is not finished,
Ke i gbundéa ma.	But she embraced her.
Ke ngi lōi i lēa ndia,	And her child was cut in half,
Ke i kūtī (kutu = short) na i lọ̄ ngeleya.	And part remained above ground.

Ke navọ̄i i gbia,
Ke i maluvéa a kọ̄nde gutī
na kambé ma.
Nyapọ̄i na ge na mia wọ
Tọ̄lọ̄ ī nyandeni.

And the money came out,
And it changed into half of the
mortar on the grave.
That was the fate of that woman.
Jealousy is not good.

XVII.

The Dream that vanished through Disobedience.

<table>
<tr><td>Tamo mia wo̱.</td><td>There was once a man.</td></tr>
<tr><td>Ta ngi mbanga ti li njei hũ.</td><td>He and his friends went to the water.</td></tr>
<tr><td>Ti kpele kahã ti yeya.</td><td>All of them had baskets.</td></tr>
<tr><td>A mba-lē kpẹ̄i.</td><td>It was cutting time.</td></tr>
<tr><td>Ti hijia,</td><td>They got up,</td></tr>
<tr><td>Ti li,</td><td>They go,</td></tr>
<tr><td>Ti fọ̄ njeima.</td><td>They reach the water.</td></tr>
<tr><td>Do̱le gbongo ngi la.</td><td>His mouth was very hunger.</td></tr>
<tr><td>I kpohũi gbia ngi gaheí mahũ,</td><td>He took the flour from the top of his basket,</td></tr>
<tr><td>I me,</td><td>He ate,</td></tr>
<tr><td>Ngi gọ̄i ve.</td><td>His belly was filled.</td></tr>
<tr><td>I li,</td><td>He went,</td></tr>
<tr><td>Ke i ligbi ngi gaheíma,</td><td>And he leaned against his basket,</td></tr>
<tr><td>Ke i ya,</td><td>And he went,</td></tr>
<tr><td>Ke i yīṅga.</td><td>And he slept.</td></tr>
<tr><td>A yini ke i hengá.</td><td>As he slept he dreamt.</td></tr>
<tr><td>Ke i gbia tawaihũ.</td><td>And he went out of the town.</td></tr>
<tr><td>Ke i ya ta mahei gama.</td><td>And he went to the king of the town.</td></tr>
<tr><td>Ke ta māi i lọ̄nga angië.</td><td>And the king of the town liked him.</td></tr>
<tr><td>Ke i ngi gonga a nyaha.</td><td>And he gave him a wife.</td></tr>
<tr><td>Ye, mu hei na mbe.</td><td>He said, You stay here with us.</td></tr>
<tr><td>Ye, bā yā li wu yei.</td><td>He said, Do not go back to your country.</td></tr>
<tr><td>Fa, nya lọ̄i ji jo̱.</td><td>So marry my daughter.</td></tr>
<tr><td>Dọ̄pọ̄i belango.</td><td>The girl is full grown.</td></tr>
<tr><td>Ta mōi ye, ngi kurua.</td><td>The man said, I accept.</td></tr>
</table>

Ke ta be mani yatemo angië.	Now he was a trap setter.
I li dogboi hũ.	He went into the bush.
I mani yate hũ guhango.	He made a trap far away.
Jiei ji nyo̱ko na a li Takwa.	The journey was as far as Tarkwa (*i. e.* from Sekondi[1], Gold Coast).
Ke i ya,	And he went,
Ke i ko̱tu wai maléa.	And he met a large rock.
Ko̱tī belengo	The rock was bearded
Kea nu vu na.	Like a living person.
Ke manī i yatéa,	And he constructed the trap,
Ke i gbo̱yoa.	And it was finished.
Ngelewo i li na.	At daybreak he went there.
Ke i hũeí wā pu a ngendé na.	And he killed ten beasts on that morning.
Ke i lewéa la.	And he passed on.
Ke i gbianga ko̱tī mahũ.	And he came out on the rock.
Ko̱tī ye, Kpana !	The rock said, Kpana !
I wō̱te.	He turns.
I mo̱li, ye,	He asks, saying,
Yo njiei leni ?	Who spoke ?
Ye, nya le.	It said, It is I.
Ye, bia bi ye ?	He said, Who are you ?
Ye, nya na ko̱tī.	It said, I am the rock.
Ye, gbele ?	He said, What is the matter ?
Ye, bā li a hũeí na.	It said, Do not take away that meat.
Ye, gbe ? nya kei.	He said, What is it, my father ?
Ye, fe be gi me.	It said, Give it here for me to eat.
Ye, ga bi baté lo.	It said, I will make you rich.
Hingdei na dogboi na hũ i gua na fō̱ yira ;	(That affair in the bush had lasted now one year ;
Numu gbi ta ngu ta gbahama.	Everybody got tired of trying to wake him.)
Ye, hũei ve ngi me.	It said, Give me the meat to eat
Ga bi baté lo.	I will make you rich.
Ye, nya keí !	He said, My father !

[1] The story was told me at Sekondi.

Ye, nga hũei ji fe biye.	He said, I give you this meat.
Ye, ngi wā lo jiei hũ.	He said, I killed it on my journey.
Ta mahei i ngi lọi vea mbe,	The king of the town gave me his daughter,
Ye, ngi jọlo.	He said I should marry her.
Ke nya va navō gbī nī yeya (= nya yeya).	And as for me I have no money.
Mani yatemo bama angē.	I am a poor trap setter.
Hũei ji mia ga pa,	It is this meat I kill,
Ga fe mahei we.	So that I may give it to the king.
Tamia nga pile nya hingdei a ne ngi līhũ,	Therefore I (try to) make my work (lit. affair) please his heart,
A gbwe ngi lọi ji hinda ma mbe.	(Because) he has left alone (said nothing about) his daughter's affair.
Ye, bā gili a ná.	It said, Do not trouble about that.
Ke ndakpalọi ke i hũei vea kọti ye, hũa pu.	And the young man gave the meat to the rock, ten beasts.
Kpele gbĭ kọtī a na wile a dakpalọi na.	Every time the rock did so with that young man.
Ke ti ndakpalọi nyahei wua Sandihũ.	And they put the young man's wife into the Sandi bush.
Gau nani i Sandi hũ.	She was four months in the Sandi bush.
Hani gbī dakpalọi i fe nyaha gami.	The young man gave nothing for the woman.
Dakpalọi i wa dogboi hũ kọtī gama.	The young man came into the bush to the rock.
Ye, keke,	He said, My father,
Ye, bē wọ ba nya baọlo.	You said before you would set me up (lit. cure).
Ye, tia nya nyahei gbiama Sandi hũ.	He said, They are bringing my wife out of the Sandi bush.
Ye, bā gili a ná.	It said, Do not trouble about that.
Ye, ndọle ji gbele, ye, tọkọ nya yeya.	It said, All this country, he said, their hand belongs to me.
Kọtī i nde ndakpalọi ma,	The rock said to the young man,
Ye, bi ya hũ-i-yi fele,	He said, Go away for two days,
Bi wa nya gama.	(And) come to me.
Ke i ya hũ-i-yi fele.	And he went away for two days.

Ke fọ̄lī ji nyaha ta Sandi gbia.	And this day the woman comes out of the Sandi bush.
Ke i ya ko̱tī gama.	And he went to the rock.
Ye, keke!	He said, Father!
Ye, bē wo̱, bē, ngā gili a na.	He said, You said before, saying, I was not to trouble about it.
Ye, ngi wa.	He said, I come.
Ye, ma ye pe nā?	He said, What are we to do now?
Ko̱tī ye, ngē wo̱ ga bi bawọ̄ lo.	The rock said, I said before I will save you.
Ye, bā gili a ná.	It said, Do not trouble about it.
Ye, bi yama lī (= līwī).	It said, Shut your eyes.
Ye, bi bawo vọ̄lọ̄-gbia ha.	It said, You will be all right at sunrise to-day.
Ke i ngi yama līwía.	And he shut his eyes.
Ye, bī yama wọ̄.	It said, Open your eyes.
I ngi yama wọ̄.	He opened his eyes.
Navọ̄ gahei hondo fere.	There were two hundred baskets of money (there).
Ye, Kpana!	It said, Kpana!
Ye, ngē wo̱ ga bi bawọ̄ lo.	It said, I said before I will save you.
Ye, bi bawọ̄ volo-gbia ha.	It said, You are all right at sunrise to-day.
Ye, bi yama wọ̄,	He said, Open your eyes,
Mbogbe wa ngeya.	There was a big cutlass in his hand.
Ye, bi nguli lē hondo fere.	It said, Cut two hundred sticks.
I nguli lē hondo fere.	He cut two hundred sticks.
Ye, bi yama lī.	It said, Shut your eyes.
I ngi yama lī.	He shut his eyes.
Nū vu hondo fele na.	(And) two hundred living persons were there.
I maluvía hinga hondo yira;	It changed them, one hundred were men;
Guru hondo yila i pekeí na kpele ti maluve a nyahanga.	The other hundred sticks all changed into women.
Ye bi yama wo.	It said, Open your eyes.
Ke Kpana i ngi yama wo.	And Kpana opened his eyes.
Ti kpele nunga atie.	They were all persons.

Kọtī i nde Kpana ma,	The rock said to Kpana,
Yē, ngē wọ	Saying, I said before
Ga bi bawo lo.	I would set you up.
Ye, nu vu hondo fere ji,	It said, These 200 living persons,
Ye, li a tie.	It said, Take them.
Ye, navọ̄ gahei ji kpele,	It said, All these money baskets,
Ye, li atië,	It said, Take them,
Li bi nyahei gwela (= gọ̄li la).	Go and pay for your wife with them.
Ke i ya a kpi tei hũ.	And he took them all into the town.
I li.	He goes.
I nyahei gọ̄li a navọ̄i na.	He pays for his wife with that money.
Kọtī i nde Kpana ma, ye,	The rock said to Kpana, saying,
Nyahei na, ye, ti fenga biye,	It said, That woman that they have given you,
Ye, wa ta a la lọ wayakpa,	It said, You and she lie together eight days,
Bē soro.	(But) you must not join with her.
Ye, Bi sọlonga,	It said, If you join,
Ye, bē gbate.	It said, You will not be rich.
Ke ta ta ti ya ti la.	And he and she went and lay down.
Ti yī lo wọ fela ē soro.	They slept seven days, and he did not join with her.
Yi wayakpa bindi ma	On the eighth day at night
Ngi nyahei ye,	His wife said,
Bī nya jole (= joloi).	If you do not join with me
Nga gbele lo bima,	I will leave you,
Ke i songa,	And he joined with her,
Ke i wunga.	And he woke up.
I heni kahei bu njela.	He sat under the basket at the waterside.
Aye i ngi wọ̄ma gbele,	When he looked behind,
Kula gahi na wọ ngi wọ̄ma,	His cloth and the basket that he had before on his back,
Kpele i lula,	Had all rotted,
Kahibui lulanga wọ̄ma.	The bottom of the basket had rotted on his back.

Na mia, nū layia gbialahũ ī nyandeni.	So it was, disobedience was not good.
A kọtī na layiahũ wọ̄	If he had listened to the Rock's word
A gbate lo.	He would have been rich.
Ke ī ngi layia-hũī wọ̄.	But he did not listen to what it said.
Tamia i wile i nyani.	So it came about that he became poor.
Na wọ̄ma yira, i hengá wo ē lọ̄ma.	Once again what he dreamed of did not remain.
Dapoi i hengá wi'e (= wile) na a lọ̄ma wọ,	If what the young man had dreamed of had remained,
Hengá gbĭ numu a pi'e (pile) a lọ̄ma.	Everything a person dreamed of would remain (as a fact).

XVIII. Songs.

Nos. II. to VIII. by a Panguma man.

I.

Dogbọi a ye jiji mua le.	When you see the bush shake it is we.
So ! bī wanī-oh, ˀeh !	So ! you have not come !
Ke bi lọ̄a, kere ?	And you are left, is it not so ?

(Sung by women in the Bondo bush.)

So, an important personage in the Bondo bush.

II.

Lines 2 to 7 *in a monotone.*

Yia wi yandova i hi !	Ah ! he sings, my lover, yes, indeed !
Mua bọ̄wo lọ̄pọ̄ mua pebu,	We are an ignorant boy, we come into the house,
i wọ̄te pema ;	(he turns to the wall ;
i nọwe yange we ;	he scratches his craw-craw ;
i we wa.	he does so plenty.)
Kā ī nyama, nya nje nya le wọ,	No dirt is on me, my mother bore me long ago,
Kā ī nyama nya wui lani	No dirt is on me, my head lay
Kia guli hũ (*in bass voice*)	As in a pillow
Guli wango (*even low voice*).	Spotlessly clean.
Yia wi yandova i hi (*high-pitched voice*).	Ah, he sings, my lover, yes, indeed !

yia wi = ? precise rendering.
i hi = e hiye, indeed.
craw-craw = a skin disease.

III.

Mba nyā.	My fellow wife.
Langa vali ga gbia ga hema fele.	I pull cassada, I do so twice.
Gbengbe kunya, kunya, kunya !	A big bundle, it comes ! it comes ! it comes !

Nyā = nyaha.

Kunya, a word used when pulling up something by the roots that breaks the ground.

IV.

Jọ̄-le hīnde na-oh!	There is a deserted place there!
Jo-li na ge!	Show me that deserted place!

Line 1 by a man; line 2 by a woman.

Jọ̄le, joli = different pronunciation of definite form of njọ̄la, desolation, etc.

V.

A lekpe mbe gĭ nya yengele goe je yakáma.	Give me a chance (or place) to pick my "crincre" at the water side.
Nyahei ī le ngeleya.	The woman cannot climb up (a tree).

VI.

Bola tọ̄we, bola tọ̄we, kpa-ngba ta!	O pumpkin neck, pumpkin neck, O big pumpkin!
Di mbe-oh, gemoi! dimbe! ga li dogbo̱ ma.	Beat me, drummer, beat me. I am going into the bush.

Translation is as given by the singer.

neck may be rendered *vine* or *runner*.
di = ndewe.
kpangba ta = doubtful.
gemoi = doubtful.

VII.

Sombo! bia na, i ye, ey e, e? (*deep voice*).	Sombo! how are you?
Bagoë! Sombo! biana i hiye?	Bagoe! Sombo! how are you indeed?
Jama! bia na ey e, e?	Chief, how are you?
Nyahali jama! bia na i hiye? (*rising voice*).	Jealous chief, how are you indeed?

Sombo, woman's name. *Bagoë*, man's name.
ey e, e has no meaning.

VIII.

O ma ngewo gē jondu gelema hongē!	O God! I swear not by heaven, O God!
Nyangbawula! ba to gei jondo ngilime hongē.	Nyangbawula! you see I swear not by heaven, O God!
Ngi namubo, gā gula ko̱tī-ma be, hongē!	If I slip, I do not fall on the stone here, O God!
O ma ngewo, gē jondu gilima, hongē!	O God, I swear not by heaven, O God!

Nyangbawula = a man's name.

IX.

Ngī gbate-oh, nga ha lo.	I am rich (and) I shall die.
Bi nyani-oh, ba ha lo.	You are poor and you will die.

X.

Sung at the Skipping Rope.

E, E, ye! e, e, ye! e Gbwando.	E, E, ye! e, e, ye! Eh! Gbwando.
Mu gbē go, e, e, ye! e, e, ye!	Let us play, e, e, ye! e, e, ye!

Gbwando = a man's name.

XI.

Sung at the Skipping Rope.

Ko̱ Kọndọ! Kọndọ!	Hi! Grasshopper! Grasshopper!
Ma wuë! mu dọnga-oh.	I and you, we stand up (together).

XII.

Sung at the Skipping Rope.

Gbo! Nina a pe a ko̱ ve a hũgbe lo i hīte.	What! the rat looks into the iron pot before getting into it.

Ko̱ = ko̱lu, iron.

XIII.

Sung at the Skipping Rope.

Hagbe̥ wu' go nyenye vi i!	O you with a leg as thin as a gazelle's!
Reply—I yale! gbe i ya'e.	If it break, let it break.
Nya mbe!	It is my own!
I yale! gbe i ya'e.	If it break, let it break.

Hagbe wulọ̄i go̱we. Ya'e = yale.

Vi i = ?